# The Body Collected in Australia

# The Body Collected in Australia

## A History of Human Specimens and the Circulation of Biomedical Knowledge

Eugenia Pacitti

BLOOMSBURY ACADEMIC
LONDON • NEW YORK • OXFORD • NEW DELHI • SYDNEY

BLOOMSBURY ACADEMIC

Bloomsbury Publishing Plc, 50 Bedford Square, London, WC1B 3DP, UK
Bloomsbury Publishing Inc, 1359 Broadway, New York, NY 10018, USA
Bloomsbury Publishing Ireland, 29 Earlsfort Terrace, Dublin 2, D02 AY28, Ireland

BLOOMSBURY, BLOOMSBURY ACADEMIC and the Diana
logo are trademarks of Bloomsbury Publishing Plc

First published in Great Britain 2024
This paperback edition published in 2025

Copyright © Eugenia Pacitti, 2024

Eugenia Pacitti has asserted her right under the Copyright,
Designs and Patents Act, 1988, to be identified as Author of this work.

For legal purposes the Acknowledgements on pp. ix–x constitute
an extension of this copyright page.

Cover image © Tramond mounted exploded skull (Maison Tramond, c. 1900)
Harry Brookes Allen Museum of Anatomy and Pathology, Melbourne

All rights reserved. No part of this publication may be: i) reproduced or transmitted
in any form, electronic or mechanical, including photocopying, recording or by means
of any information storage or retrieval system without prior permission in writing from
the publishers; or ii) used or reproduced in any way for the training, development or
operation of artificial intelligence (AI) technologies, including generative AI technologies.
The rights holders expressly reserve this publication from the text and data mining
exception as per Article 4(3) of the Digital Single Market Directive (EU) 2019/790.

Bloomsbury Publishing Plc does not have any control over, or responsibility for,
any third-party websites referred to or in this book. All internet addresses given
in this book were correct at the time of going to press. The author and publisher
regret any inconvenience caused if addresses have changed or sites have ceased
to exist, but can accept no responsibility for any such changes.

A catalogue record for this book is available from the British Library.

A catalog record for this book is available form the Library of Congress.

| ISBN: | HB: | 978-1-3503-7372-3 |
| --- | --- | --- |
| | PB: | 978-1-3503-7375-4 |
| | ePDF: | 978-1-3503-7373-0 |
| | eBook: | 978-1-3503-7374-7 |

Typeset by Integra Software Service Pvt. Ltd.

For product safety related questions contact productsafety@bloomsbury.com.

To find out more about our authors and books visit www.bloomsbury.com
and sign up for our newsletters.

# Contents

| | |
|---|---|
| List of figures | vii |
| Acknowledgements | ix |
| Glossary of medical terms | xi |
| | |
| Introduction: Bones of contention | 1 |
|     The history of medicine and medical museums in Australia | 4 |

1   Dissecting the culture of anatomy    9
    Collecting the human body    10
    The Melbourne Medical School    16
    The anatomists    20
    Cadaver poems    25

2   From patient to specimen: Collectors and networks    33
    Nineteenth-century collecting activity    35
    Harry Brookes Allen and the collecting network    36
    Transforming patient into specimen    38
    'The battle of the brains': Public views of a clandestine network    41
    Why did they collect?    43
    Amateur versus paid collecting    49

3   The anatomy of a museum    53
    From grotesque body parts to pedagogical tools    55
    The museum as an encyclopaedia of the body    60
    Specimens as pedagogical tools    62
    Private and public anatomy    69

4   Unrealized lives: A collection of foetal specimens    75
    Medical authority and the foetal specimen    77
    Specimen collecting and medical discourse    86
    Foetuses preserved in isolation    87
    Foetuses preserved in situ    90

| | | |
|---|---|---:|
| 5 | War pathology specimens | 97 |
| | War specimens and the development of military medicine | 100 |
| | Displaying the collection | 109 |
| 6 | Moving parts: Repatriation and bioethics | 119 |
| | The persistent culture of anatomy | 121 |
| | Moving parts within the context of decolonization | 124 |
| | The Berry Collection | 134 |
| | Moving parts within a changing bioethical climate | 135 |

| | |
|---|---:|
| Conclusion: Afterlives | 143 |
| Notes | 149 |
| Bibliography | 191 |
| Index | 211 |

# Figures

1 Hydrocephalus skeleton, 531–008101, Harry Brookes Allen Museum of Anatomy and Pathology, University of Melbourne. Photograph by Gavan Mitchell     2
2 Early dissection class, with Richard Joseph Bull, MHM 00422. Image courtesy of the Medical History Museum, Faculty of Medicine, Dentistry and Health Sciences, University of Melbourne     23
3 Hydrocephalus specimen, showing cracks in the enlarged cranium, 531–008101, Harry Brookes Allen Museum of Anatomy and Pathology, University of Melbourne. Photograph by Gavan Mitchell     34
4 Corrosion cast of kidney, 516–500011, Harry Brookes Allen Museum of Anatomy and Pathology, University of Melbourne. Photograph by Gavan Mitchell     56
5 Lecture Class Anatomy, 1898, MHM 02129, Medical History Museum, University of Melbourne     64
6 Medical Students of 1876–80, c. 1880, MHM 00460. Image courtesy of the Medical History Museum, Faculty of Medicine, Dentistry and Health Sciences, University of Melbourne     66
7 Medical Students' Society display for the University's Jubilee procession, 1906, *Speculum*, no. 65, May 1906, 15     67
8 Auzoux model of heart, Maison Auzoux, c. 1890, 516–500277, Harry Brookes Allen Museum of Anatomy and Pathology, University of Melbourne. Photograph by Gavan Mitchell     68
9 Extra-uterine pregnancy, 516–101852, Harry Brookes Allen Museum of Anatomy and Pathology, University of Melbourne. Photograph by Gavan Mitchell     82
10 Bronchus, mustard gas poisoning c. 1914–1918; Stomach, mustard gas poisoning c. 1914–1918, 531–003784 and 531–003783, Harry Brookes Allen Museum of Anatomy and Pathology, University of Melbourne. Photograph by Gavan Mitchell     98

11 Sphenoid bone with bullet, 531–003663, Harry Brookes Allen Museum of Anatomy and Pathology, University of Melbourne. Photograph by Gavan Mitchell     98

12 Lung, poisoning, 531–003617, Harry Brookes Allen Museum of Anatomy and Pathology, University of Melbourne. Photograph by Gavan Mitchell     99

# Acknowledgements

This book started out as a doctoral thesis, so I would first like to thank my PhD supervisors. I am very grateful to Associate Professor Paula Michaels for her unfailing enthusiasm for my work from the very beginning, her intellectual engagement with my ideas, as well as her ongoing support as I revised my thesis into this book. I would also like to thank Professor Christina Twomey for her generous and constructive feedback on my ideas and writing, and her kindness and encouragement as I navigated different stages of this project.

Without the assistance of the curators of the Harry Brookes Allen Museum of Anatomy and Pathology, this project would simply not have got off the ground. My deep thanks to Dr Ryan Jefferies, who first introduced me to the collection and encouraged me to pursue my research, and to Rohan Long for facilitating my visits to the museum and discussing the collection with me.

Research for this book took me to many libraries, archives and museums around Australia. I am grateful to the countless staff at these institutions whose assistance, whether hauling boxes of documents to reading rooms or showing me through museum collections, made this book possible. On the editorial side of things, my sincere thanks to the editors and anonymous reviewers at Bloomsbury, especially Maddie Holder and Megan Harris who were so encouraging, helpful and patient as they guided me through the publishing process. I would also like to acknowledge the editorial work of John Mapps, whose keen eye and constructive suggestions have strengthened the book.

I have benefitted greatly from the camaraderie of fellow historians through years of research and writing. I am very grateful to the members of our wonderful writing group in Historical Studies at Monash University, particularly Margaret Coffey, Jackie Hopkins, Bernard Keo, Jenny Lord, Rosa Martorana, Alex Potočnik, Anisa Puri, Julia Smart, Hannah Viney and Kyly Walker, who shared their knowledge and wisdom throughout this project. I must give special thanks to Bernard Keo who has not only been immensely generous in reading many drafts and offering advice, but also so steadfast in his encouragement and friendship, and to Julia Smart and Jackie Hopkins for keeping me motivated, even in the rough patches. The support of my wider group of friends has also been invaluable, and I am particularly grateful to Georgie Steggall and Monica Cronin for always lending me an ear.

To Jackson, whose patience and belief in me have meant so much throughout this journey. Thank you for celebrating my achievements along the way, providing timely doses of perspective, and helping me find the courage to persevere when I needed it most.

And finally, thank you to my family – especially my sister Caterina, aunt Christine, (Piper!) and parents Nick and Elizabeth – for your unwavering support as I worked on this project and in all my endeavours. Thank you for nurturing my love of reading and learning, and for giving me, throughout my life, a space to talk about my ideas and foster my imagination.

# Glossary of medical terms

**Achondroplasia** is a bone growth disorder characterized by a trunk of normal length with disproportionately short limbs and an enlarged skull.

**Anencephaly** is a serious developmental defect in which major parts of a foetus' brain, skull and scalp do not form completely.

**Aortic aneurysm** refers to an abnormal swelling of the wall of the aorta (the major blood vessel that feeds blood from the heart to the body).

**Boro-salicylic powder** was an antiseptic compound used to dress wounds during the nineteenth and early twentieth centuries.

**Corrosion casts** are produced by injecting the vessels of an organ with a solidifying material, such as wax or resin, then corroding or macerating away the flesh to leave only the cast created by the hardened material.

**Craniotomy** is, with reference to this thesis, an emergency procedure in which a doctor fatally perforates the skull of a foetus, before crushing and removing the foetal remains, to save the life of the mother.

**Dissection** refers to the act of cutting open a dead body, or cadaver, for the purpose of studying or displaying its structures, as opposed to a **post-mortem examination.**

**Dry specimens** are body parts, typically skeletons, skulls, but also organs, prepared through being dried or injected with a material such as wax.

**Extra-uterine foetation**, now commonly known as an extra-uterine, or, ectopic, pregnancy, refers to an instance when a fertilized egg implants itself outside the uterus, usually in one of the fallopian tubes.

**Fibrodysplasia ossificans progressiva**, or FOP, is a rare disorder in which the body's soft tissues, such as muscles, ligaments and tendons, turn permanently into bone.

**Glisson's capsule** is a layer of connective tissue that surrounds the liver.

**Gigantism** is a disorder in which the pituitary gland produces an excess of growth hormone during childhood, before the growth plates in the legs have fused, resulting in accelerated growth.

**Hydatid cysts** can occur following the ingestion of the tapeworm parasite *Echinococcus granulosus*, usually from hand-to-mouth transfer of its eggs in animal faeces.

**Hydrocephalus** is a condition characterized by an enlarged skull as the result of an excess buildup of cerebrospinal fluid (CSF) on the brain.

**Lithotomy** is the removal of kidney, bladder or gallbladder stones. It also refers to a position commonly used in medical examinations involving the pelvis and lower abdomen, as well as during childbirth.

**Meningoencephalocele** refers to an abnormal sac of fluid, brain tissue and membrane that extends through a defect in the skull.

***Mycobacterium ulcerans*** is a bacterial infection that affects the skin and subcutaneous tissues, resulting in nodules and lesions that can ulcerate if left untreated.

**Omentum** refers to a thin sheet of fatty tissue that connects and protects internal abdominal structures.

**Podalic version** is an obstetric procedure in which the foetus is turned inside the uterus so that one or both feet can move through the cervix.

**Polydactyly** refers to the occurrence of one or more extra fingers or toes.

**Post-mortem examination**, or, a post-mortem or autopsy, refers to a medical examination of a dead body, to ascertain the cause of death.

**Prosectors** are people who prepare or dissect bodies in readiness for demonstration or illustration.

**Quickening** refers to the moment when a pregnant woman first feels foetal movement, typically between fifteen and twenty weeks' gestation. The term is rarely used nowadays, but has historically had significant medical, legal and social connotations.

**Wet specimens** consist of body parts prepared through being submerged in a preservative liquid, such as a formaldehyde or alcohol solution, and contained within a sealed glass or Perspex vessel.

# Introduction: Bones of contention

In July 1907, a skeleton arrived at the University of Melbourne. With deformed bones and an enlarged skull, the skeleton exhibited signs of hydrocephalus – a pathological condition marked by an excess of cerebrospinal fluid on the brain. The skeleton was that of a recently deceased twenty-eight-year-old man who had spent the final eight years of his life confined to a 'soft bed with his head on a soft pillow', unable to move due to the weight of his head.[1] The limbs, contracted in death as they were in life, evoked the discomfort the man must have felt during these years. There is no record of his name, birthplace or former history. In contrast, the man who retained the skeleton and sent it to Melbourne from the University of Adelaide, Professor Archibald Watson, was well known in the Australian medical scene. He flouted convention in both his medical practice and social life and attracted controversy for his legal misdemeanours.[2] The man to whom Watson sent the specimen, Professor Harry Brookes Allen, was also prominent in the medical profession and, importantly, the curator of a large collection of human anatomy and pathology specimens. Once the skeleton entered Allen's care, it was prepared and articulated at the Museum of Victoria before being placed in a custom-built wooden cabinet in the anatomy and pathology museum at the Melbourne Medical School, where it remains today.[3]

The story of the hydrocephalus skeleton (Figure 1) encompasses some of the people and places at the centre of human specimen collecting in late-nineteenth- and early-twentieth-century Australia. It also reveals the deceased pathological human body to be a valued object among members of the medical profession, which raises a number of important questions. What conditions enabled Watson to take this man's skeleton and send it across the country to a colleague? Why would this anatomist want to retain such a specimen? And, what was the skeleton used for once it came to rest in the Melbourne Medical School anatomy and pathology museum?

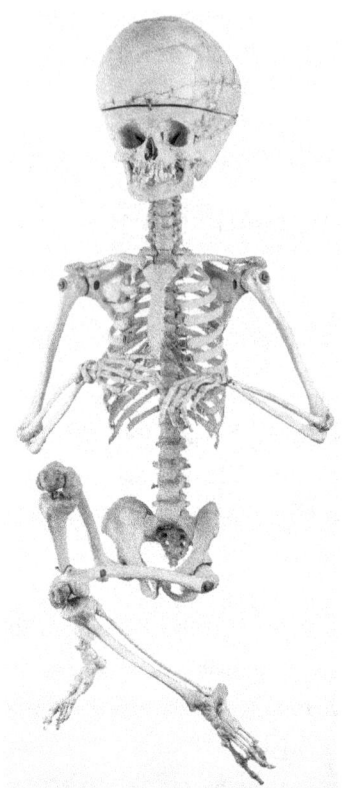

**Figure 1** Hydrocephalus specimen, 531-008101, Harry Brookes Allen Museum of Anatomy and Pathology, University of Melbourne. Photograph by Gavan Mitchell. (This image may not be copied, reproduced or distributed in any way unless authorized by the Curator, Harry Brookes Allen Museum of Anatomy and Pathology, the University of Melbourne.)

The hydrocephalus skeleton was but one of many human specimens collected, deliberately and specifically, in late-nineteenth- and early-twentieth-century Australia. Of particular significance is the collection and repatriation of Indigenous Australian Ancestral Remains, which has garnered substantial attention from scholars and the public alike. During the same era, however, thousands of other specimens – taken mostly from vulnerable members of society, such as the indigent and infirm – ended up in university collections and public museums around the country. Such collections have come to be literal and figurative bones of contention. And yet, the way they have been used by anatomists, medical students, scientists and museum professionals for instruction and research has not been the subject of thorough scholarly enquiry. Rather, as historians Lisa O'Sullivan and Ross Jones note, 'once incorporated into collections, specimens often become static' and their culturally and historically contingent meanings obscured by their biological attributes.[4]

The relative stasis of such specimens within the historical literature speaks to a wider absence of discussion about how the living have engaged with the collected dead body to develop medical and scientific knowledge in Australian history – an oversight which this book intends to remedy. *The Body Collected in Australia* is the first in-depth study to investigate the complex social and cultural roles that collected human remains in anatomy and pathology museums have assumed in the narratives of medicine and collecting in Australia. It contends that collected specimens at the Melbourne Medical School anatomy and pathology museum should be 'read' as sources in their own right which reveal how Australian physicians have used the dead to better comprehend the intricacies of the human body in illness and good health. The specimens raise questions about how physicians and other collectors accumulated human bodies and body parts within a developing medical culture in turn-of-the-century Australia and why they did so. They also provide a window into changing perceptions of the human body which allow for investigation into the complex and evolving relationships between the nation's medical profession and the public. By examining the lives of collected specimens in Australian anatomy and pathology museums, I look beyond their biological features to recast them as cultural materials that are deeply embedded in Australian medicine's past and present.

Further, I show how these materials fit into a traditional system of understanding the human body within the Western biomedical world based upon learning directly from the body itself. My analysis also reveals a distinct national context characterized by a medical profession that paradoxically wanted to conform to established norms in prominent centres of knowledge production in Britain, Europe and the United States, while at the same time sought to resist them and develop its own image on the international scene.

Finally, in this volume, I make the case that historic specimen collections in Australia are not obsolete remnants of an earlier era of medicine; they are active pedagogical tools in medical education, and materials that continue to shape practices and attitudes concerning uses of the deceased body. While focusing mainly on specimens and cadavers collected for educational use, I also examine how the legacy of collecting Indigenous Australian bodies continues to affect the medical profession and the museum industry in the present day. These strands of analysis enable a holistic interrogation of collected specimens: to reconsider their position in the history of Australian medicine and to recover the social and cultural processes that underpinned their collection and continuing use in medical education and research.

To explore these lines of questioning, this book centres primarily on the collecting activity that surrounded the Melbourne Medical School during the period between 1862 and 1926. Embracing one city in lieu of a sweeping study allows for a more intimate investigation.[5] The School is the ideal case study and serves as the quintessential model for understanding the ways in which both collectors and the act of collecting operated. As the first medical school in colonial Australia to teach medical students, and home to one of the nation's largest teaching collections of human specimens, it was a centre for Australian medical teaching, research and practice in the late nineteenth and early twentieth centuries, as well as a site of colonial exchange with the British imperial medical profession. Further, the University of Melbourne occupies a noteworthy place in the history of repatriation in Australia, as one of the institutions which began to negotiate the return of Ancestral Remains to the Traditional Owners in the 1980s. The two other colonial-era medical schools in Sydney and Adelaide, also examined in this book, offer insight into the broader narrative of specimen collecting in Australia. The years in question were a formative period for the medical profession in Australia and represent the height of specimen collecting activity. The year 1862 signifies the opening of the Melbourne Medical School, while 1926 marks the death of Harry Brookes Allen and the subsequent end of his tenure as curator of the medical school's anatomy and pathology museum.

## The history of medicine and medical museums in Australia

This book breaks new ground in the history of medicine in Australia by drawing collected human remains and their presence in medical museums from the periphery of scholarship to the centre. The establishment of Australian medical schools and hospitals, along with the achievements of prominent medical men, has been well chronicled.[6] These studies have built a picture of the nation's medical profession, from the early days of colonization to the introduction of formal medical education marked by the opening of medical schools in Melbourne (1862), Sydney (1883) and Adelaide (1885), often emphasizing the synergies between the British medical education system and these new colonial schools.[7] In the last twenty years, historians such as Helen MacDonald, Paul Turnbull and Ross L. Jones have considered the social and cultural dimensions of anatomists' work with dead bodies in colonial Australia. These scholars show how legislation afforded anatomists the corpses they required, and how the anatomists used it to attempt – often unsuccessfully – to subdue public anxiety over their interactions with the dead. They have also contributed to a deep understanding of the conditions in which collectors accumulated the bodily remains, and particularly skulls, of Indigenous Australians between colonization in 1788 and the middle of the twentieth century, and how such materials became highly sought after within the international scientific world.[8] Woven through these works, alongside significant scholarship concerning the British, European and American contexts, is evidence of the role that anatomy as a discipline has played in the professionalization of medicine, and the medical profession's developing authority over the body, on a local and national scale.[9]

Anatomy and pathology museums have often been overlooked in histories of nineteenth- and twentieth-century medicine. Scholars, including Samuel Alberti, Jonathan Reinarz and Erin McLeary, have begun challenging this convention, instead positioning the medical museum as a site where physicians and medical students created meaning out of fragmented bodies and standardized the terminology of bodily abnormality.[10] During what Reinarz labels 'the age of museum medicine', from the mid-nineteenth to early twentieth centuries, these museums possessed instructional qualities for students and also provided material that contributed to research in the broader medical profession.[11]

Historians have often denoted the mid-to-late nineteenth century as the heyday of museum medicine in Western medical schools, following which specimen collecting, and anatomy and pathology museums, experienced a sharp decline.[12] But, the story did not end there. Not only did many specimen collections in Australia remain intact and active past their ostensible heyday and into the late twentieth and early twenty-first centuries, but so, too, did the ideals, practices and power structures that enabled their assembly. Despite shifting attitudes and improving technology, this book shows that specimens in Australian collections continue to inform a constantly evolving understanding of the human body.

The place that Australian anatomy and pathology museums occupy in local and global systems of collecting, education and knowledge production has not yet been fully investigated. Often working within networks, a range of collectors accumulated thousands of body parts and sent them to those who managed the museum collections. This activity shares features with the collecting culture and circulation of knowledge detailed in literature that focuses largely on the field of natural history.[13] While such studies provide a critical underpinning for understanding the nineteenth-century drive to classify and make meaning of the world through collections and museums, the nature of collecting human remains yields a distinctive narrative in the history of collecting worthy of its own attention.

Further, spotlighting Australia reveals a flow of anatomy and pathology specimens, as well as other medical and scientific material and ideas, from the small colonial universities to prominent knowledge centres in Britain, Europe and the United States. Historians have shown that Australia's association with British knowledge centres was vital to the growth of the colony's medical and scientific professions domestically. Conscious of their physical isolation, practitioners in these fields – many of whom had come directly from Britain – sought to 'soften … the tyranny of distance' through connections to their British contemporaries.[14] Australia was also deeply embedded in global schemes of collecting and knowledge production, many of which placed a high value on Australian material.[15] At the same time, physicians and scientists carved out careers as producers of distinctly Australian knowledge, particularly as the number of Australian-born practitioners, such as Allen, increased.[16] My analysis shows the collecting network that surrounded the anatomy and pathology museum to be at neither the centre nor periphery of the British Empire, but one that occupies what historian Tamson Pietsch terms a 'sub-imperial space'.[17] It was a self-sustaining network that nurtured local personal and professional ties, while also engaging with the field of medicine at large.

How can we recognize the specimens, too, as subjects in this history, alongside the collecting network and the anatomy and pathology museums it inspired? Signalling a dissatisfaction with traditional divisions between people and things, and their subsequent treatment as separate entities, historians and cultural anthropologists in the last several decades have begun to examine how material objects convey meaning within the world around them.[18] To articulate the relational nature of people and things, this book reflects an approach that considers the social and cultural 'lives' of human biomedical specimens.[19] They are materials whose histories are entangled with human actions; they have influenced and informed those who engage with them, and continue to evoke strong emotional responses.

*\*\**

The following chapters trace the journeys of collected specimens through time and place to show how the tradition of anatomy and its cognate disciplines developed in Australia throughout the late nineteenth and early twentieth centuries. Chapter 1 brings to life the culture of anatomy in this era through the people who collected the deceased body and the places in which they worked. Anatomists collected cadavers and specimens within a set of social, cultural and legal norms inherited from Britain, but adapted for the colonial Australian context. Amid challenging conditions, stoked by public concern over anatomists' work with morbid materials, the dissecting room emerged as a critical site for developing medical knowledge. It was also a place where students grappled with the anatomist's attempts to reconcile a desire to heal and the need to dissect the human body, which they sometimes viewed in oppositional terms.

Whereas most cadavers were disposed of once medical students had dissected them, many collected body parts had afterlives that continue to the present day. Chapter 2 moves beyond the cadaver to collected specimens, to explore the personal and professional networks that enabled anatomy and pathology collections to grow, and to probe how collectors shifted the value of the human body from potential medical waste to useful object within the field of medicine. Continuing along specimens' journeys, Chapter 3 enters the medical school anatomy and pathology museum – the site where anatomists and medical students transformed specimens from disordered body parts into valuable educational tools. Medical language and ideas also entered the public sphere in late-nineteenth-century Melbourne through public anatomy exhibitions. These ventures laid bare the tensions within the medical profession as well as the complexities of the relationship between the medical profession and the public.

Outside the realm of medical education, collected specimens assumed significant roles in the broader Australian medical profession. Chapter 4 considers how the collection of foetal specimens at the Harry Brookes Allen Museum reflected the evolving concerns of women and doctors alike about pregnancy and miscarriage amid the professionalization of medicine in the late nineteenth and early twentieth centuries. By rethinking the presence and value of female bodies in the museum collection, this chapter fills part of the discursive void that accompanies the material culture of pregnancy loss in Australian history. Chapter 5 provides a close analysis of a collection of pathological specimens from the First World War to show how it contributed to the Australian medical profession's growing sense of identity during a period of great social hardship. Drawing on comparisons with similar collections in overseas contexts, it considers what the Australian collection's absence from the public sphere for more than a century reveals about the limits to the visual representation of the soldier's body in national narratives of war commemoration.

The final chapter centres on the Indigenous-led repatriation movement that began in the 1980s. It shows that a growing emphasis on bioethics and decolonization within medicine and the museum industry in the late twentieth and early twenty-first centuries has forced institutions with historic collections to confront the colonial conditions under which the material was acquired, and to decide how to address the legacies of their predecessors. While some collections have been disassembled and others remain intact, specimens continue to accumulate histories within shifting cultural contexts long after they were collected.

Woven together, the collective impact of these chapters delivers an account of medical specimen collecting in Australia that charts both development and stasis over time, as well as draws out the distinctive identity of the Australian medical profession during its formative era amid the broader global historical narrative.

\* \* \*

The way that members of the Australian medical profession collected and engaged with human bodies and body parts in the late nineteenth and early twentieth centuries matters. Through their engagement with specimens, individual practitioners developed knowledge of the body that led to improved healthcare. Further, specimen collecting created a sense of shared purpose among physicians in Australia's developing medical scene. It also enabled the Australian medical profession to participate in global networks of knowledge transfer and to break out of its image as a consumer of medical knowledge, to become itself a producer. More than that, late-nineteenth- and early-twentieth-century specimen collecting set in place a culture of anatomy that in many ways endures today. Confronting the legacies of past collecting has not only prompted reflection on the deep-seated power structures that led to the exploitation of vulnerable bodies; it has also influenced the development of regulations for acquiring and handling human tissue that are in place today. While thousands of specimens have been removed from collections to be repatriated or destroyed, thousands more remain within Australian museums and repositories.

Many specimens, such as the hydrocephalus skeleton, continue to be used in university medical education, just as their original collectors intended. To consider these specimens as only biological objects, however, is to disregard their wider significance. Looking beyond the physical collected body or potted specimen presents a deeper understanding of the historically contingent and socially constructed relationship between the living and the dead – one that can inform decisions about the future of the specimens that comprise the body collected.

1

# Dissecting the culture of anatomy

The process of anatomical dissection fragments and explores its object of interest; it opens the human body to reveal layers of tissue and bone. After making an incision over the sternum of the cadaver, the anatomist moves carefully and methodically through the body's interior. They come upon the heart, its smooth walls no longer rhythmically contracting and dilating with each living breath. The organ's value has shifted from its necessary role in sustaining life, to instead educate the living about themselves and their anatomy. The anatomist continues to dissect, opening the chambers of the heart, following the delicate ribbons of dark blood vessels that lead in one direction, towards junctions with vessels going in another. Behind the heart, hidden out of sight past the borders of the ribs, lie pale nerves that the dissector must draw downwards into view to reveal their structure. Finally, the anatomist might move along the body to perceive the tension of the ligaments that bind the bones of the feet together into functional arches. In exploring the connections, detachments and hidden recesses of the human frame, the anatomist breaks the body down into parts to then reconfigure them as newly defined anatomical knowledge.[1]

Like dissection, the culture of anatomy in late-nineteenth- and early-twentieth-century Australia was characterized by tension, necessity, and shifting and hidden values in the historical relationship between the anatomist and their object of interest – the cadaver. This chapter brings to life the culture in which anatomists collected and interacted with the deceased human body, as a type of collected specimen, in late-nineteenth- and early-twentieth-century Australia. It discusses the people who imbued the cadaver with value and the spaces in which they worked, to offer a fresh interpretation of the essential role the cadaver has played in the development of Australian medicine.

A substantial body of scholarly work exists that focuses on the social and cultural meanings of the human corpse in Western biomedicine and society, from its position in rituals of death and burial, to its worth as a commodity and as the subject of anatomical inquiry.[2] Anatomists in colonial- and early-federal-era Australia collected and worked with cadavers within a set of norms inherited from Britain, which in turn had been influenced by a longer tradition of anatomical dissection in Europe. At particular moments in the early 1860s, however, colonial anatomists and authorities invoked the privilege of hindsight to create regulations and legislation that sent the trade in deceased human bodies on a distinct path from its forebears.

## Collecting the human body

The tradition of dissecting bodies in colonial Australia finds its roots in the fourteenth century, when, following centuries of animal dissection and vivisection, Italian anatomists began to dissect human bodies behind the closed doors of medical schools for educational and legal purposes. It was not long, however, before anatomists in Padua and Bologna drew large and enthusiastic crowds to witness them perform public dissections on human cadavers.[3] The premise at the heart of these early anatomical explorations was that one could not possibly know the body or be able to treat it surgically or otherwise without actually studying it in the flesh. The value of the corpse as a means to uncover the secrets of human anatomy lay in its verisimilitude to the living body. In death, though, the body could be opened, and the internal organs removed, held and viewed at any angle. Through this method, anatomists could comprehend how interior bodily structures worked alone and in relation to one another. Death was not an absolute, definite end; instead, the dead human body revealed facts only knowable once life had ceased and the bodily interior could be explored. Based on the opportunities it presented for the study of anatomy and surgical techniques, the dissection of cadavers became the primary means by which to uncover knowledge of the human body in Western Europe, as well as much of its overseas empires, including colonial Australia.

Dissecting criminal bodies became the norm in the British Empire when it was codified in law following the introduction of the Murder Act in 1752. As the purpose of the Act was 'better preventing the horrid crime of murder', it was necessary that 'some further terror and peculiar mark of infamy be added to the punishment of death'.[4] This further terror was that the executed body would either be left to hang in chains publicly until it decomposed or it would be given to anatomists, who were often present at the gallows, to be dissected. Typically, the anatomist would open up and display the body in front of a general audience before conducting further investigations with only medical men and students present. Due to mishaps at the site of execution, bodies were sometimes already in poor condition when they arrived on the anatomist's table. For the most part, though, the youth and good health of hanged criminals meant they made excellent dissection subjects.[5]

The legal codification of dissection had a dual effect: the law gifted colonial Australian anatomists the cadavers they required, and also purported to assist the colonial government as it sought to deter members of the public from committing heinous crimes such as murder. Colonial Australian anatomists kept few records of their dissections, but members of the press often documented the proceedings so the public would be aware of the graphic realities the punishment entailed.[6] Whereas anatomists considered the corpse to be a useful object with which to better their professional knowledge, most of the public viewed it as a sacred object to be buried appropriately. The process of dissection often disfigured the body to such an extent that many believed its integrity to be compromised, imperilling the repose of the soul. As in Britain, dissection therefore went against Christian burial practices in nineteenth-century Australia, which dictated that the deceased should be interred intact in consecrated ground.[7] Despite the affront dissection presented to contemporary sensibilities, Australian newspaper accounts echoed sentiment in Britain that 'the fear of dissection had ... no effect in preventing the crime of murder', as one Sydney newspaper noted in 1833.[8] While post-execution dissection was intended, in part, to be an instrument of social control, dissection of criminal bodies did not lower murder rates in the developing Australian colonies. It did, however, affect the relationship between anatomists and the public.

The presence of an anatomist at executions and the punitive overtones of post-mortem dissections in nineteenth-century Australia fostered an inescapable connection in the eyes of the public between anatomy, criminality and punishment. Anatomists became part of the state-authorized system of retributive justice. They commanded power over the criminal body in a manner that not only allowed them to acquire material necessary to their work, but also instilled in the public a sense of fear about the physical and spiritual effects of being dissected. When lawmakers and anatomists turned to the impoverished rather than the criminal body to accommodate a greater need for dissection subjects, such attitudes of fear and distrust only intensified as a greater proportion of the population was vulnerable to being dissected.[9]

With plans well underway from 1857 to open the first colonial Australian medical school for teaching students in Melbourne, anatomists and authorities created regulations and legislation to control the trade in cadavers that was distinct from that in Britain. Noting the prestigious past of dissection in constructing anatomical knowledge, those charged with establishing the new medical school knew it needed to offer dissection classes to attract students. The number of corpses coming from the gallows was not sufficient for students to undertake dissection classes, so anatomists had to find another source to accommodate this increased demand for cadavers and human specimens.

Faced with the same concern amid decreasing executions thirty years earlier, British anatomy schools had turned to body-snatchers, or 'resurrection men', to fill gaps in supply.[10] These men often worked in bands, stalking burial grounds at night and digging up freshly buried corpses to sell to medical schools. Perhaps the most infamous instance of illicit corpse trafficking was an extreme case in Edinburgh in 1828. Over a period of ten months, William Burke and William Hare murdered sixteen lodgers in Hare's house for the purpose of selling the corpses to renowned anatomist Dr Robert Knox at the Edinburgh Medical School. Following the revelation of their criminal activities, Burke was convicted and hanged and Hare fled, never to be heard from again. The incident created considerable outrage at not only the murderers' actions, but also the complicity of Knox and the anatomists at the medical school.[11]

As historian Helen MacDonald states, 'after 1828, everything came back to Burke and Hare', whose murderous crimes had become the 'enduring reference point' for the moral culpability of anatomical work in the British Empire.[12] For instance, when passers-by discovered 'a portion and fragments of a human body' in the ground behind a newly built private anatomy theatre in Aberdeen in 1830, their minds turned to the case that had caused such anger just two years prior. Fuelled by revulsion, a group of local Aberdonians stormed the anatomy theatre and burnt it to the ground, as a crowd of 20,000 cried out, 'burn the house! – down with the Burking-shop!'[13] ('burking' had become a common term in Britain for a murder committed with the intention of selling the corpse). Riots of a similar nature occurred elsewhere in Britain, and also in the United States, around the same time.[14] Informed by local news reports that reached the outposts of empire, audiences in Australia were well aware of British anatomy riots and incidents of body-snatching.[15]

Amid a distrustful society still reeling from the Burke and Hare episode, British authorities expedited the implementation of an Anatomy Act. The new legislation, passed in 1832, provided written assurances to the public that it was now safe from 'burkers', body-snatchers and resurrection men, whose fearsome figures loomed large in the public imagination; Mary Shelley's tale of an ambitious young doctor who becomes a resurrectionist in the hope of finding a way to overcome the finality of death, and Robert Louis Stevenson's short story, 'The Body Snatcher', which features characters based on the students of Dr Robert Knox, are but two examples from popular novels and works of gothic fiction in the nineteenth century. The Anatomy Act effectively put body-snatchers out of work and created a regulated system to provide the medical schools with a consistent supply of cadavers that the bodies of executed criminals could not meet. But in doing so, according to nineteenth-century English surgeon William Roberts, the Act '*covertly*, but not the less specifically, and exclusively' targeted a new type of body: the impoverished body.[16]

The practice of anatomizing executed murderers all but stopped in Britain when the Anatomy Act offered up the workhouses as a new source of bodies, but as colonial Australia did not yet have a medical school in this period, the bodies of hanged criminals provided an adequate supply to the colony's trained anatomists. Dissections from the gallows continued in Australia throughout the 1850s.

Anticipating the Melbourne Medical School's need for a consistent supply of cadavers, while wanting to prevent the development of a covert body trade as had occurred in Britain, the Victorian colonial government introduced *An Act for Regulating Schools of Anatomy*, or the Anatomy Act, in 1862 as the first piece of legislation to regulate the collection and use of human remains in colonial Australia. Taking cues from the British Act of 1832, the Victorian Anatomy Act was based on an implicit understanding that knowledge of the afflictions that affect the human body 'cannot be acquired without the aid of anatomical examinations'.[17] It therefore permitted any 'legally qualified medical practitioner or any professor teacher or student of anatomy medicine or surgery to receive or possess [a body] for anatomical examination', provided they waited a minimum of twelve hours to confirm that the body was indeed unclaimed.[18] By introducing the Anatomy Act in anticipation of the medical school's needs, rather than in response, the colonial government avoided the emergence of a body-snatching trade. On paper, at least, the procurement of cadavers was regulated.[19]

The Anatomy Act functioned primarily to benefit the Melbourne Medical School, which opened in 1862, and other licensed anatomy venues, by enabling them to receive lawfully the requisite supply of cadavers for students to perform dissections. The legislation attempted to mitigate moral panic over dead bodies being snatched and traded in moonlit, backdoor deals. It did not, however, protect the most vulnerable members of society. Soon after the Victorian parliament passed the Anatomy Act, it also brought into effect the Electoral

Act, which disenfranchised 'any person ... receiving relief as an inmate of any eleemosynary [charity] or charitable institution'.[20] Without being able to vote to prevent the legislation passing into law, the poor effectively had no say in the disposal of their bodies. It is little surprise that the main source of subjects in Victoria was the unclaimed bodies of the friendless poor left in hospitals, benevolent asylums and lunatic asylums. The implementation of the Anatomy Act imbued the corpse with new significance. Where it had once been a subject at the centre of trained anatomists' explorations of the bodily interior, the Act legitimized its place as an integral part of medical students' education. This shift in utility and value did not, however, alleviate the public's concern over how their bodies would be treated after death.

While few doubted that doctors and medical students needed to look to the body's interior to understand human anatomy, the long-standing association between dissection and punishment for criminality meant that many members of the public found the notion of their own body being dissected entirely disagreeable. It was incompatible with contemporary death and burial ideals, and now it unfairly targeted those living in poverty. Although the poor in the post-goldrush slums of late-nineteenth-century Melbourne were not pushed into workhouses as they were in England, they were still subject to similar poverty politics, which considered the contribution of one's body to medical advancement in utilitarian terms as the repayment of debt for the moral and pecuniary burden one had imposed on society during life. As Ruth Richardson argues eloquently in her influential work *Death, Dissection and the Destitute*, where dissection had once been a punishment for criminality, it was now also a punishment for poverty.[21]

In reality, colonial anatomy acts did little to quell the public's fear of the anatomist's work with the dead body – and with good reason. Amid a climate already characterized by historical tensions between anatomists and the public inherited from Britain, several objectionable incidents involving prominent anatomists further heightened the distrust of anatomists' work with dead bodies. For instance, in 1892 Dr James Thomas Wilson faced scrutiny for removing the bones 'of a Chinaman' from the post-mortem room of Sydney's Prince Alfred Hospital during his work as pathologist to the hospital.[22] Originally from Dumfriesshire, Scotland, Wilson had arrived in Sydney in 1886, having trained under famed anatomist William Turner, and been a demonstrator at the prestigious anatomy department at the University of Edinburgh from 1885 to 1886. Faced with threats of exposure from a disgruntled hospital worker, Wilson defended his actions to the Chancellor of the University of Sydney, where he was appointed Professor of Anatomy in 1890. Wilson detailed what he considered to be his gentle treatment of what remained of the body after he removed the skeleton, and noted that he had 'carefully left [the man's face] intact' so that the man's friends could view the body before burial.[23] Wilson added that he had 'always taken extreme precautions against publicity and consequent scandal', suggesting that in his prominent position, he was well aware of the disparity between what the public and the medical profession viewed as a proper way to treat dead bodies.[24]

In another serious incident, William Ramsay Smith, who had been appointed the Adelaide City Coroner and South Australian Inspector of Anatomy in 1899, was accused in 1903 of treating bodies indecently over the course of his coronial work. Reports state that Smith shot and stabbed dead bodies in the morgue to see the effects of weapons on the body – acts that blurred the lines between undertaking a dissection (an act intended to explore the body's anatomy) and an autopsy (an act intended to determine the cause of death).[25] Smith also faced charges of illegally retaining heads and other body parts from subjects that should have been buried on consecrated ground.[26] Smith fervently defended himself against the accusations, which he believed constituted a 'deliberate perversion of the facts' intended to 'insult and damage' his reputation.[27] After a lengthy investigation, which included the examination of twenty-five witnesses, the court eventually found that Smith had not contravened the somewhat vaguely worded South Australian Anatomy Act, which had been introduced in 1884.[28] He remained the city's coroner, but had to relinquish his hospital duties as a result of the incident.

Despite his vindication, Smith's actions brought the medical profession's treatment of cadavers into the public eye well after legislation had been put in place ostensibly to manage its interactions with corpses. An Adelaide newspaper stated that the 'public have manifested deep interest in the matter', and that they awaited the enquiry into his actions 'with great anxiety'.[29] The threat of these acts becoming exposed to the public was a serious matter that required anatomists to act to preserve their personal integrity, and that of their profession.

Lower-profile incidents also played on social anxieties about dissection. The decency clause in the Victorian Anatomy Act, mandating that after dissection bodies must be encased in a 'decent coffin or shell' and 'decently interred' in consecrated ground, was not always followed. There are recorded cases in which anatomists buried mismatched body parts with other human, or even animal, remains, or left human body parts to be eaten by dogs or burnt on an open fire.[30] A newspaper article published in *The Herald* in January 1895 states that a chaplain at the Melbourne Cemetery 'candidly' admitted that 'bodies after doing service as "subjects" at the medical school' were 'invariably interred without the rites of the church'.[31] In other instances, anatomists retained bodies far longer than the maximum six weeks permitted by the Act; sometimes bodies were simply missing when friends and family arrived to claim them within the twelve hours after death mandated by law.[32] By contravening parts of the Anatomy Act, anatomists opened themselves up to criticism, and the press obliged in publicizing their transgressions. The anatomists and their supporters did their best to affirm a commitment to the respectful treatment of the dead through the same channels, but public concern was not without cause. Despite the distinctly proactive implementation of an Anatomy Act in Australia to regulate the body trade, the colony's medical profession faced a negative public perception akin to that of their counterparts in Britain.

Although supposed contraventions of anatomy acts were met with public condemnation, as was the case for William Ramsay Smith, or even riots, as in the case from Aberdeen, there were rarely legal repercussions. Not only was it impossible for the inspectors of anatomy to keep an eye on every licensed anatomy venue, but the self-satisfying, tight-lipped nature of the elitist anatomy fraternity was also seemingly impervious to even the perception that they could be punished. On occasions when the public did call for inquiries into potential breaches of an anatomy act, anatomists in the British Empire engaged in 'professional non-cooperation' until the issue subsided.[33] The impunity with which the anatomists flouted the ambiguously worded anatomy acts only augmented the powerlessness of the poor.

Australian anatomists working in the late nineteenth and early twentieth centuries procured cadavers amid inherited traditions and anxieties stoked by new causes for public concern over their work. While the colonies of Victoria, New South Wales and South Australia introduced Anatomy Acts in this era as a measure to regulate the trade in dead bodies before it entered into the hands of resurrection men, as in Britain, the public bemoaned the fact that it overtly targeted the impoverished, and that anatomists repeatedly failed to comply with its conditions. Anatomical science and its practitioners, the anatomists, were therefore 'regularly at the centre of scandal and dispute'.[34] So, too, was the space in which most dealings with the dead occurred: the medical school.

## The Melbourne Medical School

Little fanfare accompanied the opening of the Melbourne Medical School in 1862. As the first medical school in colonial Australia to teach students, it was to be the crowning jewel of the University of Melbourne, which itself had only been established nine years earlier. But, following protracted debates over its cost and viability, the medical school came into existence with only the bare bones of the infrastructure, equipment and staff needed to function. There were no complete buildings until 1884, so the school's first professor, George Britton Halford, held dissection classes in a converted stable in the backyard of his house until a more appropriate location became available.[35] Three inaugural students enrolled in the course consisting of classes in general anatomy, physiology, pathology, *materia medica*, Latin, Greek and chemistry, as well as dissection in the second and third years.

Forming a medical school in a colonial city was no easy feat and the initial staff faced significant challenges. During the establishment phase, the Chancellor of the University, Redmond Barry, sought the advice of prominent English anatomists Richard Owen and James Paget regarding how to develop a curriculum that would provide students with the best medical education possible.[36] The pair had also endorsed Halford as professor, with Paget stating he was 'one of the most distinguished experimental physiologists of his day' and 'his name would give distinction to any University'.[37]

The original medical programme was five years long, compared to shorter four-year courses on offer at prestigious schools in London and Edinburgh. Students complained that the course was expensive, too long and too literary, with one student labelling it a 'weakly little curriculum prematurely born'.[38] They wanted 'more instruction in diagnoses, in operations, in fact, in the great mass of knowledge that comes not from books, but can only be gained from the wards'.[39] The first year contained almost no practical work, instead including subjects like Greek, Latin and Natural Philosophy, which most students detested. It was only in the second, third and fourth years that students began to study anatomy and take up what little clinical experience was on offer in the city's hospitals. The opportunity to gain clinical experience was among the most acclaimed features of medical courses in Britain during this era, so it is unsurprising that students wanted to receive the level of education they admired from afar. Compared to overseas offerings, the Melbourne Medical School course was lambasted as 'splendid in theory, but lamentably lacking in practice'.[40] Despite the medical school's youth and initial difficulties, however, in the decade that followed the number of students increased steadily.

In the early days of dissection classes, the Melbourne Medical School relied almost exclusively on the Melbourne Hospital for cadavers.[41] Halford arranged for a fee of £2 to be paid per subject to cover the expense of transporting the body to the medical school and the subsequent burial of the remains.[42] Historians who have skilfully pieced together the histories of those dissected in Australia and Britain note that dissection subjects were mostly adult, male, of low social standing and had often succumbed to respiratory diseases like tuberculosis and pneumonia. People of this demographic were well-represented in the Melbourne population – in the benevolent asylums in particular – owing, in part, to the gold rush of the mid-nineteenth century.[43] It is worth remembering that each cadaver that ended up on the anatomist's table represented a human being who lived within a social and cultural context that placed value on their body in a specific, medicalized manner.

Tensions emerged at times between the hospital and the university, and like the British Anatomy Act, the Victorian Anatomy Act did not specify the institutions from which corpses should be procured. This lack of detail meant that no institution was compelled to hand over the unclaimed dead. There was also a provision in the Act that if a person 'expressed … desire either in writing at any time during his life or verbally in the presence of two or more witnesses', anatomists would not be permitted to retain or dissect their body.[44] In the pervading atmosphere of suspicion and fear over the medical profession's treatment of dead bodies, the task of procuring cadavers for teaching and learning amid a growing cohort of students presented a considerable challenge from the outset.

Ambiguity over where anatomists should obtain bodies, an opt-out system and the occasional lack of cooperation from the hospital led medical students to complain about an 'insufficient and intermittent' supply of cadavers, which impeded their ability to dissect and learn from the body itself.[45] Sensing this problem, Halford sought a solution. He wrote to the committee of the Melbourne Benevolent Asylum – which was home to some of the city's most impoverished – numerous times between 1869 and 1873 to request that the unclaimed bodies of residents be channelled to the medical school.[46] Halford acknowledged that the request 'may be repulsive' to the asylum's staff, but expressed fear that the medical school would have to close if the dearth of dissection subjects continued.[47]

At first, the committee acquiesced to Halford's requests so long as his work was done 'without wounding the feelings of any person living'.[48] Not long after the committee's decision, however, the asylum residents expressed their strong opposition to having their bodies used for anatomical purposes after death. So vociferous was their resistance that the committee of the Benevolent Asylum could not ignore them. *The Argus* newspaper reported in August 1869 that 402 residents petitioned against the resolution, stating that they 'felt that their last moments would be made more painful by their minds dwelling on the horrible and repulsive uses to which their remains might be subjected'.[49] One committee member, Mr Wild, reflected that the asylum could hardly call itself a well-managed charitable institution if it 'disregarded the feelings of the inmates in such a matter'.[50] Several letters to the editor of *The Argus* similarly expressed public condemnation of the idea that the bodies of the poor and infirm could be claimed and dissected by the medical school, and of the heartless manner in which the medical school had asked for the bodies.[51] Some residents even stated that they would rather leave the asylum and take their chances on the streets than risk the prospect of being cut open after death by anatomists and medical students.[52] Siding with the residents, the committee rescinded the resolution and continued to deny Halford's appeals for bodies for the next decade.

Despite an anatomy law specifically designed to provide bodies to the new medical school, staff struggled to obtain a sufficient supply of cadavers for medical students. There were apparently no bodies in 1887, and what students described as a 'subject-famine' continued into 1888.[53] According to students, in 1894 there were as few as 'four bodies for one hundred men' and a subsequent 'prevailing depression … invaded the dissection room'.[54] Students paid 4 pounds and 4 shillings – a significant sum for students – for the opportunity to dissect a whole body during the winter months, but in many cases did not receive what they paid for.[55] One student reflected that 'if only two parts, double-handed at that, can be given to each student, it is not honest to charge for a whole body to himself'.[56] In this situation, students would have been lucky to see a cadaver at all, let alone gain hands-on experience dissecting – and without this experience students would be at a disadvantage when they sat examinations that questioned their knowledge of body parts that they had not seen or dissected. The problem was exacerbated when women were permitted to enter the course in 1887. For reasons of decency, female students performed dissections in separate rooms to the men. Simply due to their smaller number, the women had a greater opportunity to dissect, often with a subject to share between just three students.[57]

As medical student numbers increased in the 1880s, the university council finally granted the medical school the buildings and equipment it needed to function efficiently, and to continue to attract new students. The new medical school building (originally called the Anatomy Building, then the Old Pathology Building, and now the Elisabeth Murdoch Building) was completed and opened for classes in 1885. Despite the many difficulties in acquiring a sufficient supply of cadavers, when bodies were obtained, they were taken to the dissecting room, which lay behind the striking bluestone and red brick façade of the new medical school, alongside laboratory spaces and a lecture theatre.

## The dissecting room

In the nineteenth century, the medical school dissecting room emerged as a critical site for an evolving understanding of the human body in Australia. Here, students learnt about human anatomy, and gained the practical and emotional skills needed to dissect the human body.

Popular press from the era often depicted the dissecting room as an unregulated, fear-inducing space of horror. The existence of bodies floating in tanks of methylated spirits was 'well known' to the men lodging at the Melbourne Immigrants' Home, and speculative talk emerged of 'cellars where sightless eyes stare up from the cavernous depths below, and outlines of legs and arms, and occasionally a human trunk, which float round in a confused mass'.[58] While these accounts may be more reminiscent of an imaginative shilling shocker than reality, they demonstrate how the dissecting room was described to the public in late-nineteenth-century Melbourne. Faced with such images, it is little wonder they feared what went on behind the closed doors of the dissecting room.

In reality, the layout and activity that occurred inside the dissecting room was somewhat less lurid than these popular depictions. Contemporary architectural plans and written accounts tell us that the dissecting room in the new medical school building was around fifteen by eight metres, with six-metre-high walls. It was well-lit through tall, south-facing windows, which also ensured that a breeze could enter the room. A staircase entry at the back of the building serviced the room, so that bodies arriving at the university did not need to be carried through multiple rooms or the front entrance to their destination.

A group of unnamed visitors to the dissecting room in 1864 reported that it was 'certainly the noblest dissecting room' they had ever seen, and that if only the anatomical diagrams were removed from the walls it could be taken for a ballroom.[59] Years later, in 1887, following significant building improvements, a student even noted that the room's 'light and airy appearance' meant that one was 'almost prepared to see the corpse on the table smile'.[60] While the public perceived the dissecting room as a gothic space full of suspicious activity, the students and staff at the medical school considered it a place where they could conduct their necessary educational work with the dead out of sight.

## The anatomists

Throughout the course of study at the Melbourne Medical School in the late nineteenth and early twentieth centuries, students undertook what one of their own described in 1887 as a 'systematic training of the senses' – learning how to see, listen and speak in a medical manner.[61] They attended lectures that exposed them to the medical and anatomical language of disease, symptoms, biology and surgical techniques.[62] Under what has been termed the medical, or clinical, gaze, patients became knowable bodies, disease became a series of symptoms and students learnt to interpret health, illness and the body according to the social and cultural norms that are distinctive to the medical profession.

It was students' participation in dissection classes, however, that brought them into contact with the human body, enabling them to learn both the practical and emotional skills necessary to become a physician. In this setting, students became acculturated to the medical gaze; they learnt to suppress or suspend many of the normal psychological and physical reactions experienced when dissecting a cadaver, such as revulsion, anxiety and guilt. The act of dissection was a rite of passage for those wishing to enter the medical profession, and it played a significant role in students' socialization.[63] While there undoubtedly positive, constructive elements of dissection, nowhere did the behaviour of medical students arouse the public's concern more than in the context of their actions towards cadavers in the dissecting room.

Despite the long history of dissection in medical schools, when students stepped up to the table, they often lacked sufficient knowledge, skills and guidance in how to undertake the task. Historian Rachel N. Ponce provides evidence that students in early-nineteenth-century North America regularly made 'false starts' when dissecting; they made a cut in the wrong place or with an incorrect technique.[64] To make matters worse, students often had only blunt scalpels and dull knives with which to work. Supervision of the dissecting room was also inadequate, so students did not always know what to do or how to behave when confronted with the difficult task of cutting open the body of a recently deceased human being. Similar issues existed at the Melbourne Medical School, where one student recounted having to work with 'faulty appliances' of an inferior quality to those available commercially.[65] In one recorded instance, 'the first plunge of [a student's] knife went straight through the sternum', and in another, 'the first cut of the saw took the calvarium [the upper portion of the skull] almost completely off'.[66] These examples suggest that, despite published dissection guides, such as Cunningham's *Manual of Practical Anatomy*, being regularly available, many student dissections were, as Ponce writes, 'more akin to butchery than artistry'.[67]

The dissection experience of late-nineteenth-century Australian medical schools was not only characterized by students' lack of practical skills, but was also punctuated by episodes of poor behaviour and alarming attitudes towards the corpse. During this era, much of the public viewed medical students in a poor light. Contemporary newspapers contained reports of medical students engaging in riotous conduct, being arrested for drunken behaviour, vulgarity and displaying contempt for authority.[68] For instance, *The Argus* reported an incident in August 1888 in which 200 students arrived at the Melbourne Exhibition Building, dressed in cap and gown, to carry out a practical joke during a concert. The students held aloft a banner emblazoned with their well-known emblem of the skull and crossbones and carried with them 'about 30 femurs, or thigh bones, vouched for as human', but of origins unknown.[69] The 'youthful Galens' sang as they marched through the building until a 'collision with the police' resulted in the destruction of two chairs and a table, as well as the threat of prosecution.[70] The students displayed their penchant for mischief again the following year when they disrupted a public performance of *Hamlet*. They reportedly sang loudly, 'with the time marked by the beating of long thigh bones with skulls swaying pendulum-wise'.[71] While some audience members thought their 'exuberance of youth' endearing, others were less amused.[72] News reports about the poor behaviour of medical students, coupled with the suspicion that already surrounded the work of anatomists with dead bodies at the medical school, compounded the negative public perception under which they laboured.

Colonial Australian medical students appear to have inherited part of their poor public perception from their British contemporaries. British medical students were commonly depicted in nineteenth-century popular fiction and satirical periodicals as boorish, ignorant and frequently drunk. For example, a series of articles in *Punch* portrays London medical students as 'a dissipated and irreligious set of young men' with an assortment of unappealing traits.[73] Scholars also point to Charles Dickens' novel *The Pickwick Papers*, with its unattractive characterization of the two fictional medical students as 'slovenly' and 'mildewy', as a salient example of the depictions that permeated the popular imagination.[74] Historian Keir Waddington argues that London medical students came to embody the anxieties and proclivity for vice that accompanied the city's growing urbanism in the mid-nineteenth century.[75] While many Australian colonial medical students brought negative attention upon themselves through their behaviour, the parallels between public perceptions of medical students in Britain and the far-flung colony suggest that the Australian public shared many of these social anxieties.

The medical school worked hard to promote a positive image of its students and their actions, despite such antics and disturbing rumours about dissecting room behaviour. Richard Berry, who was Professor of Anatomy between 1905 and 1929, told *The Argus* in 1907 that the 'conduct of students in dissecting rooms ... is most orderly'. He resented the public's 'foolish fallacy' that medical students were 'filled with levity' while dissecting and commented that their work was so neat that it 'could well be performed in a drawing room'.[76] Berry's remarks concur with several staged photographs of the dissecting room in late-nineteenth-century photographs, which depict small numbers of students standing around a neatly-posed dissection subject (see Figure 2). These photographs present the scene that the medical school wished to project to the public, rather than spontaneous insight into dissecting activity.

While some dissecting classes may have mirrored the scene depicted in the staged photograph, reports of a poor learning environment in *Speculum*, the journal of the Melbourne Medical Students' Society (MSS), demonstrate a culture of behaviour more aligned with the public's sentiment towards the medical school and its inhabitants. There are accounts of disorderly 'meat fights' in which 'students sometimes threw at each other bits and pieces' of decaying, cadaverous flesh, as one student later recalled.[77] Another student, writing in *Speculum*, told

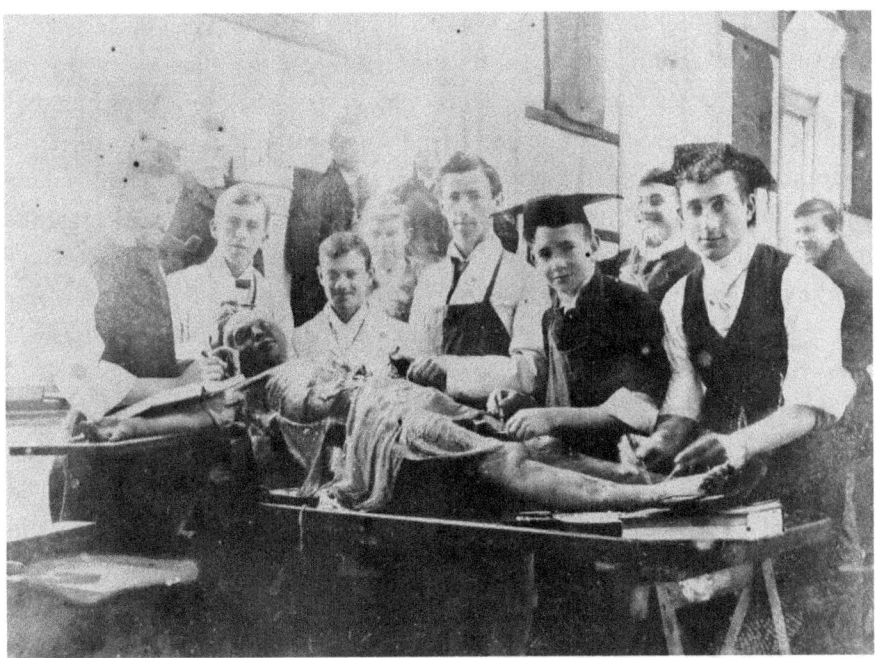

**Figure 2** Early dissection class, with Richard Joseph Bull, MHM 00422. Image courtesy of the Medical History Museum, Faculty of Medicine, Dentistry and Health Sciences, University of Melbourne. Copyright © The University of Melbourne 2022.

of 'almost being "knocked out" by a large and heavy deltoid muscle thrown the whole length of the room'.[78] Sometimes a student might have pocketed a femur or a pelvis to complement their own sets of bones at home, and in the dissecting room, a suggested remedy for cleaning up the cadaver's post-mortem expulsion of fluids was simply to 'mop up the superfluous moisture' with the tassels of their hats or the hems of their gowns.[79] Episodes of pranks and crude behaviour hardly present a scene of decorum or focused learning, and instead harken back to the colourful images found in *Punch*, *Melbourne Punch* and other satirical works of the nineteenth century.

These unfavourable views of medical students are reflected in historical scholarship, where damning stories and characterizations are frequently repeated.[80] That said, the actual lived experiences of medical students, particularly their engagements with dissection subjects, have proved difficult to recover from the historical record. Despite this difficulty, recent studies have shed light on the experiences of British, Irish and North American medical students from the late eighteenth to mid-twentieth centuries, analysing their attitudes towards learning, their beliefs about their role in society and their conduct in the dissecting room. In her study of British medical students, Hurren portrays dissection as rather monotonous work, involving long hours labouring over a cadaver while inhaling tobacco and snuff to alleviate the unappealing odours and noxious fumes emitted by the decaying corpse and preservative fluids.[81] Michael Sappol presents a more lively scene regarding North American dissecting rooms, one that includes tales of smoking, joking, 'alcoholic jollity' and acts of initiation.[82] Adding to this discussion, Laura Kelly suggests that the morbid humour in dissecting room episodes such as those described above can be thought of not simply as unruly or apathetic behaviour, but as a way of coping with the emotional difficulties students experienced in what was an overwhelmingly homosocial environment.[83]

Medical students' voices have often been relegated in favour of the version of history told from the perspective of those in power. They were not silent, however, with their voices recorded in the pages of *Speculum*. First published in July 1884, the journal aimed to bring 'students of all years into contact, and to foster a kindly feeling' within the student body.[84] As the journal's inaugural editor, H. R. Salmon, declared in the first issue, students intended that *Speculum* would 'reflect ideas of the Melbourne medical student among his fellows'. They also hoped it would 'imbue … the public mind with a totally different opinion of medical students to what ha[d] been its wont in the past'.[85] The journal boasted a wide readership among Melbourne Medical School students; in 1898, there were already seventy-seven paid-up subscribers. *Speculum* also claimed a 'large circulation among Medical Men in and around Melbourne and throughout the Commonwealth', and a reciprocal relationship between it and the *Australian Medical Gazette* ensured student voices gained exposure in the wider profession.[86] Although the Melbourne Medical School faculty maintained the power to discipline, and even remove, members of the editorial committee who had been voted in by their peers, the medical school supported the publication in essence and in finance. It was the students, however, who brought it to life through submissions that ranged from reports of the latest meetings of influential members of the medical sphere to creative writing, and from complaints about the curriculum to advertisements for the society's social events.

## Cadaver poems

Before the introduction of formaldehyde as a preservative in 1893 prevented cadavers from succumbing to quick decay, the dissection room was an especially unappealing place, light on air and heavy with tension. In this space, Melbourne Medical School students learnt to develop what famed Scottish anatomist-surgeon William Hunter called the 'kind of necessary inhumanity' needed to dissect.[87] Despite students' acculturation to the medical gaze, poems about cadavers they published in *Speculum* reveal that they contended emotionally with this difficult undertaking. They felt anxiety, fear and, at times, great empathy for their dissection subjects, and projected this wide spectrum of emotions, imagined identities and narratives onto the corpse through their writing.

Student-written cadaver poems featuring fictional encounters with corpses provide a window through which to examine students' affective responses to their experiences of dissection. By the late nineteenth century, there existed a strong tradition of creative writing within the medical school milieu in the British Empire.[88] Much of this writing explored both the social anxieties and practical difficulties students faced during their medical education, and during dissection classes in particular. Student authors drew on tropes and themes of contemporary gothic fiction, such as vengeful corpses, malefic spirits and degenerate doctors, to explore the anxieties and unresolved tensions they faced during dissection, as well as the contentious aspects of the medical profession that they would soon enter. These tropes are more than just literary devices. Fictional encounters with apparitions were grounded in doctors' roles in determining the boundaries of life and death, and the concerns they held over their work with human remains.

The living and the dead in the late nineteenth and early twentieth centuries were entangled; anatomy was, in the words of historian Fay Bound Alberti, 'not merely a biomedical discipline, but also a philosophical endeavour'.[89]

One illustrative example is the 1889 cadaver poem, 'A Night in the Dissecting Room', written under the pseudonym 'Femur' that depicts an episode in which several cadaverous dissection subjects come back to life to seek revenge on a medical student. In the poem, the student character finds himself unexpectedly locked in the dissecting room for the night, when the spirits of five dissection subjects 'rise and waken' to take part in a 'swelling chorus'.[90] They recount the turn of events that led to their deaths, before the Chief Spirit directs them to 'fling away [their] sadness' and join together in a lively dance. As the spirits embark on a furious waltz around the room, they stumble upon their visitor who, until this point, has been hiding. Upon recognizing the visitor as a student, they proclaim that 'to men [they] are vicious … But to students most malicious', and begin to inflict upon him the suffering they themselves had endured. One spirit pronounces:

> And, for once about me joking,
>    (I was far too stout to please you),
> In my side your finger poking,
>    By the snout I now will seize you.[91]

The student is saved from further suffering when a chirping bird signalling dawn causes the spirits to flee.

The student in the poem is terrorized by the cadaver he had left 'dissected on the table/In the piercing winter weather'. The spirits inflict physical torment on him – grabbing him by the nose, then binding him 'quickly to the earth' as they prepare to dissect him alive. Murderous spirits of the student's own making have come back to harm him in retribution for his past actions towards their bodies. He must come to terms with these monstrous, vengeful creations, much like Victor Frankenstein's confrontation with his monster in Mary Shelley's iconic novel about the struggle between life and death – allegory for an anatomist's battle with the power and responsibility that comes with their work. In addition to his fear of the cadaver's reanimation, the author was also likely reflecting on the dangers, particularly of contagion, that the dead body presented to the living during dissection. As depicted in Figure 2, students in late-nineteenth- and early-twentieth-century dissecting rooms did not wear gloves or other protective equipment. They were, therefore, directly exposed to the putrefying corpse and any fluids that it may have expelled, as well as errant scalpel blades.[92]

This interpretation of the spectral cadaver in the poem as a representation of medical students' fear of the dissection process and the cadaver itself reveals something about how students felt about engaging with the social afterlife of the deceased body.

'A Night in the Dissecting Room' provides insights into the genuine anxieties grounded in historical reality held by medical students, and also reflects the struggle they faced coming to terms with their future responsibilities as arbiters of life and death. In the late nineteenth and early twentieth centuries, not only did doctors have little knowledge about the scientific mechanisms behind cell death, brain death and organ failure, but hurried mass burials during outbreaks of infectious diseases like cholera led people to fear being buried alive while in a minimally conscious state.[93] The circulation of published manuals of resuscitation techniques and common methods to confirm death reflect this apprehension. By the nineteenth century, such methods had been in use for centuries. Family and friends of the deceased usually took part in 'waking', or watching the presumably deceased body for several days, to ensure there was no movement. They sometimes pricked the wrists or toes of the apparently dead to check for twitching or blood circulation that might indicate life.[94] In an Australian case from 1866, for instance, a man who was 'to all appearance dead, the body being cold and seemingly stiff' was found to be alive when the undertaker, who had arrived to measure up his coffin, placed 'a looking-glass … to the lips of the supposed corpse' and saw breath emerge from his body.[95]

These measures demonstrate that there was the possibility of 'reawakening' for bodies thought to be deceased, as they do in the cadaver poem, if doctors did not accurately establish the moment of death. Reports in *Speculum* reveal that students knew of and internalized the gravity of the duties that awaited them as physicians.[96] Indeed, in an article published in December 1901, one student shared his thoughts about the 'frightful responsibilities' and 'unutterable importance of forcible and definite attention to the serious nature of the task' that lay before him and his peers.[97] The cadaver poem, therefore, represents another outlet through which students developed cultural meanings of what it meant to be a doctor and engaged with the complex and morally contestable elements of their chosen profession.

Students confronted these fears and concerns about mortality in writing they shared with their peers. The student-written cadaver poem suggests that dissection could also be an uncanny, haunting experience. The spirits represent the reappearance of what the student thought of as 'securely consigned to the past': cadavers that had been dissected and felt aggrieved at his hands.[98] As the spirits haunt the student over his dismemberment of their bodies, he describes the return of forgotten feelings of guilt about his lack of 'words and deeds atoning' for past actions.[99] Although serendipity saves the student from suffering, the encounter prompts him to reflect on the difficulty of his task – to dismember the deceased body of another human being, while maintaining a connection to his humanity.

Cadaver poems also convey how medical students negotiated their need to subvert normal moral behaviours in the dissecting room. In the 1908 cadaver poem 'The Wail of the Wraith', the student character is startled when a dissection subject 'moved its brainless head' and comes back to life while the former is eating lunch in the dissecting room.[100] The wraith '[took] up its tale', describing the way it had been treated by medical students. It recounts:

> They were rude and too familiar when they brought my body in,
> Though I own 'twas cold and formal in the trough of formalin;
> But they put me on this table, and the students came and gazed,
> Then my rigid limbs distended for lithotomy they raised.[101]

The student listens on as the cadaver continues to lament:

> There are other things … things which vex my inmost soul,
> If they must expose my thorax, can't they keep my tissues whole?
> When they'd teased out my spermatic cord, they tossed it in the sink,
> As they've cut my motor oculi, I cannot even wink.[102]

The poem evokes the process by which students became desensitized to a subject's humanity during dissection and began to view it as an object of anatomical knowledge. Bodies that had sometimes only hours earlier been living lay in front of students, exposed on the dissecting slab to be cut open. To impose violence on the body through dissection, students learnt to adopt a medical gaze in which they objectified bodies and considered disease to be a series of symptoms rather than an embodied experience. They needed to see and act in a manner that Melbourne-based surgeon Dr G. A. Syme told students in 1906 was 'different altogether from the principles which regulate the behaviour of ordinary people'.[103] The wraith in the poem bemoans this reality; he conveys that he felt pathetic and undignified due to the insensitive way that students probed, pulled at and exposed his body during dissection. Indeed, the wraith was so aggrieved by his handling that he cried for 'pity at the sight' of his body, and 'tugged at [his] omentum … to draw it as a veil … over all their words and actions'.[104] Through humanizing the cadaver in this manner, the author empathizes with its plight and reflects on the pain and distress that students inflicted on their dissection subjects. Furthermore, the wraith's final request to 'let [him] rest in peace or pieces' suggests the student's unease at the prospect of this corpse not finding solace after death as a result of dissection at his hands. The poem demonstrates that, although students learnt to objectify the corpse in order to undertake dissection, they did not do so without considering the effects of their actions. As such, it presents medical school dissection as an emotionally loaded experience of self-discovery about death, dying and human mortality.[105]

The encounter depicted in 'The Wail of the Wraith' between a medical student and his dissection subject had a profound impact on the student. When the wraith speaks, it takes on human qualities that challenge the student's approach towards the 'anatomical ethics' of the era, which includes the respectful and dignified treatment of human subjects.[106] Inspired by the wraith's lamentation, the student 'took [his] fountain pen in hand, with courage on [his] brow' and signed a pledge to treat cadavers better in the future.[107] Even in death, the cadaver has the ability to affect the student emotionally. As such, the poem demonstrates the cadaver's crucial cultural role in medical students' development of a moral code within a medical culture required the corpse to be objectified.

The author of the poem was likely influenced to reflect on his treatment of the corpse by ideals imparted to him during his education. In the early twentieth century, the Melbourne Medical School went to great lengths to ensure that students learnt about the professional conduct and ethics that would help them on their journeys into medical careers. Students took part in practices of moral enculturation, such as attending lectures and presentations, where they began to appreciate the medical profession's normative behaviours and mores. For example, in the aforementioned address to students about medical ethics in 1906, Dr Syme emphasized the need for the next generation of physicians to 'practise an art' rather than 'drive a trade', and to demonstrate good etiquette at all times.[108] In another lecture, titled 'Our Duties and Responsibilities', Dr P. W. Farmer reminded his students that their 'influence for good or evil [was] very great' and adjured them to 'treat poor patients as if they were the wealthiest in the land, remembering that position is largely a matter of accident'.[109] Farmer continued that 'kindness, politeness, and gentle manners' towards patients were of the utmost importance during professional practice.[110] These guiding words of professors and well-respected medical professionals appeared in the pages of *Speculum*, which ensured that even students who did not attend lectures in person would be able to engage with the ideas presented.

Student voices in the journal echoed their teachers' words about the importance of adhering to a strong moral code in professional endeavours. For instance, in May 1903 the editor of *Speculum* wrote that 'a doctor is not to be regarded as a mere concocter of prescriptions, and a surgeon is not a man who uses a scalpel only'.[111] He encouraged his peers to treat patients as people, not 'as pathological specimens pure and simple'.[112] These sentiments show that medical students thought deeply about their conduct throughout their time at medical school, and expressed their ideas to others in their cohort as part of their socialization as doctors.

There is no doubt that due to the difficulty and physical dangers it presented, dissection was a formative experience for student doctors – one that stayed with them for the rest of their lives. It also harboured an emotional effect that has often been overlooked in historical literature about medical education. While conversations students may have had in person about these matters are lost, their creative, insightful writings in the pages of *Speculum* show that they reflected on their role in correctly diagnosing death, their fear of the dissection subject and their anxiety over how to objectify and humanize the body simultaneously. The cadaver poem can, therefore, be considered as another form of literary text in which the worlds of popular culture and science meet. Amid humorous elements and gothic overtones, the poems reveal that the dissecting room was a site of deep tension and reflection.

By moving away from a dominant medical discourse of dissection to one that incorporates its cultural elements, the cadaver can be conceived of as more than a functional material object that students dissected as a medical school rite of passage. The dead body did not simply lose its ability to affect the living. Rather, it was an entity that evoked strong and varied emotional responses in the students who encountered it. Although the title *Speculum* appears to be a tongue-in-cheek choice at a time when all medical students were male, the journal's full motto encourages readers to 'look into the lives of all men as into a mirror, and thence to take example'.[113] The speculum, then, signifies a mirror with which students are encouraged to reflect on the humanity and dignity of those they dissect and treat, as well as their own. Such a message is fitting when considering the rich vein of insight it provides into students' emotional responses to dissection.

\* \* \*

By the late nineteenth century, a culture of anatomy was well established in Australia. Anatomists worked with cadavers in a cultural climate of inherited traditions that valued the corpse, entangled with local distinctions and tensions. The introduction of anatomy acts and other regulations consolidated the relationship between the collected cadaver and medical education, but exacerbated social anxieties about the treatment of cadavers, specimen collecting and the medical profession's growing authority over bodies. The next chapter moves beyond the body as a whole to consider the cultural history of the collected body in parts.

2

# From patient to specimen: Collectors and networks

To Melbourne Medical School students and staff, the skeleton displaying hydrocephalus in the wooden case has become a familiar presence. Positioned near the entrance of the anatomy and pathology museum, it is in full view of any visitor who walks through the space. Upon close inspection of the articulated bones, which are held in place by screws and bolts, a small clasp allows the hinged skull to be opened to reveal the enlarged inner cavity that characterizes hydrocephalus (see Figure 3). Upon even closer inspection, the skull contains many cracks where pieces of bone have been glued and pinned back together. How the skull came to be cracked and in need of repair constitutes one part of the skeleton's journey from patient to museum specimen. So, too, do the social and interpersonal dynamics that led to the specimen's collection and placement in the anatomy and pathology museum. These aspects of the hydrocephalus skeleton's history remain overlooked despite its long residency and familiarity to those who frequent the museum today.

When Dr Archibald Watson retained the patient's skeleton in 1907, he fashioned the human body into a divisible, dehumanized object that could be transported across the country, from its original location in Adelaide to Professor Harry Brookes Allen at the anatomy and pathology museum at the Melbourne Medical School. These traceable movements reveal Watson's and Allen's motivations for collecting human remains. They also provide insight into the way in which the anatomists' acquisition of the skeleton erased the patient's identity and replaced it with a new set of values that were regarded highly within the medical profession.

Collecting biomedical specimens in the nineteenth and early twentieth centuries was a collaborative venture. It involved many hands, each with different roles, skills and contributions. The hydrocephalus skeleton is one of thousands

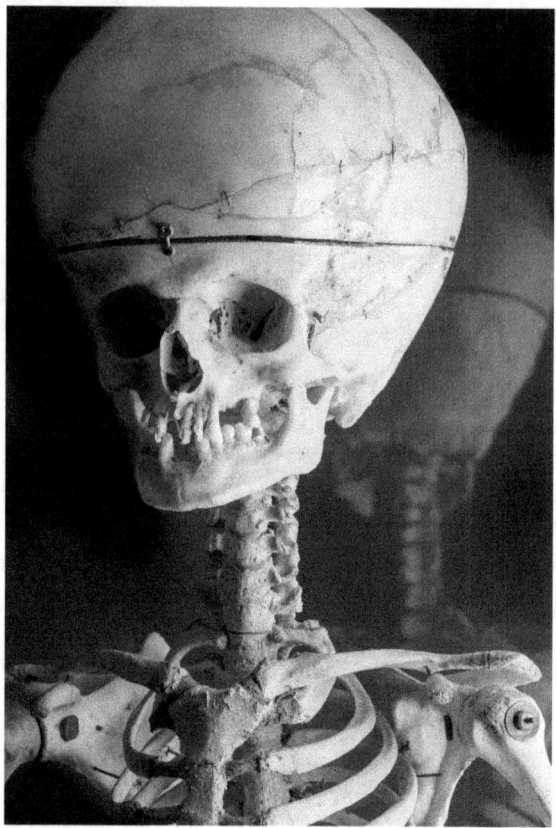

**Figure 3** Hydrocephalus specimen, showing cracks in the enlarged cranium, 531-008101, Harry Brookes Allen Museum of Anatomy and Pathology, University of Melbourne. Photograph by Gavan Mitchell.
(This image may not be copied, reproduced or distributed in any way unless authorized by the Curator, Harry Brookes Allen Museum of Anatomy and Pathology, the University of Melbourne.)

of specimens in the Harry Brookes Allen Museum of Anatomy and Pathology that underline the fact that 'collecting did not begin in the museum'; instead, the museum is often the end point of an object's journey.[1] How was the human body transformed in parts, from patient to objectified museum specimen? What characterized the network of collectors who rendered the diseased dead into parts? And what motivated collectors to do so? By focusing on the interactions between people and objects, collectors and the collected, I aim to reach a renewed understanding of the values with which medical professionals in Australia imbued the collected human body, and the position of human specimen collecting in the broader collecting dynamic of the nineteenth century.

## Nineteenth-century collecting activity

The 'splendidly capacious and well-lit' museum containing thousands of specimens at the University of Melbourne was not the work of any one individual.[2] Though now named in honour of Sir Harry Brookes Allen, the museum was created by a network of collectors and museum preparators, each inspired to contribute to the museum for varied reasons.

Collecting in this era was encyclopaedic in its scope, and was pursued in a particularly vigorous way in the field of natural history. Collecting often formed part of imperial expeditions in what were considered exotic places, and frequently involved the dispossession and exploitation of native peoples in colonized lands.[3] Collectors embarked on vast journeys and faced significant challenges when collecting and transporting materials susceptible to decomposition and damage, such as skin, flesh and fur, over long distances. The development of effective and widespread methods by which to fashion specimens into stable forms that could be easily transported was a catalyst for a more thriving natural history trade in Australia and abroad.[4] The Australian anatomy and pathology collecting network was plagued by similar issues concerning preservation, as discussed below.

Some collectors in this era turned their work into a profession, but many were amateur, lay members of the public. Until the mid-1800s, amateur collecting was a respectable activity. It was undertaken largely by the middle class as a leisurely exercise in self-improvement, and as a way to contribute altruistically to the burgeoning field of scientific knowledge.[5] Prominent collectors, like Victorian Government Botanist and director of Melbourne's Botanic Gardens Ferdinand von Mueller, sometimes placed newspaper advertisements asking interested members of the public to collect on their behalf.[6] Other collectors lodged specimens of all kinds with passengers and transport crew for journeys to distant destinations.[7] In the context of the anatomy and pathology collecting network, however, the distinctions between amateur and paid collectors are blurred.

In the last twenty years, historians of medicine and science have begun to examine the dynamic interpersonal webs that enabled objects and knowledge to circulate locally and globally.[8] Networks could be complex; they were not often solely a matter of centre and periphery, as was commonly argued in mid- to late-twentieth-century scholarship on spatial connections in the British Empire.[9] Instead, collecting networks were vibrant systems which facilitated the exchange of materials and ideas, and involved people and places around which power formed and dispersed at distinct times. This shift in focus and methodology gave rise to studies that use archival and museum documentation to consider the complex dynamics and relational aspects of nineteenth-century collecting and museum collections.

Collectors do not always leave traces of their work, but this chapter pieces together extant correspondence between doctors, museum catalogues, and medical journals to reveal the network that centred around the Melbourne Medical School. I analyse the network's relational nature and discuss the motivations behind collectors' decisions to collect, within an episteme characterized by a will to collect specimens from the natural world to generate new knowledge. As there are undoubtedly many undocumented interactions between collectors and curators, these sources do not provide a complete picture of human specimen collecting in this era of Australian history. They do, however, allow us to shift away from thinking of collectors and the objects they collected as separate poles, to consider instead the 'biographical possibilities' of them both.[10] This approach reconfigures our understanding of activity in Australia to collect human body parts and fashion them into specimens on two fronts: first, by characterizing it as a relational project carried out between a set of interconnected collectors, albeit with significant distinctions from natural history collecting, and, second, by identifying the motivations behind collecting to reveal the shifting values of human bodies within the medical profession and public sphere.

Because my focus is the collecting network during Allen's tenure as Professor of Anatomy, I do not discuss material the museum acquired under the leadership of his successor, Richard Berry. Similarly, I do not refer to collections of skeletal remains, mainly of Aboriginal origin, amassed for purposes of comparative anatomy and anthropology, which are discussed in Chapter 6.

## Harry Brookes Allen and the collecting network

The network within which collectors amassed specimens was centred around Harry Brookes Allen, Professor of Anatomy and Pathology at the Melbourne Medical School and curator of the anatomy and pathology museum. Born in Geelong in 1854, Allen studied at the Melbourne Medical School between 1871 and 1876, where he consistently topped the class. Upon finishing his Bachelor of Medicine degree, Allen worked as a demonstrator in anatomy at the university and as a pathologist to Melbourne Hospital. Allen wrote that while working at the hospital, he 'soon found the nucleus of a museum', made up of anatomy and pathology specimens from hospital cases, 'growing under [his] hands'.[11]

Seeing 'no room for its storage and expansion' at the hospital, he suggested the specimen collection be relocated to the medical school, where it would be put to better use.[12] Allen had just become Professor of Anatomy in 1882, and declared it his 'ambition ... to leave hereafter an excellent pathological museum as [his] permanent memorial to the Medical School'.[13] A tall, bearded man, 'stiff and rigid as a ramrod', Allen was known for getting things done. He was described as 'correct, methodical' and 'so irritatingly exact that folk gr[ew] tired of opposing him', that when he set out to make change, he succeeded.[14] It is therefore no surprise that his wish for a museum was granted at the end of 1883, when the collection was transferred by deed of gift to the university.

Those who contributed specimens to the museum were interdependent actors working within the social world of the medical profession. According to his extant written correspondence, Allen received specimens from at least fifty-one individual collectors.[15] The contributors were all staff at medical institutions, and all were male, except for Dr Grace Vale of Ballarat. In most cases, the doctor who performed the surgery or post-mortem examination retained and sent a specimen to the medical school. Many of these contributors may have known Allen personally through attending the same university or moving in the same professional circles. Several medical professional societies emerged in Victoria in the nineteenth century, including the Medical Society of Victoria from 1855 and the Victorian branch of the British Medical Association (BMA) from 1879. Allen was particularly active in the latter organization; he frequently delivered papers of case studies encountered in practice at branch meetings, using collected specimens to illustrate his presentations. Many members of the collecting network were also members of the Victorian Branch of the BMA when they donated specimens to the museum and may have come to know about Allen's museum by attending meetings or through word of mouth among members of the association.

Some collectors, such as Franke Legge, Mark Lidwill and W. L. Mullen, had studied under Allen prior to gaining employment in Swan Hill, Ballarat and the Kew Lunatic Asylum, respectively. Despite his circumspect and somewhat frigid demeanour, Allen gave his students earnest attention and kept track of their careers and endeavours once they had graduated. The familiar tone of their correspondence intimates an existing relationship between a teacher and his former students, and that they respected his position in their common profession. Archibald Watson also wrote to Allen amicably when he sent the hydrocephalus skeleton, referring to Allen as his friend and teacher and noting when they would next meet in person.[16] It appears the trust and shared worldview that doctors developed through face-to-face interactions, in both professional and educational settings, encouraged them to contribute to the collection. The network that formed around these shared values may also have helped maintain a connection to the centre of the profession for collectors who practised in distant locations.

On occasion, a post-mortem room attendant or assistant sent in a specimen on behalf of their superior. There is little evidence in the historical record of the work of these contributors. Their absence speaks to a wider limitation for reconstructing collecting networks; there is often recorded information for wealthy established professional white men in nineteenth- and early-twentieth-century Australia to the exclusion of many others, such as amateur collectors and women, whose stories and contributions are difficult to find.[17]

As many of Allen's professional acquaintances worked in Melbourne, the main source of specimens was the city's major hospitals: the Melbourne Hospital, which had a long-standing relationship with the university; St Vincent's Hospital; the Children's Hospital; and the Women's Hospital. These hospitals were located within a few kilometres of the university, granting specimens easy passage from one institution to the other. The trusting professional relationships that Allen developed with local hospital staff proved instrumental in the formation of the collection. To put their scale and significance into perspective, in 1892 alone, no fewer than 222 specimens came to the anatomy and pathology museum from these hospitals. Although the collecting network was largely centralized around Melbourne, there were important outliers in distant parts of the state of Victoria, elsewhere in the country and even overseas. From the hospital or private practice, the specimens began to move along their trajectories to the museum.

## Transforming patient into specimen

For most specimens the path to the collection began with a patient seeking out the assistance of a physician. Most patients represented in the specimens obtained by the collecting network attended a hospital or private practice in Melbourne; others went to regional Victorian hospitals, and some to hospitals located elsewhere in Australia, and even beyond. As is common, doctors' written records do not include substantial information regarding the identity or biography of the patient from whom a specimen was taken. We do know that patients ranged in age from young children to the elderly. There are also examples of foetuses and stillborn babies, the subjects of Chapter 4.

Physicians retained specimens in their professional capacity – which involved a position of power over patients – during surgeries and post-mortem examinations. As was the norm in Britain, too, there is little to suggest that patients knew a doctor had retained part of their body, or that they granted consent. Nevertheless, medical staff took body parts from patients they encountered in practice, to send to the Melbourne Medical School. This removal began the process of fragmenting the body and dissociating the body part from its original identity and sense of humanity.[18]

With few options for preventing decomposition, doctors lost many specimens that otherwise would have been beneficial to medical students' education. Thomas Shearman Ralph, who procured specimens for the Melbourne Hospital pathology collection from 1859, reported that he faced many difficulties in preserving the material. He noted that 'the decomposition especially during the warmer months … proved injurious to specimens which had been removed'.[19] In Ralph's time at the hospital, and until the introduction of formaldehyde in 1893, biomedical specimens were commonly preserved in spirits or alcohol. This method sometimes had detrimental effects on the body parts; alcohol could have discoloured a specimen or caused it to lose its shape – sometimes to such an extent that it was no longer clear exactly what condition was being displayed.[20] In such a state, specimens had limited educative value and were of little use to the museum.

Improvements in preservation techniques towards the end of the nineteenth century proved crucial in enabling physicians to transform body parts from biological material into useful, educational museum specimens. In 1905, for example, Terang doctor Norman Dowling sent to Allen a specimen of a foetus that he had 'dusted … in Boro Salicylic powder' to 'leave the specimen the same colour etc. as present and at the same time preserve it' until it reached the university.[21] Several other contributors wrote that they had placed specimens in a formalin solution before sending them to Allen.[22] The uptake of new preservation methods that could suspend the decomposition of specimens meant there was less wastage and need for replacement specimens to be procured.

Also imperative to the growth of the collection was an increasing number and expanding distribution of collectors. Medical personnel in the network acted as the eyes, ears and hands of the museum's curator, who simply could not be in every local and distant hospital, post-mortem examination or morgue to lie in wait for interesting specimens. For example, as the Sydney Medical School began to form an anatomy and pathology museum, the curator and Professor of Anatomy J. T. Wilson wrote to a colleague in 1890 that only

'30 per cent of all the specimens which [they] ought to receive' ever reached the university.[23] Potential educational tools and museum exhibits were lost to burial or disposal because he did not have enough collectors to 'prowl about the hospital and other places when specimens are to be had'.[24] Curators like Wilson and Allen relied on collectors with shared values and commitment to the cause to procure and deliver specimens to their respective museums.

It was, however, no easy task to send human body parts around the country. There needed to be appropriate transportation infrastructure and routes between regional practices and the university, and knowledgeable personnel to ensure that preserved specimens could move from their point of departure to their destination.[25] Doctors' correspondence reveals that most specimens destined for the museum arrived by train at Spencer Street Station (now Southern Cross Station), located near the docks of Melbourne. Some packages, like Watson's hydrocephalus skeleton, came to Melbourne by ship before being brought to the train station by a trusted associate. In 1888, Allen made arrangements with transport authorities to facilitate the 'supply of subjects for anatomical examination from country districts'.[26] As part of this arrangement, the Railway Department agreed to 'carry the bodies [from] special sites' to Spencer Street Station, where an undertaker named Gulliver would act as Allen's agent to receive the consignments and bring them to the University.[27] Some contributors gave Allen written warning a few days prior to forwarding a specimen, while others sent specimens 'by the same train' that brought their letter.[28] Although the collecting network was localized largely around the medical school, it relied on sufficient transportation and informed associates working at various locations, particularly for collectors located outside Melbourne.

Even with logistics in place to allow the passage of specimens from hospitals and private practices to the museum, the journeys themselves were often fraught. While retaining body parts was not illegal under the Victorian Anatomy Act, there was still a high level of public suspicion regarding anatomists' work. Collectors like Dr Walter Fowler appreciated the risk that the exposure of a box of morbid anatomy presented. When he sent specimens to the museum, he asked Allen to 'please acknowledge their arrival, for we would be a bit anxious lest they go astray'.[29]

Many members of the network that surrounded the Melbourne Medical School took precautions to ensure the contents of packages would not be revealed to unsuspecting commuters. For instance, the bag containing the hydrocephalus skeleton that Watson sent to Allen was seemingly deliberately mislabelled as 'Personal Effects' of J. S. Kidd.[30] Watson had employed Kidd to 'forward the case intact' to the university once it arrived aboard the SS *Kanowna*.[31] The case was likely thus marked so as not to arouse suspicion during its transportation from Adelaide to Melbourne. The consequence of simply labelling the case with 'hydrocephalus skeleton', or the skeleton being exposed, would have been further public distrust of anatomists and their necessary work with dead bodies and body parts. As two prominent anatomists of the time, Allen and Watson followed procedures for transporting specimens in a manner that would protect their reputations from potentially being tarnished through the revelation of the package's contents. That physicians contributed to the collecting project in spite of these difficulties indicates the value they placed on developing the collection and their commitment to the cause.

## 'The battle of the brains': Public views of a clandestine network

The covert nature of the specimen collecting network centred around the Melbourne Medical School provides stark contrast to natural history collecting networks of the same era. For the most part, specimens of anatomy and pathology that entered the medical school collection had not been bought in shop-front trades or auction houses.[32] The trajectories that specimens took from patient to the anatomy and pathology museum were almost entirely overseen by the medical profession. While some transport workers, undertakers and associates assisted at times, members of the public did not have ready access to patients and body parts, and so were not an integral part of the human specimen collection process.[33]

The public was, however, aware that the specimens existed, mainly due to reports in the press. Well before Allen's tenure at the museum, the public had been exposed to the university's work with human specimens. Such precedents warned specimen collectors of the risk that public exposure presented to their work. For example, in mid-1864, the execution of three convicted murderers in Melbourne set in motion the events that *The Argus* newspaper dubbed 'the battle of the brains'.[34] Melbourne Medical School founder and anatomist George Britton Halford claimed that convicted murderer Christopher Harrison had specially bequeathed to him his body following execution. Halford had assisted Harrison in seeking a lesser sentence by claiming insanity, albeit unsuccessfully, and wanted to study the brain for physical signs of insanity.[35] Despite Halford's claim to the brain, it had in fact been put aside for government doctor John Macadam.

When it emerged that Halford had taken the criminal's brain for examination, a sheriff went to the medical school to reclaim it as the 'Government's brains'.[36] The scene that confronted him involved Halford surrounded by 'a brilliant array of medical and surgical talent', handing the brain around the room and pointing out particular structural elements of interest.[37]

Newspaper reports of this incident evoked strong public reaction over the university's use of body parts. One letter to the editor expressed outrage at the anatomists' quarrel 'over the ghastly heap of dead man's brains', and a poem in *Melbourne Punch* responding to the incident quipped that regardless of 'Which side had reason in the fight / Both *should* have brains enough to know / Such disputations are not right'.[38] Through the open acquisition of body parts without regard for public sensibility, Halford put the Melbourne Medical School's dealings with specimens under a negative spotlight.

Equipped with such cautionary tales, those who collected during Allen's curatorship went to great lengths to maintain the clandestine nature of the operation and to promote a positive image of the museum in the news. Glowing reports of the anatomy and pathology museum often featured in the press following a visit from an invited guest. In 1905, following a recent tour of the museum, *The Argus* quoted the unnamed visitors as stating that 'no such widely instructive demonstration has ever been afforded the medical men of the city and suburbs'.[39] Similar stories emerged during the Australasian Medical Congress in 1908, just as they had when the University of Melbourne hosted the Intercolonial Medical Congress of Australasia in 1889.[40] Skirting off-putting details of how Allen had amassed the collection, newspaper reports presented the museum to the public as an asset to the colony's developing medical scene.

Despite efforts during Allen's tenure to keep specimen collecting covert, or at least recognized for its positive educational value, newspaper articles reveal that suspicion continued to linger over the activities of those forming and using the anatomy and pathology collection – including medical students. In September 1906, the grisly find of mutilated human remains in inner-city Albert Park Lake gripped Melbourne. Allegedly, a group of young boys were by the lake hunting for yabbies when they came across two brown paper packages that had floated to the surface. They brought the packages ashore and opened them to find in one a 'large piece of flesh' and in the other 'a heart and other internal organs of a human body'.[41] Among the initial theories about how the body parts had ended up in the lake was that medical students had pitched them into the lagoon to carry out a 'ghastly joke'.[42] In remarks to the press, government pathologist Dr Crawford Henry Mollison quickly dismissed these rumours on the grounds that 'no student of anatomy could accomplish such a clumsy dissection'.[43] Although the investigation ultimately became a murder inquiry rather than a search for a medical student, the episode reflects the public unease concerning the medical school's specimen collection and its use by medical students.

## Why did they collect?

What motivated anatomists to go to such lengths to collect human specimens? Why did they acquire specimens and what did they think they were achieving? Correspondence sent to Allen at the Melbourne Medical School yields four main motivations to collect body parts from patients and transform them into specimens: to contribute to the teaching apparatus of the medical school, to engage in an exercise of collaborative diagnosis, to provide the museum with rare or curious objects, and to improve one's professional standing through specimen donation. Not every specimen encountered was worth keeping; understanding what motivated collecting reveals the value collectors placed on the material they collected, and how their actions shaped the composition of the museum.

Value is determined and contested within a 'field', or social space, such as the medical profession. Like other fields, the medical profession has its own internal factors, from which cultural value is determined and recognized. However, cultural value within the field was not always stable during the era in question. Rather, specimens, as cultural products, were subject to 'processes of (e)valuation'; collectors decided what was worth retaining and sending to the medical school, where Allen deemed what was necessary for the collection and whether a specimen's state of preservation diminished its value as an educational tool.[44]

The transformation of human body parts into collected anatomy and pathology specimens used as educational tools provided value, or cultural capital, to the medical school. Students in the late nineteenth and early twentieth centuries spent significant time learning from specimens in the medical school museum, my focus in Chapter 3. For now, suffice it to say that the medical field viewed the possession of anatomy and pathology specimens as a mark of prestige and a commitment to the future of medical education. Large collections that developed in eighteenth- and nineteenth-century Britain, such as John Hunter's collection, now the Hunterian Museum at the Royal College of Surgeons, London, the anatomy museum at the University of Glasgow founded on the collections of John Hunter's older brother William, and the collection at St Bartholomew's

Hospital, had long provided examples to which smaller colonial schools like the Melbourne Medical School could aspire. As personnel and ideas transferred readily from Britain to Australia in this era, colonial schools inherited a tradition that placed cultural value on the possession of specimens for use in lectures and demonstrations.

To enable this type of specimen-based learning, doctors who performed operations or post-mortem examinations retained specimens from their patients, which embarked on an afterlife in the medical school museum. In 1898, Dr B. Stewart Cohen sent in an 'excellent specimen of hydrocephalus' that he thought would be 'an instructive specimen for the Midwifery class'.[45] Midwifery was on the medical school's first list of proposed subjects drawn up in 1858. Students also completed rounds at the Women's Hospital to learn about women's health and the complications of childbirth.[46] Experience with a rare condition like hydrocephalus, however, would not have been common, so this specimen may have deepened students' education in the speciality. Similarly, several years later Dr Kelly of the Echuca District Hospital forwarded a specimen of what he believed to represent 'the death of the foetus in utero by hooking of the umbilical cord', which he thought 'may be of interest to [Allen] and students'.[47] Kelly also deemed this to be an unusual cause of death that students might not come across in their regular exposure to midwifery cases. By retaining specimens that demonstrated uncommon pathologies and complications, and sending them to the medical school, Cohen and Kelly altered the course of what may have ended up as medical waste, giving it new purpose as a teaching specimen.

Patients' body parts that doctors removed and retained as specimens helped develop a comprehensive array of common pathologies and elements of anatomy at the museum. Some doctors appear to have known of deficiencies in the collection and remained alert to cases that might yield specimens not represented already. Dr Louis Ashworth, for example, chose to send in a tumour specimen taken from a three-year-old boy who had been treated at the Brisbane Hospital for Sick Children, because he did not believe there to be anything like it already in the museum.[48] Other doctors, like resident surgeon at the Bendigo Gold District Hospital Walter Fowler, clarified whether the museum needed a particular specimen before directing it there. Fowler wrote to Allen that he had removed a 'most splendid specimen [of] cystic disease of the kidney' and was willing to 'send it to [Allen]' ... 'if [he] would like it'.[49] He also wondered how to pack and address the kidney. As one of Victoria's leading provincial surgeons, Fowler may have come across numerous cases of cystic disease of the kidney. He sent this particular specimen to Allen, though, because he considered it to be an excellent example of the disease and therefore of benefit to medical students.

As historian Samuel Alberti notes in the British context, some collectors may have even begun the process of objectifying medically interesting parts of a patient's body as a potential specimen while the patient was still undergoing treatment.[50] In a disquieting episode that occurred in Melbourne in 1904, Dr J. R. H. Willis wrote to Allen that he 'had a most unusual obstetric case ... and thought that [Allen] would like to secure the specimen: the child, which [was] still living', and had been born with severe abnormalities. Willis continued that the 'parents [were] quite willing to give [him] the child when it die[d]', and requested Allen telephone him with instructions on how to 'prevent the body passing into the hands of an undertaker'.[51] While collectors like Ashworth and Fowler were quietly vigilant for potential specimens for the museum, others, like Willis, acted upon their position of power over patients more brazenly to contribute to the collection. Most body parts that doctors removed from patients would have been disposed of as medical waste. In these cases, however, individual doctors chose to fashion them into specimens that would develop a comprehensive museum of the human body in parts. In doing so, they aimed to contribute to bettering knowledge of human anatomy and pathology for the benefit of medical education, and the medical profession as a collective.

A second key motivation for taking body parts from patients and transforming them into specimens was to enable doctors to take part in the collaborative development of medical understanding and perceptions of the human body in illness and good health. The nature of the colony of Victoria in the 1880s and 1890s meant that hospitals and physicians' practices were dispersed over a wide geographical area. Apart from the major city hospitals, there were key regional hospitals in the Goldfields region, Echuca, Sale, and Warrnambool, and asylums at Yarra Bend, Kew, Beechworth and Ararat had doctors on staff to treat the confined. The distances between medical institutions meant that it was difficult to have a second physician consult on a patient or on the findings of a post-mortem examination. Many cases, however, merited clarification. In these instances, doctors sent specimens out of the hospital or private practice to medical experts, like Allen, for advice and help with diagnosing the patient's condition. When Norman Dowling sent in the foetal specimen dusted in a preservative powder as a contribution to Allen's museum, he also sought clarification of a pathology unknown to him that he described as a 'peculiar diseased condition of the spine with malformation of head'.[52] Perhaps feeling isolated in Victoria's Western District, Dowling wrote to Allen that he could 'throw no light on the causation' of the foetal abnormality and would be 'very interested to learn what [Allen's] opinion [was] as to the pathological condition'.[53] He sent the preserved foetal specimen, alongside the patient's case notes, for Allen's inspection and acceptance 'if of any value' for the museum collection.[54] Through their correspondence about the specimen, Dowling and Allen engaged in a form of collaborative diagnosis to better understand what appeared to them to be a rare foetal pathology.

In many cases, physicians collected specimens to seek a second opinion on more common pathologies. For example, in 1905, Dr Frank R. Legge sent in a lung specimen taken from an eighteen-year-old boy. Legge had been Allen's student during his time at the Melbourne Medical School, and he asked his former professor 'if the lesion of lung was bronchiostasis' and if an abscess on the specimen was 'secondary to the lesion in the lung'.[55] Although Allen's response no longer exists and there is no way of knowing exactly what he wrote in reply, we know from Legge's return letter that Allen asked for further notes about the patient's condition. Legge wrote that 'there were no pleural adhesions' and that he 'had not noticed any falling in of [the] chest wall at any part'.[56] He also provided some detail of the boy's previous illnesses, in the hope that it might help Allen confirm the initial diagnosis. This example demonstrates that specimens did not circulate in isolation; instead, they accompanied an exchange of facts and ideas about aetiologies and treatments of disease. Specimens assumed a central role within the collecting network, which became a valuable and productive site for professional development, and the improvement of diagnostic techniques in the formative years of the medical profession in Victoria.

A third reason doctors collected parts of the body was for their rare or curious nature. In 1902, a doctor in Strahan, Tasmania, sent a 'foetus, presumably about 8 months old which [he] consider[ed] a curiosity'. He added that Allen 'may value it' for precisely that reason.[57] An article in the *Medical Journal of Australia* in 1926 stated that 'each specimen [in Allen's collection] was a masterpiece and every one told its own peculiar story'.[58] Writing about early modern European medical collections, historian Rina Knoeff suggests that 'often the story was the first reason for preserving a specimen', and this was no less true in turn-of-the-century Victoria.[59]

The hydrocephalus skeleton Watson sent to Allen in 1907 also fits into this category. Although it may have had some educational potential, Watson appears to have retained the hydrocephalus skeleton specimen for its rarity. In the early twentieth century, treatment for hydrocephalus was not well developed, which meant that most sufferers did not survive infancy or early childhood, let alone live to the age of twenty-eight, as Watson's patient did. The skeleton was, therefore, an uncommon and curious specimen.

Writing in the late 1940s following his graduation from the Melbourne Medical School, physician and medical historian Bryan Gandevia also linked the hydrocephalus skeleton with another case of collecting based on curiosity that had occurred 125 years earlier. He reflected that 'the manner in which the skeleton of the little hydrocephalic, familiar to every student, was obtained was said to be highly reminiscent of anatomist John Hunter's acquisition of the Irish Giant'.[60] In this notorious case, Charles Byrne, known as the Irish Giant for his abnormal height of around 231 centimetres – which we now know was the result of a pituitary gland tumour which caused acromegaly and gigantism – requested his body be weighed down and buried at sea after death in order to escape the looming grasp of the anatomists. Following Byrne's death in 1783 at the age of just twenty-two, an associate of Hunter is said to have bribed a man along the coffin's journey to the docks and managed to acquire the body and deliver it to Hunter at his London residence for display as a curiosity in his museum. Byrne's skeleton remained in a glass case on public display at the Hunterian Museum in London for more than two hundred years. Following a years-long campaign to fulfil Byrne's dying request, the Hunterian Museum Board of Trustees announced on 11 January 2023 that Byrne's skeleton would no longer be displayed when the museum reopened following a five-year closure. It will still be available, however, for 'bona fide research'.[61] Although curios represent a small part of the Melbourne Medical School collection, they show that collectors placed value not only on specimens that provided educational benefits, but also on those that were simply rare or were accompanied by a good story.

A final motivation for collecting and contributing to the museum was to win favour with Allen, who was a prominent and respected anatomist. During his time at the university, Allen received numerous letters from students asking him to 'testify to [their] capabilities' or for the 'favour of [his] influence in obtaining work'.[62] Correspondence with hospital administration also reveals that Allen was occasionally involved in authorizing hospital appointments on behalf of the university.[63] In other words, Allen had considerable influence within the medical profession, and sending specimens to the Melbourne Medical School could return a form of social capital – defined by French sociologist Pierre Bourdieu as an individual's accumulation of means or contacts 'by virtue of possessing a durable network of … relationships of mutual acquaintance and recognition' that allow that individual to negotiate and navigate a social system in order to move up a social hierarchy.[64]

Some doctors collected specimens for Allen as apparent gestures of goodwill that would enhance his opinion of them and their professional capacities. For example, when Dr Mark Lidwill sent two specimens to Allen in October 1903, he also offered his services to Allen, stating that he would be 'very pleased to save [specimens] and send them down' to the university.[65] In August of the following year, Lidwill again assured Allen in writing that if he wanted 'any specimens in particular … [he] would source them for [him]'.[66] Lidwill was a young doctor working in Ballarat who had graduated with his Bachelor of Medicine at the Melbourne Medical School the year before he began sending specimens to the university. As a new graduate and a relatively recent migrant to Australia living in a regional city, Lidwill's contributions to the museum collection enabled him to maintain a connection to Allen, and the centre of the profession. Lidwill demonstrated his capacity to identify and procure valuable specimens for the collection, which may have boded well for securing demonstratorships or other professional appointments. He may also have had his name recorded in the museum catalogue alongside the listings of specimens he sent in; it was common practice across the developing museum sphere to acknowledge not only the specimen but also the collector in catalogues and registers. Whether to make a name for himself as a specimen collector or to maintain a presence in professional circles despite his location, Lidwill's actions suggest that there was a sense of positive exposure to be gained in return for contributing to Allen's growing collection. Lidwill went on to become a celebrated medical innovator, designing a portable machine for delivering anaesthetic to patients in 1913, as well as being credited with carrying out the first successful use of a cardiac pacemaker.

Collectors also sent preserved specimens to Allen with the hope that in return they could use his name to lend legitimacy to their findings and research reports based on the specimen. For example, in 1901, Dr John Ramsay asked Allen to provide a short description of a specimen he had sent to the museum because it would 'add greatly to the value of the report' he was about to submit to the *Intercolonial Medical Journal of Australasia*.[67] Featuring written and visual depictions of collected specimens in medical journals and correspondence was common, and provided doctors with a means to overcome the difficulties involved in transporting human body parts across great distances. Rather than transport the literal specimen, doctors transposed the ideas about aetiology, diagnosis and treatment that accompanied a specimen into words and images in the pages of the journal. In this format, specimens were not confined to one physical setting; they moved beyond their material forms to become a type of mobile currency in these long-distance relationships.[68] Ramsay, who published prolifically during his career, leveraged Allen's name to bring greater recognition to his work, but perhaps also to promote research emerging from the growing Australian medical profession. Through disseminating knowledge about specimens by means of journal articles, Australian specimen collectors partook in the circulation of knowledge throughout local and global networks.

Despite the small size of the network, and the distance between the intellectual centres of Britain and its colonial Australian outposts, Australian scientific and medical research was not undertaken in intellectual isolation. Australian doctors engaged deeply in research and intellectual ideas that emerged from the British medical and academic spheres, and also worked to bring greater exposure to their own findings. In particular, their published findings and subscriptions to major medical and scientific journals held in the medical school's voluminous library facilitated the establishment of 'links with "universal" learning'.[69] Such connections thereby helped to stimulate the growth of the medical profession by lessening the tyranny of distance sometimes experienced in colonial universities. Through the exchange of specimens for professional support, the work of Australian physicians could gain greater legitimacy in the broader medical sphere. Collected anatomy and pathology specimens, then, were bound up in social interactions that extended beyond the exchange of physical material.

## Amateur versus paid collecting

The systems and practices through which members of the collecting network preserved body parts as specimens and sent them to the museum complicate the distinction between amateur and paid collectors. Physicians worked in a professional capacity to procure body parts, but their correspondence reveals little evidence of a direct system of payment for their contributions during Allen's time at the helm. In fact, one collector even 'enclosed a cheque of four guineas' to cover the return transportation cost of two specimens for which he had requested the professor's advice.[70] Specimens were not stock-in-trade of a large-scale 'manufactory of pathology', as Alberti suggests of the British context.[71] There had long been a marketplace of body parts in the United Kingdom, as well as in Europe and the United States, where anatomists and other collectors bought and sold biomedical specimens. Records indicate that in eighteenth-century London, William Hunter paid out handsome sums to those who procured specimens, sometimes illicitly, for his growing museum.[72]

Smaller museums, too, engaged in a large-scale trade of human specimens.[73] Although many of these overseas museums also relied on donated specimens, their curators purchased specimens from collectors who expected payment in a manner not experienced at the Melbourne Medical School.

As discussed earlier in this chapter, collectors received non-monetary reward for their donations to the museum. In return for contributing specimens to a project that Allen and other prominent physicians valued, some collectors gained social recognition that may have enabled them to advance their standing within the medical profession. They may have been able to move in professional circles, which could have had a positive effect on their career progression. For collectors like Dr Ramsay, who requested Allen's input and nominal support for a medical journal article in exchange for the specimen it featured, the reward may have been greater, such as more widespread recognition of their work within the field. Collectors may not have received or been motivated by monetary payment, but they engaged in a system of exchange in which they received discernible reciprocal benefits. As such, these exchanges blurred the distinction between amateur and professional collecting activity.

For other collectors, the benefit of collecting lay in the knowledge that they had contributed valuable specimens to the museum, in an era when such collections became a cornerstone of medical schools in the Antipodes, following the example of esteemed schools in Britain. Such an attitude is reminiscent of amateur collecting in the first half of the nineteenth century, in which there was a sense of nobility associated with unpaid amateur collectors who donated objects to the developing field of natural history. Paid collectors, on the other hand, were thought of as tradesmen, motivated by profit rather than contributing to the greater scientific good.[74] This changed in the second half of the nineteenth century, when the prestige associated with amateur collecting diminished, and many scientists turned their backs on the 'informal army of … [amateur] enthusiasts' who they now looked upon as 'dabblers'.[75] Although working in a professional capacity, physicians in the Melbourne Medical School network embodied many of the attitudinal attributes of amateur collectors. The medical profession continued to view their actions as honourable, despite the shifting dynamics of the wider collecting project away from the input of amateur collectors. For physicians who donated specimens for their educational properties, the reward lay in contributing culturally valuable specimens that would advance the state of medical education in Victoria rather than in payment. In other words, the act of exchange was the source of value.[76]

The Melbourne Medical School collecting network was not a binary of amateur and paid collectors, but a system that exemplified the characteristics of both. While collecting networks in the late nineteenth and early twentieth centuries often relied on auctions, private sale and barter, the Melbourne Medical School collection formed largely through informal exchanges of cultural and social capital between a group of collegial, dedicated doctors.

The collection of anatomy and pathology specimens is a narrative of objects in motion, bound up with the motivations of individual collectors, and shifting values attributed to human remains within the medical profession. Whereas most cadavers were disposed of once medical students had dissected them, many parts of the body had afterlives that continue to this day. Doctors retained and preserved body parts from their patients and fashioned them into stable, partible objects that could be transported to the medical school to improve its educational qualities, to enable a collaborative diagnosis of disease, to improve one's professional standing and to accumulate rare or curious specimens. The next chapter follows the specimens into the museum, to discuss how medical students and professionals used them once in this space.

3

# The anatomy of a museum

Human specimens arrived at the Melbourne Medical School's anatomy and pathology museum as disrupted bodies. They were disfigured and decomposing body parts that, in some cases, had little accompanying information. In the museum, they were redefined as pedagogical tools, to be used in medical education and the development of discourse about the human body within the medical profession.

The way doctors and medical students transformed, used and controlled specimens within the anatomy and pathology museums that housed them has received less historical attention than more coherent and evocative depictions of the body, such as cadavers. However, since historian Jonathan Reinarz wrote in 2005 that scholarship on anatomy and pathology museums generally consisted of a 'snap-shot usually depicting a parade of skeletons and as many jars as could be found in the average eighteenth-century apothecary's shelf', historians have begun to explore their role in the sphere of medicine.[1] In the British context, scholars such as Samuel Alberti, Elizabeth Hallam and Reinarz contend that the primary purpose of these museums was to provide an educational space for medical students and professionals to further their knowledge of human anatomy and pathology.[2] Writing about the Leiden anatomical collections, historian Hieke Huistra shows that non-medical audiences also interacted with specimens physically and emotionally, often relying on the collection's catalogue and tour guides to interpret the material.[3] Erin McLeary adds further that the typical North American medical museum during this era was not 'simply a storehouse, classroom, or library', but also a site of medical research and experimentation.[4]

This chapter follows specimens into the anatomy and pathology museum at the Melbourne Medical School to discuss how the living interacted with the dead in the museum space. Specimens were not simply pieces of flesh in jars that sat idly on museum shelves; they were educational tools that established the medical school as the primary site of learning for late-nineteenth- and early-twentieth-century Australian medical students. Like the cadaver, they were objects that formed a site of contestation for students over the meanings of the human body. Once possessed and categorized in the museum, specimens could be understood within the broader narrative of the growing museological world of the nineteenth century. By revising our understanding of these institutions, this chapter remedies the scholarly trend to privilege 'research over teaching and laboratory over museum'.[5] In this way, it embeds the museums that have been termed 'anatomical accessories' into the fabric of Australian medical history.[6]

By the early twentieth century, the specimen collection at the medical school was well-established, containing over 5,000 wet and dry specimens, including large skeletal specimens, small examples of hydatic cysts, rarities such as a foetus with meningoencephalocele (an abnormal sac of fluid, brain tissue and membrane that extends through a defect in the skull) and displays of commonly encountered pathologies, such as an aortic aneurysm. Neat rows of tall wooden display cabinets lined the museum space, with specimens in sealed glass jars of different sizes also positioned on benches at the end of each aisle.

In the nineteenth century, anatomy and pathology museums had become commonplace in European and North American medical schools. The tradition was particularly strong in Britain, where in the second half of the eighteenth century there existed around forty such museums. This number grew up to one hundred over the following half-century as the Medical Act of 1858 standardized medical training.[7] No comparable laws existed to govern the first three colonial Australian medical schools that opened in Melbourne, Sydney and Adelaide between 1862 and 1885, but as noted in Chapter 1, each school was modelled, in part, on prestigious private anatomy schools in England and Scotland. The colonial Australian medical schools acted upon the belief that museums of anatomy and pathology formed an essential part of medical training, and followed this convention to establish their own museums. As early as 1857, the Council at the University of Melbourne assigned funds to form the 'nucleus of a Museum' in preparation for the opening of the medical school in 1862, and architectural plans from 1885 reveal space set aside in the medical school building for a large museum.[8] Although the Australian colonies did not have the legacy of private anatomy schools as in Britain, those who founded colonial medical schools attempted to emulate their British counterparts.

The museum became a site of teaching for medical school staff and was often the first site of learning students encountered during their education.[9] The Melbourne Medical School museum originated from a specimen collection that had been transferred from the Melbourne Hospital in 1883. Over the next two decades, with some financial assistance from the University Council and the efforts of a network of dedicated collectors to source specimens, the museum grew to be a valuable asset to the medical school that 'furnish[ed students] with the means of studying preparations of morbid structures'.[10] It even caught the attention of Sir Henry Loch, Governor of Victoria, who favourably observed the 'careful arrangement' of museum specimens during a visit to the medical school in 1887.[11] While this chapter focuses on the anatomy and pathology museum at the University of Melbourne, I also draw on evidence from the Sydney and Adelaide contexts to show that in the museum, staff and students acted upon specimens in ways that transformed them from abstract to comprehensible iterations of the body that played a significant role in the development of medical education in late-nineteenth- and early-twentieth-century Australia.

## From grotesque body parts to pedagogical tools

Despite physicians' efforts at preservation during the collection process, specimens still entered the museum as dismembered, degrading body parts that were often decontextualized from the body as a whole. Their appearance subverted the recognizable, classical imagery of the body characterized by the Vitruvian ideals of perfect proportions and symmetry, familiar to anatomists and students through the long association between the fields of anatomy and art. Indeed, students at the Sydney Medical School in the early twentieth century took part in a series of lectures entitled 'Anatomy and its Application to Art' that imparted to them an understanding of anatomy based on classical imagery of the body in art.[12] Similarly, the anatomical atlases and guides, such as Henry Gray's *Anatomy of the Human Body*, to which students referred in this era, presented idealized, standardized representations of the body that avoided 'true to nature' imperfections.[13]

Compared to this imagery, collected anatomy specimens, such as a heart in isolation, represented what literary critic Mikhail Bakhtin labels 'ugly, monstrous, hideous', grotesque versions of the body that were no longer 'closed, completed unit[s]' bound by order.[14] Pathology specimens, such as examples of sarcoma (cancer) of the brain and 'Pott's curvature of the spine' (spinal tuberculosis), by their very nature demonstrate abnormal bodily manifestations. To render these individual grotesque body parts into comprehensible specimens for medical education, they needed to be altered and contextualized in the museum space.

Specimen preparators had many methods of preservation at their disposal; human specimens could be injected, immersed, dried, stained or articulated in the case of skeletal mounts. Submersion in spirits had been undertaken since the seventeenth century, as had corrosion casting – a process whereby the veins and arteries are injected with a hardening substance before the surrounding tissue is removed through immersion in an acid solution to leave only the cast of the vascular system behind (see Figure 4).[15] In the eighteenth and nineteenth centuries, anatomists experimented with different 'recipes' for preservatives as they honed their specialized skills. The uptake of formalin, a solution of formaldehyde, as a fixative in the 1890s proved particularly significant. Formalin

**Figure 4** Corrosion cast of kidney, 516-500011, Harry Brookes Allen Museum of Anatomy and Pathology, University of Melbourne. Photograph by Gavan Mitchell. (This image may not be copied, reproduced or distributed in any way unless authorized by the Curator, Harry Brookes Allen Museum of Anatomy and Pathology, the University of Melbourne.)

retained the colour and shape of tissue more accurately than alcohol, and it provided a cheaper option when alcohol costs were often prohibitive.[16]

Some accomplished specimen preparators and anatomical model makers, including Frederick Ruysch and Joseph Towne, were quite secretive about their methods – often taking them to the grave. Wendy Moore notes, however, that William Hunter gave periodic lectures in which he shared his knowledge about specimen preparation techniques.[17] In contrast, there were few opportunities to learn these skills from trained practitioners in late-nineteenth- and early-twentieth-century Australia. Poor wages on offer deemed 'not sufficient to attract applications from other colonies', and the fact the British General Medical Council did not recognize all Australian medical courses right away, likely contributed to the relative lack of experienced preparators.[18] Written records note that Allen undertook most of the specimen preparation at the Melbourne Medical School during this era. He likely learnt how to prepare specimens from numerous published manuals and guides, as well as from reading medical journals and interacting through written correspondence with those at the forefront of research into preservation techniques.[19] While the young colonial medical schools struggled to attract esteemed practitioners who could impart their knowledge and train new specimen preparators, physicians like Allen worked tirelessly, independently and with few resources to become proficient in this field.

Upon arriving at the museum, anatomy and pathology specimens underwent various processes, such as staining, injecting and potting, that transformed them into effective educational objects. Allen's notes reveal that he stained sectioned specimens with colours that would emphasize important structures to students. He described one method for preparing a microscopic specimen of a 'lardaceous liver' as follows: 'harden in spirit. Stain twenty-four hours in 25 per cent gentian violet; wash with 1 per cent acetic acid till the colours differentiated; place in 50 per cent glycerine until the dye ceases to soak out. Mount in Farrant's Solution'.[20] He explained that, through this method, the 'gentian violet colours the lardaceous parts a rosy-pink and the rest of the tissue slaty blue', and that with a low power setting on a microscope, the 'pink colour is not seen in the centre of the lobules, near the intralobular vein, nor at the margins of the lobules near Glisson's capsule'.[21] Allen's written interpretation demonstrates how his preparation visually enhanced this specimen's pathology (the lardaceous, or fatty, parts) to render it a useful example for teaching. He also diligently handwrote and attached paper labels to each new mounted specimen to ensure that students and physicians knew what they were observing, and so they could navigate the museum efficiently.

Some specimens did not need to be stained or injected with coloured dye, but were instead carefully positioned in pots and cases so they could be studied effectively. The placement of the hydrocephalus skeleton specimen, and a similarly sized skeleton displaying fibrodysplasia ossificans progressiva (a rare pathological condition in which muscle and connective tissue, such as ligaments and tendons, are eventually replaced permanently by bone), in custom-built wooden display cases attests to the care taken to best exhibit the noteworthy features of each specimen. Carefully preparing collected body parts ensured that each individual specimen within the museum collection was stable and comprehensible; it was the first step in creating an ordered, educational collection, rather than a mere assemblage of degrading body parts.

Although the benefits of properly prepared specimens appear obvious, Allen faced significant difficulty in securing support from the university for his endeavour. In 1914, he wrote an exasperated letter to the University Council and Vice-Chancellor stating that in the thirty-seven years of his involvement with the museum he had never received any 'special assistance, qualified or unqualified'. He had worked for years with the help of two unqualified laboratory attendants, but these two workers also concurrently had to assist three other staff within the faculty, so their time in the museum was limited. The lack of support forced Allen to do most of the labour by himself – a workload he stated rendered the 'permanent organisation of the museum impossible' and left at least 7,000 specimens awaiting permanent mounting in mid-1914. Not only did the university withhold financial assistance for a museum attendant, but Allen could not 'find a man with special experience available in Australia' after advertising locally and making enquiries in Sydney and Adelaide.[22]

Allen was not alone in his struggles. At the University of Adelaide, even the vocal Professor of Anatomy, Archibald Watson, had his funding requests for the museum rejected by the university's Finance Committee. Despite the Medical School Committee declaring in 1887 that the purchase of glass jars 'absolutely necessary' for the museum to grow and function, Watson was left to scavenge some hand-me-down jars from Adelaide's public natural history museum.[23] The shortage of skilled preparators and institutional reticence to support made the task of developing museum collections in nineteenth-century Australia a difficult undertaking.

To overcome the discrepancy between the number of specimens arriving at the museum from members of the collecting network and Allen's capacity to prepare them, students at the Melbourne Medical School prepared specimens during practical classes. A handwritten table from 1892 lists specimens and pot numbers alongside a column that states 'work done by class'.[24] The table notes that students dehydrated and mounted specimens for use in the museum, and also learnt how to place specimens in acetic acid or Farrant's solution to prepare microscope slides for histology classes. While students generally appear to have performed adequately, Allen did describe one attempted preparation as 'not a satisfactory section' and another as simply 'not very good'.[25] Curriculum records from the Sydney Medical School demonstrate that students undertaking practical classes in the late 1880s also had to dissect, prepare and preserve specimens in the classroom like their contemporaries in Melbourne. Further, staff at both the Adelaide and Sydney medical schools appointed fourth- and fifth-year students who showed promise in the dissecting room as 'prosectors'. These students helped their professors prepare specimens for demonstration in the classroom – a role that provided them prestige rather than remuneration.[26]

Comparatively little evidence exists of students being taught preparation techniques in the British context, where it was usually 'elite practitioners' who undertook such work.[27] At Leiden University in the Netherlands, however, a 'lids off and hands on' approach saw students prepare specimens, sometimes working on one body part for several weeks. A small number of students may have kept these specimens to develop their own personal collections, and deserving student preparations became part of the university's teaching collection.[28] The dangers and difficulties of this work should not be underestimated. Specimen preparators often experienced serious physical and emotional side effects from working with strong chemicals, death and disease. They dealt with headaches, severe coughs, pricks and cuts from sharp tools and, in some cases, life-threatening infection.[29] Australian students contended similarly with the harmful effects of using methylated spirits, formalin and 'absolute alcohol' in their preparation work.

Colonial Australian medical students' involvement in preparing specimens may reflect the smaller number of specimen preparators there compared to Britain. Allen and his contemporaries needed help to develop their museum collections, and so taught their students the requisite skills. Specimen preparation also provided medical students with the opportunity to engage closely with idiosyncratic, imperfect bodies to complement their book-based learning, which favoured standardized depictions of the body.

Despite Allen's best efforts, and those of his students and the collecting network, many specimens could not be rendered comprehensible for use in the anatomy and pathology museum. Allen's written records reveal that some specimens arrived in an irreparably distorted state and had little potential as museum exhibits. For instance, Allen described a specimen listed in the museum catalogue as 'some growth ... [possible] carcinoma?'.[30] Without any case notes or further clarifying information, even an experienced practitioner like Allen could not identify what pathology the specimen presented, and it was 'put aside' as unusable.[31] Similarly, when Dr J. Ramsay sent a specimen to Allen in December 1901, he was 'afraid that [he had] spoiled the specimen for museum purposes by the strength of the alcohol' in which he had preserved it; in another instance three years later, Dr Walter Fowler expressed a fear that specimens he sent from the Bendigo Gold District Hospital 'ha[d] "gone off" a bit' due to preservation difficulties.[32]

While these incorrectly packaged specimens had succumbed to decay and could not be used, they bring to light the challenging nature of Allen's task – to draw meaning out of unintelligible body parts. They also demonstrate that, despite their grotesque appearance, specimens that ended up in the museum had been subjected to a range of procedures that changed them from degrading body parts into stable, contained and viable heuristic devices that generations of medical students would be able to use to develop their knowledge. Faced with many challenges, Allen and his contemporaries persisted in their efforts to ensure that medical students and professionals in this era had access to a comprehensive collection of biomedical specimens.

## The museum as an encyclopaedia of the body

Even though preparation rendered specimens individually understandable objects, they remained devoid of context and connection to the body as a whole. In the museum, however, Allen categorized, ordered and arranged the many thousands of specimens taken from disparate bodies, which demonstrated a wide array of anatomy and pathology, into a newly imagined whole.

One student wrote in the first issue of *Speculum* in 1884 that the museum did not have 'any system of arrangement so far'; however, written records present evidence to the contrary.[33] A rough plan drawn in Allen's hand depicts the museum space organized by body system. Allen's immense handwritten catalogues also indicate that the museum was structured visually by body part and body system, as it had been when the collection was located at the Melbourne Hospital. For instance, specimens demonstrating 'Diseases of the Nervous System' are listed together, and within this category the two specific cases of hydrocephalus in the collection feature one after the other.[34] Considering the catalogues and hand-drawn blueprint together, the museum would likely have appeared as a three-dimensional encyclopaedia of the body, in which students could essentially walk around the body to see internal parts in relation to one another as they moved through the space.[35] Historian Elizabeth Hallam notes that 'anatomical practices take bodies apart to analyse the internal relations between those parts'; in the anatomy museum those same practices also recreated it anew.[36]

Allen's categorization, cataloguing and systematic placement of specimens within the anatomy and pathology museum can be understood as part of the broader 'museological world' of the nineteenth century.[37] Although scholars commonly trace the origins of formal collecting to the early modern era, it was not until the nineteenth century that the museum institution as a repository of the natural world developed in earnest. Prior to this development, collections often consisted of assemblages of unusual or curious objects arranged without an intelligible order. Aimed at inspiring curiosity, such collections are termed *Wunderkammern*, or 'cabinets of curiosities'. Most cabinets of curiosities were owned by wealthy men, who collected items during their travels or employed collectors to bring back objects from distant lands. When long-distance travel became increasingly common in the late eighteenth and nineteenth centuries, collections grew in number and variety. At the same time, collecting began to assume a crucial role in representing and understanding objects that comprised the natural world. Part of this shift saw the purpose of collecting change from amassing a series of curiosities and oddities to classifying and ordering objects into comprehensible, and often narrative, displays. In contrast to earlier collections, nineteenth-century natural history collections – like the anatomy and pathology museum – seldom constituted mere accumulations of rare items.[38] Instead, they represented what historian Steven Conn terms the 'Victorian rage for order'.[39]

Allen's work in the museum shifted specimens – both natural specimens and artificial models – from a state of chaos to one of order. Just as natural history collectors worked to categorize objects of the natural world, Allen desired to possess and classify the constituent parts of the human body. He catalogued the collection meticulously from the earliest days of his time in charge and continually updated his records as new specimens arrived. Through this process, Allen made manifest the essential order of human anatomy and pathology. The specimens assumed a shelf position and catalogue number that effectively effaced their former personhood and gave them a new identity and meaning within the museum. They were no longer individual body parts in isolation, but instead formed part of what Alberti aptly terms the 'dividual' body – that is, a body composed of 'distinct but interlocking' parts.[40] For instance, a student could view a specimen of a healthy aorta next to an aorta with a blood clot, and other parts of the circulatory system, to comprehend how these fragmented pieces of anatomy fitted together.

Understandably, despite collectors' best efforts, the museum did not have specimens to depict every part of the human body and every pathology that affects it. In such cases, wax and papier-mâché models provided substitutes for difficult-to-find body parts.[41] Correspondence from 1899 between Allen and the Maison Tramond – one of the most reputable modellers of anatomical waxworks in the late nineteenth century – reveals that the medical school paid a significant sum for over a dozen wax anatomical models to complement human specimens in the museum. The development of the anatomy and pathology museum occurred as part of a distinct movement to classify objects of the natural world within institutional repositories. Through the ordered placement of multiple parts in the museum space and museum catalogue, the human body could be viewed as a unified system. This enabled medical students to gain a holistic understanding of anatomy and pathology as they moved through the space.

## Specimens as pedagogical tools

Prepared specimens did not sit inactively on the museum shelves; they constituted pedagogical tools for late-nineteenth- and early-twentieth-century medical teachers and students. Such specimens provided ancillary visual and tactile aids that represent a shift in medical education in this era, from abstract to practical learning – a shift that emphasized medical knowledge based on what a physician felt or observed, rather than what the patient described about their condition. Eighteenth- and early-nineteenth-century British students customarily attended didactic lectures that offered a formal introduction to medical terminology. This style of learning mirrored the medical profession at large in this era, which, according to Reinarz, had entered a literary, theoretical phase that 'discounted touch'.[42] Historian Susan C. Lawrence suggests that such lectures had the effect of 'educating the senses not training them', and that lecturers often found words insufficient to convey specific information about the body.[43]

The tradition of lectures lingered as the Melbourne Medical School opened in 1862, but students frequently complained towards the end of the 1880s that the curriculum on offer was too theoretical. They wanted to gain hands-on experience, rather than just read textbooks and endure lengthy lectures that one student described as consisting of a professor standing before one hundred students who were 'for the most part dozing contentedly'.[44] Professor Allen may have been partly to blame for the students' apathy; his 'curious sing-song intonation' and method of speech during lectures were said to have 'rob[bed] him of all chance of admiration' and exposed him to ridicule and imitation.[45] The faculty's teaching methods were seemingly so ineffective that the student asked, 'Where is the student who can lay his hand on his breast and truthfully declare he has kept wide awake through one third of the course?'[46] The same student wrote in *Speculum* that English medical schools had begun to replace lectures with practical demonstrations, and that he and his peers desired a similar change. In his words, 'with a good textbook and well-selected supply of specimens, surely there is no necessity for compulsory lectures'.[47]

Whether as a result of students' pressure or due to broader shift in attitudes within medical education towards practical learning, by the late nineteenth century medical students engaged with specimens during classes in what Hallam terms 'embodied encounters' that trained the hand and eye to work together in pursuit of anatomical knowledge.[48] This shift from theory to practice saw Melbourne Medical School professors take specimens out of the museum to complement their lectures. For example, a photograph from the mid-1880s depicts Allen lecturing to a class of around forty students, including three women, with a selection of specimens on the table in front of him and a skeleton hanging to the side (see Figure 5). The image shows that Allen integrated specimens into his classes and referred to them as he lectured. Similarly, at the Sydney Medical School curriculum records show that staff used 'wet and dry preparations freely … to illustrate and explain the subjects of Lectures'.[49] The inclusion of specimens as visual aids would have assisted lecturers in imparting information to students where language proved inadequate. However, while this may have been an effective didactic teaching method that trained the students' eyes to see and understand specific elements of anatomy and pathology, it did not provide students with the practical, hands-on experience they would need in order to treat patients as their careers advanced.

As the nineteenth century progressed, education at the Melbourne Medical School began to include more practical work that put students in direct contact with human bodies. While a large part of this shift saw students gain clinical experience in hospital wards and undertake dissection, the curriculum reflects an increased hands-on use of specimens in formal learning. In 1892, for instance, a series of tutorial demonstrations in the museum replaced a pathology course consisting of seventy-eight formal lectures.[50] Further, at the University of

**Figure 5** Lecture Class Anatomy, 1898, MHM 02129, Medical History Museum, University of Melbourne. Reproduced with permission.

Adelaide, specimens could be 'taken out of their jars if necessary to be handled and examined by students', and records for the 1889 University of Sydney academic year show that in Descriptive Anatomy and Practical Histology classes, 'each day, three or four preparations ... [were] explained and exhibited'.[51] The introduction of classes that brought students into close contact with specimens reflects their perceived benefits as teaching and learning tools. The professors of anatomy and pathology at these universities believed that direct experience with specimens enriched students' learning. Such was Allen's enthusiasm for the specimen as a tool for learning that historian Kenneth Russell writes that the whole of Allen's teaching revolved around his 'old and treasured friends' (the specimens) in the museum.[52]

One of the main benefits of working with specimens was that they made up for some of the cadaver's shortcomings. Unlike cadavers, which could only be dissected in the winter months due to their swift decomposition in warm weather, the specimens Allen and his students prepared and stabilized through submersion in a preservative could be used throughout the year for teaching. While the nature of dissection meant that opening or removing one part of the body naturally obscured the view of another, specimens could be handled, passed around and viewed from all angles. Similarly, specimens could be used time and time again to benefit hundreds of students over many years, whereas a cadaver could only be fully dissected once. At the University of Adelaide, Archibald Watson believed that specimens also provided a suitable learning tool for some first-year students, whom he deemed 'not yet ready to dissect as they had first to learn the bones'.[53] Cadavers could be 'too real and too complex' for medical students to learn from effectively, and specimens may have given students a manageable introduction to a more straightforward version of the body before attempting to dissect.[54]

While one Melbourne student complained in 1890 about odours and the 'often unsavoury' nature of working with specimens, students appear to have largely embraced the opportunity for practical engagement with specimens during their education.[55] Acknowledging that there may be a discrepancy between intended and actual use, architectural plans of the Melbourne Medical School from 1907 demonstrate that students were encouraged to learn actively with prepared specimens. The plans show a large table alongside the cases of specimens around which students likely observed and discussed the specimens they removed from the shelves.[56] The plans also depict a 'museum work room' down a nearby corridor, where students would have undertaken practical examinations in pathological histology and morbid anatomy that included testing on 'mounting and examination of specimens … from the Museum'.[57] Students even chose to engage with specimens outside their formal curriculum of lectures and tutorial classes, and asked for a room in which to do so.[58]

The Melbourne Medical Students' Society regularly held meetings with presentations of specimens for discussion and display. When the society lay down rules at its foundation meeting, Rule XIX stated that meetings were to include 'the reading and discussion of papers, reports of cases' as well as the 'exhibition … of microscopical, physiological, or pathological specimens'.[59] Summaries of meetings published in *Speculum* demonstrate that members of the society stayed true to this initial intent; around half of the society's meetings between 1886 and 1896 included the presentation of biomedical specimens. In these meetings, students also discussed papers published in medical journals and delivered by visiting medical professionals, many of which included specimen demonstrations. This activity affirms that medical students valued opportunities to learn from prepared specimens, rather than through older, more didactic methods. Such was their affinity with specimens that they even adopted them as symbols of their status as medical students, with photographs from the late nineteenth and early twentieth centuries depicting students posing with assortments of individual bones, such as femurs and skulls, full skeletons and even what appears to be a preserved foetal specimen (see Figures 6 and 7).

Wax and papier-mâché anatomical models also assumed a role in students' learning about the human body through touch and sight. Anatomical models often had surface colouring to demarcate bodily structures, such as arteries or veins. Modellers achieved this by wrapping coloured ribbon around wire that they glued into place on the model. Such markings enabled students to perceive intricate details of specimens with greater clarity than they could looking at an undifferentiated whole. The material qualities of wax allowed it to mimic the form and colour of the body, making wax models ideal alternatives when real specimens could not be procured.[60] Models were, however, artificial anatomies. They did not portray an individual body but, rather, constituted a representation of up to 200 dissections that could sometimes take over a year to create.[61] As such, wax models were often hyperreal representations of the body that did not always bring to light the idiosyncrasies of the body as could fleshy specimens; the mimetic ability of wax was at once its greatest asset and simultaneously its greatest failure when it came to educating medical students.[62]

**Figure 6** Medical Students of 1876–80, *c.* 1880, MHM 00460. Image courtesy of the Medical History Museum, Faculty of Medicine, Dentistry and Health Sciences, University of Melbourne. Copyright © The University of Melbourne 2022.

**Figure 7** Medical Students' Society display for the University's Jubilee procession, 1906, *Speculum*, no. 65, May 1906, 15.

Despite the shortcomings of artificial anatomies, they provided students with an opportunity to handle representations of the body. For instance, the papier-mâché 'heart and aorta' made in 1889 by French modeller Louis Auzoux for the Melbourne Medical School comprised multiple detachable parts that could be taken apart piece by piece to reveal the structures underneath (see Figure 8). Students could hold and visualize these models, known as 'clastiques' from the Greek 'klastos', or broken, to learn about the body in pieces in order to understand the whole. Although wax and papier-mâché models provided idealized bodily representations, they were highly sought-after alternatives to real body parts. Such was their utility that prominent Melbourne physician James Robertson stated in his inaugural lecture to students in 1892 that the 'road [was] made easy' for students by the 'exquisite models being used in teaching'.[63]

Using specimens and models as sensory pedagogical tools continued to be popular in the twentieth century. The arrival of the new Professor of Anatomy, Richard Berry, at the Melbourne Medical School in 1905 saw a significant increase in the use of specimens for teaching in the classroom. After setting foot inside the anatomy department, Berry bemoaned the lack of specimens at his disposal. He noted in the manuscript for his autobiography that the department

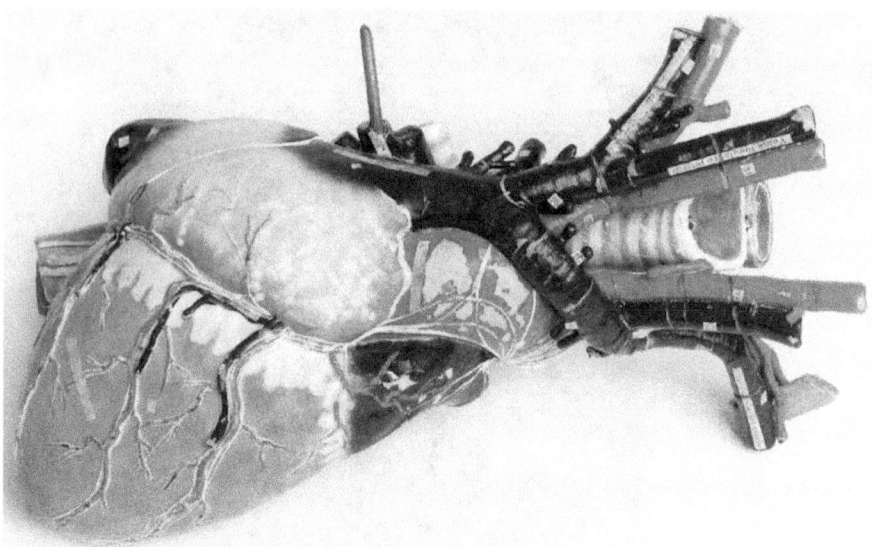

**Figure 8** Auzoux model of heart, Maison Auzoux, c. 1890, 516-500277, Harry Brookes Allen Museum of Anatomy and Pathology, University of Melbourne. Photograph by Gavan Mitchell.
(This image may not be copied, reproduced or distributed in any way unless authorized by the Curator, Harry Brookes Allen Museum of Anatomy and Pathology, the University of Melbourne.)

had 'literally nothing, not even a skeleton, though later [he] discovered quite a lot in the cupboard'.[64] Although there is anecdotal evidence to suggest that Allen had, in fact, taken the majority of the specimens for his own use in the pathology department before Berry could lay eyes on them, the collection at the university clearly failed to meet the standards to which Berry was accustomed to during his prior studies and teaching in Britain.[65] Berry quickly sought to rectify the situation, instigating a specimen-collecting spree to ensure that 'anatomy [was] no longer dry bone' for his students.[66] He also encouraged students to discuss interesting specimens they encountered in the dissecting room, and to 'cultivate ... an interest in anatomy and anthropology outside that which is necessary for examinations and purely professional success'.[67] Allen and his successor Berry acted based on the attitude that specimens constituted a fundamental component of teaching at the Melbourne Medical School. When complementing one another, human specimens and anatomical models could be used to overcome some of the deficiencies of learning solely from cadavers and books, and their portability and longevity made them ideal teaching aids in the classroom.

The incorporation of specimens into lectures and practical classes in the museum established the medical school as the primary site of medical learning in late-nineteenth-century Australia. Rather than be left to 'rest in words', as had students of the past generation, late-nineteenth-century students integrated new, practical methods into their studies.[68] The lives of collected specimens intertwined with artificial representations of the body to present medical students and teachers with a visual and material depiction of human anatomy and pathology. Museum specimens as visual and tactile aids in medical education also reflect the shifting power dynamics between physicians and their patients that occurred as the field professionalized during this era. Instead of merely listening to information, students used specimens to train their hands and eyes to garner information about the body and its afflictions. They learnt to use their senses to make authoritative judgements in a manner that they would be able to transfer to patients as their careers progressed. As such, specimens formed an integral part of medical school training – one that is often overlooked for the ever-evocative cadaver.

## Private and public anatomy

The transformative processes that turned specimens into effective learning devices occurred within an environment that was inaccessible to the public, whose bodies and body parts the collection comprised. The limited group of practitioners involved in creating and using the collection gained power over representations of the human body, and over the language used to discuss its anatomy and pathology. In particular, within the museum space physicians and medical students developed standardized terminology for pathologies. For example, in 1900 a train carrying a 'very pretty "monster"' arrived at the museum from Casterton in western Victoria.[69] The 'monster' was in fact a deformed stillborn baby recently delivered by a thirty-five-year-old woman. Several years later, Watson described the hydrocephalus skeleton he sent to the Melbourne Medical School in similar terms. He advised Allen that if the specimen was not suitable for the museum, he would 'relieve [him] of the "incubus"'.[70] While using terms such as 'monster' and 'incubus' to describe pathologies might offend modern-day sensibilities, they featured commonly in nineteenth-century medical descriptions of severe, externally visible obstetric and gynaecological pathologies. This was the era in which teratology and teratogeny (the sciences of birth defects) emerged as medical specialities. Articles in the *British Medical*

*Journal* on obstetrics and gynaecology in the nineteenth century frequently referred to 'monsters', 'double monsters' and even 'double headed monsters'.[71] Similarly, the *Australian Medical Journal* also published reports on monstrous births using similar terms. Cases published as late as the 1940s and 1950s of a 'dicephalic monstrosity' and a case of a 'uniumbilical-dibrachidicephalic monster' demonstrate how pervasive this language had become in the medical sphere.[72] In the exclusive arenas of the anatomy and pathology museum, and in medical journals, doctors worked to create and maintain control over a standardized language of pathology.

The anatomy and pathology museum shared numerous characteristics with the broader nineteenth-century museum institution. It was a space in which anatomists stabilized, ordered and began to comprehend specimens as representations of the human body. The museum did, however, elude what sociologist Tony Bennett labels in his influential work *The Birth of the Museum* the 'conception of the modern museum as a *public* museum' that emerged in the nineteenth century.[73] First, for the most part, Australian anatomy and pathology museums were not accessible to the public. They were the domain of medical students and their teachers, who used them for teaching and learning, and of visiting medical professionals, who would often be invited to tour the museum.[74] Some British medical museums allowed certain members of the public to view the specimens in a manner that brought science out of academic circles and into the general population.[75] In particular, displays of curiosities proved to be popular and easily interpretable. This was not the case in the Australian context, where few outside the medical profession had the opportunity to visit the museum.

That said, the language of pathology and monstrosity did not always remain bound within the insular medical sphere. It also entered into public spaces that catalogued, displayed and commercialized anomalous bodies, such as so-called 'freak shows', living human displays and public anatomy exhibitions and museums.[76] These ventures took 'deviant' bodies that had been framed and defined within the medical sphere to the public, forming part of the nineteenth-century 'exhibitionary complex' that spectacularized the human body.[77] They were sites in which professional and popular ideas were contested and modes of display and speech overlapped; just as those who promoted 'freak shows' used the increasing authority of medical language to attract paying customers, medical practitioners borrowed the practices of spectacle, and even pathologized bodies themselves from these shows for display in museums and discussion in medical journal articles.[78] Rather than discuss the presence of anomalous bodies in the 'freak shows' of Victorian Melbourne, I focus instead on another site in of contestation between professional and public meanings attached to bodily difference: the public anatomy museum.

Messrs Kreitmayer and Wiseheart's Grand Anatomical Museum welcomed visitors from 1861 until 1869. German-born Maximilian Kreitmayer had been an anatomical wax model maker at St Bartholomew's Hospital in London prior to opening his venture in Melbourne. Kreitmayer's public anatomy museum provided exhibits for a wider audience than medical professionals and students alone, albeit with some restrictions. A visitor generally needed to be male, educated and able to afford the one-shilling admission fee. Women were permitted to enter the museum during particular hours, and an exhibition pamphlet from 1861 states that Kreitmayer's wife gave periodic lectures for 'visiting ladies'.[79] The nineteenth-century privately owned, popular anatomy museum provides a critical point of contrast to the anatomy and pathology museums associated with the universities, which were closed to the public. It instead represents a venture closer to Bennett's conceptualization of the public museum institution as one that attempted to enact a 'benevolent and improving influence' on the public.[80]

Historians generally have understood popular anatomy museums to be 'disreputable places, catering for those seeking eroticism and coarse humour'.[81] For instance, historian Michael Mason asserts that the exhibits at Dr Kahn's Anatomical and Pathological Museum in Victorian London were 'often prurient, and the Kahn Harley Street practice was quackery'.[82] Similarly, in the Australian context, Mimi Colligan states that public anatomy museums were 'pure show business'.[83] While these contentions certainly have merit, the scholarship of Elizabeth Stephens and A. W. Bates supports consideration of Australian public anatomy museums in more complex terms.[84] Their proprietors took advantage of the medical profession's rising social status in the late nineteenth century to present a form of anatomical information to a public generally excluded from accessing such knowledge. The exhibitors claimed to educate the public about illnesses that affected the body, and sought to be a moralizing force to warn of the dangers associated with certain behaviours, all the while profiting off ticket sales and the peddling of fraudulent treatments.

The content of Melbourne's public anatomy exhibitions appears to have fluctuated between education and carnivalesque spectacle. Kreitmayer exhibited specimens under the guise of instructive entertainment, and his catalogue confidently promised guests a visit filled with 'high intellectual enjoyment'.[85] While his exhibition included some sensational content, such as models of syphilitic ulcers in both males and females, and an anatomical Venus,[86]

Kreitmayer had a good reputation and was by all accounts a skilled wax worker who leveraged his ability cleverly to capture the public's imagination. In September 1861, the exhibition toured the regional Victorian goldfields town of Bendigo so that, with 'medical jargon being carefully eschewed', even the 'most feeble' mind in the general public could access useful anatomical information.[87] The anatomical museum garnered legitimate intellectual interest and received positive reviews when it toured Sydney, where it was described as a 'most pleasing, and equally instructive' exhibition that helped the visitor 'learn … many things that ha[d] hitherto been incomprehensible to him through the more imperfect medium of books and engravings, however carefully written or prepared'.[88] These descriptions align Kreitmayer's exhibition with the aims of the public museum institution: to have a 'benevolent and improving influence' on the public through the deliberate arrangement of objects and information.[89]

In 1867, a rival museum owned by Dr Henry Jacob Jordan and Dr Samuel Beck opened its doors to the public. Despite being advertised as 'the Most Wonderful, Extraordinary, Mysterious, Marvellous, Thrilling, Exciting, and Scientific Institution' where visitors could marvel at the wonders of life, 'Dr' Jordan had his credentials publicly questioned in the local newspapers, where he was quickly labelled a quack.[90] His supposedly lurid spectacle, which mainly contained representations of diseased male and female reproductive organs, was the subject of venomous public commentary. A letter to the editor of *The Age* newspaper in September 1869 derided Jordan and Beck's museum as a 'disgusting exhibition', and accused its proprietors of 'grop[ing] the gutters for a livelihood'.[91] The author, writing under the pseudonym 'Humbug', continued in his condemnation. He stated that the 'silly prate about "science" and "intellectual improvement" [was] simple humbug' and believed that all a visitor's experience amounted to was 'half-terrified perusal'.[92]

The public campaign against Jordan was such that only a week after the letter to the editor had been published, a different Melbourne newspaper reported the exhibition of 'wax nastiness' to be a 'thing of the past' that would no longer accept visitors.[93] While many who chose to write to the newspaper about the exhibition concealed their identities, in the British context, the majority of condemnation for public anatomy museums came from within the medical profession. English medical men funded prosecutions of museum proprietors, and even invoked the Obscene Publications Act in the 1870s to have the museums shut down.[94] According to Bates, the medical profession was concerned that public museums would have a 'corrupting influence' on the populace and used legal action as a strategy to retain their 'medical monopoly of anatomy'.[95]

It is not clear if 'Humbug' was a medical professional or a concerned member of the general public, but the regulation of the profession was a major source of angst in nineteenth-century Victoria. Historian Philippa Martyr describes the earliest days of the colony as the '"golden age" of unregulated medical practice'.[96] By the 1890s, so many practitioners worked outside orthodox practice, despite legislation to prevent it, that one contemporary journalist described the medical sphere colourfully as 'The Paradise of Quacks'.[97] In 1886, one Melbourne medical student took particular issue with practitioners like Jordan. Writing for *Speculum*, he labelled unregistered practitioners as 'charlatans who infest Victoria' and worried that he would complete five years of medical training only then to have opportunities taken by 'some person styling himself' as a doctor.[98] Medical students were taught that 'most breaches of ethics arise from the introduction of a spirit of commercialism into the profession' – an element certainly present in public anatomy museum ventures, which often sold a range of ointments to treat venereal disease.[99] Despite the claim that quacks threatened the welfare of patients and the public, the real concern to physicians was more likely the loss of business in the competitive market of medical care and a will to exclude those they believed to be operating outside the realm of legitimate science and medicine.[100] Whether or not members of the medical profession played a direct part in the campaign against Jordan, they were evidently concerned about ventures that threatened their exclusive hold on anatomical knowledge, and may have acted to discredit those who sought to wrest away their authority.

Anatomy and pathology collections formed key sites of tension concerning claims to authority over the body in late-nineteenth- and early-twentieth-century Australia. Melbourne's two nineteenth-century public anatomy museums attempted to educate the public about the effects of what were considered to be immoral and unsafe behaviours, and provide them with medical terminology to describe human anatomy and pathology, while also offering an entertaining spectacle for visitors. Operating amid an indignant medical profession that tried to maintain its control over anatomical knowledge, as well as members of the public who denounced them as salacious, unappealing spectacles, these museums gained little traction. They did, however, represent spaces in which the medical terminology and interpretations of the body entered into the public sphere, albeit sometimes bound up with the motivations of profit-driven entrepreneurs masquerading as medical authorities. They should be considered a meaningful part of the marketplace for the production of medical knowledge that developed in nineteenth-century Australia.

\* \* \*

After arriving at the anatomy and pathology museum as a chaotic assemblage of disparate and degrading body parts, human specimens underwent transformations into useful pedagogical tools contained within the ordered, insular environments of the medical school and medical profession. Along this journey, anatomists and medical students fashioned grotesque body parts into stable versions of the body that, when placed alongside each other, reimagined the body as a newly defined whole.

The few existing accounts of the anatomy and pathology museum at the Melbourne Medical School place Allen at the centre, and rarely mention the many others who contributed to its formation or worked within the space.[101] This chapter and the preceding one have established that there is more to what is now called the Harry Brookes Allen Museum of Anatomy and Pathology than just Allen himself. He was surrounded by a network of actors who, with varied motivations, dedicated their efforts to building up the collection and preparing specimens for use in medical education. This work formed a vital component of the developing Australian medical scene, particularly in terms of training the next generation of doctors and establishing the medical school's position locally and globally. Among all of Allen's many accolades and accomplishments, he is notably remembered for his work in creating the museum, which helped to 'elevate … pathology to a place it never occupied before in the university'.[102] Although he had assistance, Allen's role in preparing and ordering specimens, and extracting from them their hidden secrets of pathology, cannot be overstated. It took infectious enthusiasm and immense diligence to catalogue and make sense out of the thousands of specimens that arrived at the medical school. The next chapter delves deeper into a specific collection of foetal specimens held in the Harry Brookes Allen Museum.

4

# Unrealized lives: A collection of foetal specimens

When I arrive to view a collection of foetal specimens in the Harry Brookes Allen Museum of Anatomy and Pathology, I assume that my time spent researching anatomical and pathological museums has prepared me well for the encounter. After venturing to the medical school basement storeroom, the curator opens the shelves of the compactus to reveal several dozen potted specimens. The specimens rest in jars of varying sizes. Among the neatly ordered shelves of labelled vessels is one specimen in a Le Parfait branded preserve jar. Some vessels are only a few inches tall and wide, while others large enough to hold a full-term stillborn baby. Several specimens are in poor condition; the preservative liquid that encases them has evaporated, leaving the specimen partially exposed. The foetal specimens lie in different orientations. There is a side-on view of a fifteen-centimetre-long foetus, still tethered to the umbilical cord that once sustained its developing life, and a foetus displaying anencephaly – a condition characterized by an underdeveloped brain and skull – that faces me directly. This specimen is particularly jarring; it is both extremely difficult to look at, with its flattened and noticeably shrunken head owing to a lack of cranial vault, yet also impossible to look away from.[1]

The foetuses have a distinct humanness that specimens of dismembered body parts do not have. They do not seem like detached biological objects, but developing humans in their full form. Some specimens seem quite serene, with their eyes closed, almost as if sleeping in the formalin contents of a glass womb. Others, though, are confronting to view, with eyes wide open, staring but never seeing.

The Harry Brookes Allen Museum holds around 120 foetal specimens, showing different stages of development, from as early as eight weeks' gestation, to full-term. Most of the specimens display foetal pathology, but there are also non-pathological specimens. Around a quarter of the specimens contain some element of the female body of which they were once a part – the most common examples being the uterus, fallopian tubes, ovaries and the placenta. For all the physical descriptions I can give, though, little else can be discerned about the specimens from museum catalogue records. The foetuses exist in a curious liminal space of having never been born, yet having lives within the museum as the material remnants of lost pregnancies.

When thinking of embryos and foetuses in a medical sense, one's mind might turn to modern-day debates around abortion, embryonic stem cell research and assisted reproductive technologies such as in vitro fertilization (IVF). These practices, and the legislation that envelops them, have shaped societal perceptions of the embryo and foetus and seen their intense politicization in recent decades. Well before these debates, however, in the mid-to-late nineteenth century, doctors collected and preserved foetal material to advance their knowledge, and teach students, about pregnancy, miscarriage, childbirth and foetal development in an era before medical imaging made it possible to see inside the pregnant uterus. This work supported the medicalization of gestation and childbirth in Australia as doctors' medical authority grew over what had previously been largely an event that took place at home in the company of other women. There is more to these foetal entities than the ethical and scientific debates of the past few decades.

Foetal specimens in the museum collection are material evidence of the developing medical discourse and authority surrounding the foetus, reproduction, miscarriage and childbirth in Australia. Their historical and cultural context is obscured at first glance by scant documentation surrounding the collection's origins and use. Written records that accompany the collection are largely descriptive; they contain few specifics about the method or purpose for the specimens' acquisition, or refer to the experiences of the women from whom doctors took biological material. The sparseness of the museum records means having to look elsewhere to interpret the otherwise decontextualized specimens.

This chapter establishes the social and cultural framework in which doctors collected foetal specimens in Australia. It contributes to scholarship that has begun to address the relative silence concerning the social and individual experience of pregnancy loss in the historical record more broadly.[2] Medical journals and specimens in the museum collection bring to light the types of questions late-nineteenth- and early-twentieth-century doctors and their patients sought to answer about the foetus and complications during pregnancy and childbirth. They show both a growing medical interest in the foetal body as an entity in its own right, and doctors' continuing inclination to consider the foetal and maternal bodies as an entwined pair for the sake of diagnosis and treatment. Amid a medical discourse seemingly dominated by white male physicians, women's voices and bodies emerge at critical moments to provide cultural context for the museum specimens, and insight into women's participation in the increasingly medicalized event of childbirth.

Through this discussion, the specimens are shifted away from their historical status as biological objects and recast as cultural objects. By looking beyond the potted specimens to recover their cultural context, the reproductive experiences of many women need not be reduced to an assemblage of specimens preserved in formalin on a museum shelf. Instead, through a better understanding of these 'small but culturally significant bits of flesh', the foetal specimens at the Melbourne Medical School can be included as a central part of the story of pregnancy loss in Australian history.[3]

## Medical authority and the foetal specimen

To understand foetal collecting and how it relates to doctors' rising authority over pregnancy and childbirth in this period, it is first necessary to look at the culture and prevalent attitudes of the time, including the terminology used by doctors to describe the unborn. The precision of modern technology has enabled the medical profession to produce a distinct terminology to describe the stages of embryonic and foetal development, to determine at what stage of development an embryo becomes a viable foetus, and to draw distinctions between a miscarried foetus and a stillborn baby. These terms have specific meanings in the twenty-first century, but late-nineteenth- and early-twentieth-century Australian medical literature often used them differently, and even interchangeably.

A case report from 1868 of Mrs NL, a twenty-two-year-old woman from Bathurst, New South Wales, demonstrates the variation of terms even within a single case. Mrs NL presented to the hospital with 'symptoms of a miscarriage', after which she 'had [a] female child'. Her doctor believed 'that the uterus contained another foetus' and noted that he 'discovered the feet of a second child'. According to the report, this second foetus was in fact attached to another foetus – forming a set of conjoined twins. These 'children ... lived about an hour', their 'breathing simultaneous', before succumbing. After obtaining permission from the family, the doctor proceeded to examine and dissect the bodies, which he then termed foetuses again.[4] This case not only demonstrates an interchangeable use of the terms 'child' and 'foetus' to describe the same body, but also notably labels the deceased bodies as foetuses even though they had been born alive.

Such variation in terminology is relatively common in medical literature, even into the twentieth century. When reporting on a case of possible 'ovarian pregnancy' in 1912, then Lecturer in Obstetrics at the University of Adelaide Dr Alfred Lendon noted that an 'embryo may have been lost' upon the removal of a blood clot, but that 'no trace of the foetus was found'.[5] While today it is not until the ninth week after conception that an embryo shifts in status to a foetus, in November 1893 a medical journal article describes a case of spontaneous abortion at six weeks that produced a foetus.[6] Only in 1914 did the *Australian Medical Journal* report doctors' initial discussions over what constituted an appropriate point of gestation at which they should register a birth followed by a death.[7] In light of the inconsistency of language used to describe embryos, foetuses, stillbirth and miscarriage, throughout this chapter I have chosen to use the terminology employed in the contemporary medical literature and the museum catalogue, rather than attempt to impose twenty-first-century language and understandings on the past.

Until the middle of the nineteenth century, pregnancy and childbirth were largely the domain of women, which made it difficult for doctors to come into contact with foetal remains. While in the developed world today most pregnancies are confirmed through a home pregnancy test, nineteenth-century women usually confirmed the presence of a foetus through an intuitive understanding of internal sensations. Medical case reports from this era record that women usually perceived the internal movement of a developing foetus, known as 'quickening', at around eighteen to twenty weeks' gestation, but in some cases women did not sense movement until a later stage.[8] Of course, pregnant women still experience these sensations, but they now commonly place their trust in home pregnancy tests or medical professionals to confirm pregnancy, which is possible at a much earlier stage – sometimes as little as two to three weeks after conception.

The overwhelming majority of white women in late-nineteenth- and early-twentieth-century Australia gave birth in the family home, attended by female relatives, friends and, if finances allowed, a midwife. Childbirth was perceived to be a natural event that required little or no medical oversight. In this familiar setting, women could exercise a certain level of agency over their experience of childbirth.[9] Many single or indigent women delivered in a lying-in hospital, where they would receive a doctor's assistance. Historian Janet McCalman notes that Australian women who received the charity of lying-in hospitals 'could not demand a therapy' and were more subject to the whims of the attending doctors than those who invited physicians into their homes.[10] Underprivileged women may have preferred to receive assistance rather than go through the experience of childbirth alone; however, the high risk of infection in the hospital environment, which often proved disastrous for both mothers and babies, meant that the home was the safest place to give birth during this era.[11] Without technology to view inside the pregnant uterus, early-twentieth-century doctors continued to rely on women's awareness that quickening had occurred. Towards the end of the nineteenth century, however, the promise of better outcomes in childbirth through medical intervention began to see male members of the rapidly growing medical profession attend births more regularly.

Although most births eventuated at home without major complications, when things went seriously wrong, a midwife could call on a doctor to assist. One reported case of uterine rupture in a thirty-five-year-old Melbourne woman in 1893 depicted the graphic realities of some experiences of childbirth. A midwife brought Mrs C to the Women's Hospital in 'a state of collapse', whereupon she began 'rapidly dying from haemorrhage'. Her doctor, well-known gynaecologist Richard 'Bertie' Fetherston, described blood 'flowing freely over [his] hand' at such a rate that it filled an enamel basin and completely obscured his view of Mrs C's abdomen.[12] Remarkably, Mrs C survived after receiving numerous stitches to stop the bleeding from a tear covering 'the whole length of the left side' of her uterus, but she lost the foetus in the process.[13] In this case, medical intervention and sound post-operative measures at the hospital saved the mother's life.

In many cases, however, medical intervention and the need to attend a hospital did not improve the outcome for mothers, foetuses or newborns. Surgical and non-surgical procedures, like the caesarean section and the use of forceps, put both women and foetuses at risk. High mortality rates following caesareans in the nineteenth century meant physicians viewed the procedure as a desperate action to be avoided if at all possible.[14] Indeed, Dr E. J. A. Haynes noted in the *Australasian Medical Gazette* in 1892 that he could scarcely find enough staff to help him perform a particular obstetric procedure due to the perceived 'terror of such an operation'.[15] Outbreaks of puerperal fever, scarlet fever and an intermittent 'septic crisis' made the sometimes-overcrowded midwifery wards at the Melbourne Women's Hospital a fearful environment. The wards had to be closed for disinfecting on numerous occasions, and at one point their condition became such a concern that the hospital committee thought the best solution was simply to build a new hospital and start again.[16] Poorly executed surgical procedures and the high risk of infection due to a lack of hygiene in hospital settings undermined the medical profession's assurances of safety and security in childbirth.

Improved medical training in the late nineteenth century did not produce markedly better outcomes in cases of childbirth attended by a doctor. Although the Melbourne Medical School curriculum included obstetrics alongside 'diseases of women and children' from its earliest days, in 1886 students complained that their obstetrics training could 'hardly have been in a worse state'.[17] One student half-joked that he 'knew not a syllable of *Obstetrics*, and had no knowledge of even the alphabet of *Gynaecology*'.[18] Female staff at the Women's Hospital expressed reservations at having young male students observing female patients, particularly parturient women, on the grounds of impropriety – an attitude that might also indicate the resistance of female staff to allow medical men and male students to enter the realm of what had been their profession for generations. The students responded, claiming not only that they adhered to 'scrupulous decorum' in the hospital, but that there was no point being a 'brilliant honorman' if they had 'seen little or no practical work' in obstetrics.[19]

Colonial Australian medical schools may have provided students with obstetric knowledge from textbooks and manikins, but few students graduated with practical experience of delivering babies. These examples from the Australian context support historian of medicine Jacqueline Wolf's statement that absent or inadequate obstetric training in the nineteenth century meant that the 'average doctor did not know what to do at an uneventful birth, let alone a difficult one'.[20] Despite promises of better outcomes in childbirth through medical intervention, the medical profession's supersession of women's traditional authority over the birth process in the nineteenth century was not always benign and often heightened the risks involved rather than mitigated them.

Although the risks of medical intervention in childbirth were known, doctors presented themselves as trained experts who could provide women with better treatment and assistance than a midwife. The aforementioned case of Mrs C presents just one example of the contempt doctors felt towards their 'untrained' counterparts.[21] Dr Fetherston noted the midwife's lack of training in his report. He insinuated that she had shown negligence when she 'completely left the patient' for two days after the first signs of labour.[22] The account presents Mrs C as being in a dangerously 'hopeless condition' until the moment she came into the care of doctors at the hospital. Only once in this environment, away from the midwife, could Fetherston and his assistant surgeons intervene heroically to save her life. Members of the medical profession variously portrayed midwives as 'ignorant, clumsy, and dirty', 'entirely incompetent' and participants in 'cruel and filthy practices' that caused infection.[23] These assessments were gender-based, and also strongly class-based. Many midwives in colonial Australia were not formally educated, and in many cases were illiterate. Some women who attended and assisted in childbirth were paid, but many did so in an unpaid capacity.[24] Although midwives maintained strong connections and trust among local communities, cases like that of Mrs C demonstrate doctors' increasing assumption of authority over what had been the domain of women for centuries. In doing so, they began to fracture existing female healthcare networks and reap financial benefits in the process.[25]

Doctors' growing presence at cases of childbirth at both home and hospital in the late nineteenth century presented opportunities to encounter and procure specimens for the museum collection. For instance, when thirty-eight-year-old Mrs M died suddenly while giving birth in her home in Berwick, Victoria, in September 1880, Dr John Elmes performed an autopsy in the presence of Mrs M's husband, who had requested the procedure, as well as several of her friends, and a midwife. Upon removing and examining the foetus, Elmes discovered that about two-thirds of the umbilical cord was 'rotten, infiltrated with dark blood, and very friable'.[26] He investigated the state of the foetus further to surmise that extra-uterine foetation – when the foetus forms outside the uterus – (see Figure 9) had caused its unviability, and that Mrs M had died from a ruptured cyst that covered the foetus. While it is unclear if Elmes retained the specimen or not, this case demonstrates that as medicine entered the birthing room, doctors gained access to bodies and specimens that they rarely would have in previous decades.

Opportunities for doctors like Elmes to retain foetal specimens for the museum collection also arose from nineteenth-century attitudes towards the death and burial of foetuses and babies. Burial records from the Old Melbourne Cemetery reveal that dozens of young babies were buried there between 1866 and 1917. Some had died after several months; others after only a number of days. One unnamed male infant who had lived for just four short hours before succumbing to a 'want of strength' was buried at the request of his father.[27] With regards to the need for burial, it appears to have mattered greatly if a baby was born alive, even if only for a breath. When a family could not afford a private burial, babies were often buried in communal graves, along with paupers and unclaimed bodies.[28] The same cannot always be said following the loss of a foetus. There is limited evidence to suggest foetal bodies were commonly afforded a proper burial – that is, being laid to rest in a coffin in consecrated

**Figure 9** Extra-uterine pregnancy, 516-101852, Harry Brookes Allen Museum of Anatomy and Pathology, University of Melbourne. Photograph by Gavan Mitchell. (This image may not be copied, reproduced or distributed in any way unless authorized by the Curator, Harry Brookes Allen Museum of Anatomy and Pathology, the University of Melbourne.)

ground. As a result, doctors likely had greater access to foetal bodies than those of young babies. The absence of burial does not reflect a lack of mourning, loss or emotional investment in the foetus. Some families may have buried a foetal body privately if finances allowed; others may have wanted to conduct a burial but been unable to do so based on circumstance.

There were, of course, a range of views on what the foetus, embryo and miscarriage represented. In her compelling analysis of experiences of miscarriage in nineteenth-century North America, historian Shannon Withycombe notes that the 'idea that miscarriage is somehow naturally or inherently inclusive of a death is a … recent construction' and that while the language with which women and doctors described the loss of a foetus was sometimes indicative of emotional loss, death or mourning, it commonly referred to an expulsion, or 'ejective process'.[29] Prior to the nineteenth century, miscarriage was often viewed as a healthy expulsion of an unhealthy blockage, or 'bad blood'; a miscarriage was a natural end to a pregnancy, rather than an event consisting of the loss of a potential baby.[30] While doctors were developing an embryological understanding of foetal development, nineteenth-century women described the expelled contents of the uterus from an early pregnancy variously as 'bubbly lots' or 'untoward matter', with little relation to a human infant. Others conceived of it as a personified being.[31] Women's written recollections also reveal a wide spectrum of emotions towards the loss of a foetus.[32] Many women were saddened, frustrated or disappointed with their reproductive issues. Other women expressed relief, thankfulness and even outright joy at the realization they had miscarried.[33] While the latter responses might imply that a foetus was unwanted, it might also indicate that many women considered the foetus to be biological matter rather than a distinct human being. Such interpretations would have aided doctors in their efforts to retain foetal specimens.

The lack of direct evidence for these negotiations about the meaning of the foetus in the Australian sources does not allow for this same conclusion to be made. In most medical literature, the family's sentiment towards the retention and examination of foetal specimens is conspicuously absent, and correspondence that accompanies specimens does not often disclose how or if the doctor asked for the family's approval to keep the remains.[34] Elmes' report, for instance, does not mention what Mrs M's family understood the unviable foetus to be, whether they had any objection to his inspection or retention of the remains, or if they knew that he had retained them. We cannot know from the available sources whether Mrs M had imbued the foetus with social significance, or if her family's circumstances precluded their ability to bury it. Perhaps they wished to bury the foetus and their wishes fell upon deaf ears, or maybe they considered the remains to be medical waste and did not oppose Elmes' desire to remove them. It must be acknowledged that such negotiations are rarely present in documentation concerning specimen retention in general, but the apparent power imbalances in recorded encounters between doctors and women seeking medical attention for complications during pregnancy and childbirth was one decisive factor in doctors' ability to keep foetal specimens.

Some women and their families appeared willing to hand over foetal tissues, in what might be seen as a moment of collaboration between doctors and their patients.[35] But it is also vital to consider how the shifting power dynamics that accompanied the growing authority of medicine over pregnancy and childbirth affected these interactions. These changes meant that doctors could access these bodies in ways they could not for the bodies of adults, children or babies. Moreover, doctors sometimes used subterfuge to take possession of specimens they deemed valuable. When parents objected to the doctor taking an embryo or foetus, he usually left despondently but respectfully. In one case recorded in Cincinnati in 1859, however, the doctor 'concealed [a foetus] under the bedclothes' while telling bystanders it was merely blood clots.[36] In another case several years later, a doctor who discovered that his patient was carrying a second, but deceased, foetus chose not to disclose to her this fact in order to keep the specimen for his own purposes. These incidents suggest that some doctors who attended the cases of miscarriage resorted to deception to procure specimens as valuable research tools.[37] As can be seen, many doctors had a detached response towards pregnancy loss and the retention of foetal remains. Guided by this attitude, these doctors defined deceased foetuses as medical waste that could be repurposed for research or education within a specimen collection, rather than an individual body to bury.

Decades later, in the 1930s, the collecting project of gynaecologist John Charles Rock, pathologist Arthur T. Hertig and laboratory technician Miriam Menkin continued to exemplify the lengths some researchers went to in their efforts to collect embryo specimens. The research team set out to find very early embryos by encouraging women who were scheduled for elective hysterectomies at Boston's Free Hospital for Women to engage in unprotected sexual activity in the leadup to their operation. Surgeries were scheduled on specific days to maximize the researchers' chances of finding a fertilized ovum, which, if found, was placed in a vial, and taken to the Carnegie Institute for cataloguing and documentation. Over fourteen years of this orchestrated scheme, Rock and Hertig accumulated thirty-four embryos. There is some evidence to suggest that participating women knew of the scientists' intentions, and that the health of the women involved meant that the embryos would not have been viable in any case; the work also occurred in a time when there was not yet a way of confirming such an early pregnancy. What has been termed the Boston 'egg hunt' has been criticized more recently for the somewhat deceptive claim that the specimens were 'naturally occurring', and for the ethical complications of knowingly procuring specimens from hysterectomies performed on pregnant women.[38]

Whereas the above cases highlight doctors' power over their patients and their families, not all doctors acted, or could act, on their access to foetal specimens so freely. In some cases, like that of a twenty-six-year-old Australian woman in August 1881 who suffered antepartum haemorrhage, doctors faced resistance from the patient and her family. After Ballarat doctor David Jermyn arrived at the patient's home, she 'delivered of [a] singular and unsightly mass', which Jermyn retained to forward to Allen at the university. This mass was in fact an acephalous foetus that was expelled immediately following the birth of a small but healthy male infant. Jermyn recalled having attended a similar case twenty years prior, but noted that in that circumstance, he 'was not allowed to take [the foetal remains] away'.[39] This statement suggests not only that Jermyn asked the mother and her family for permission to remove the remains, but that he honoured their decision when they opposed his request.

The dangers of surgically removing a deceased foetus from a living patient meant that doctors rarely attempted such procedures, even if the foetus may have been an interesting specimen for research or the anatomy museum collection. In July 1857, Dr John Maund had a patient present with what he suspected to be an extra-uterine pregnancy. Maund could not diagnose the patient solely through examination, and when the patient's condition improved fortuitously, she returned home. After three years of what must have been considerable discomfort, the patient summoned Maund while suffering from abdominal pain, swelling and 'derangements'.[40] She died shortly after. During the autopsy, Maund found the remains of an eight-month-old foetus within an abdominal cyst. He reflected in the *Australian Medical Journal* that when the patient first presented to him, he chose not to 'satisfy [his] mind as to the exact pathology of th[e] case' by performing a gastrotomy procedure to remove the remains of the foetus.[41] To conduct 'so dangerous and doubtful an operation' would have endangered his patient's life, so he chose to 'relinquish the idea'.[42] Although written evidence shows that doctors in hospitals and private practice around Melbourne often had the ability to access and retain foetal specimens, in some situations they were dissuaded by either the patient's family or the medical risk not to act on this instinct. Unlike the doctor in Cincinnati, who ignored a family's pleas and covertly took foetal remains away under a sheet, and doctors that historian Lynn M. Morgan characterizes as 'grave robbers of the womb', medical professionals like Maund and Jermyn exercised great caution before removing such remains.[43]

An increasing medical presence in settings of childbirth, the vulnerability of women in such circumstances and nineteenth-century notions of what the foetus represented meant that, despite occasional objections, Australian doctors had relatively unrestricted access to the material remains of miscarriage. Doctors collected foetal specimens to improve reproductive outcomes for women and better medical education, in an environment in which they wrested childbirth away from traditional female authority in favour of the sphere of medicine.

## Specimen collecting and medical discourse

How did doctors' authority over women's reproductive health manifest itself in the museum? What did they use foetal material for, and how did it contribute to the development of medicine? Australian doctors retained foetal specimens in an era when the physical constitution of the developing foetus remained somewhat elusive to both the medical profession and the general public. The composition of the collection at the Harry Brookes Allen Museum attests that they did so for largely educational purposes. The collection contains very few microscopic embryos or non-pathological specimens that display a linear evolution of development, but includes over one hundred foetal specimens at later stages of development, including many examples of pathology.

Furthermore, many of the pathology specimens have been oriented within their jars to guide the viewer's eye to notable features, and others have been dissected to reveal internal structures that would be of educational benefit. For instance, one foetus – prepared in 1925 by Dr H. O. Johnston and Dr J. O. Thorburn of the Melbourne Hospital – has been dissected to show the foetal circulatory system. Another specimen from much later, in the 1950s, displays the blood supply to the bowel and kidneys of a foetus at term. It also includes a coloured glass rod placed in the inferior vena cava of the heart to draw attention to this important feature.[44] These visual and material characteristics demonstrate that doctors used collected specimens to contribute to the emerging medical discourse in medical journals and professional circles surrounding the foetus, pregnancy and childbirth, and to bring these developments to the attention of medical students.

Collecting foetal specimens for largely educational purposes provides a point of contrast to other significant foetus and embryo specimen collecting projects in the late nineteenth and early twentieth centuries, which aimed to contribute new knowledge to the developing specialization of embryology. For example, in the 1870s, renowned Swiss embryologist William His embarked on a project to collect embryos from the first two months of development. He encouraged medics in his professional networks not to dispose of what he considered to be 'precious objects', but to instead send them to him so that he could draw, photograph, model and section the specimens with a microtome.[45] Although His' collection only numbered several dozen specimens, it provided an unprecedented opportunity to view the internal structures of the embryo and offered inspiration for the 'mania' for collecting human embryos and foetuses over the following half-century.[46]

Another embryo-collecting venture, at Johns Hopkins University in Baltimore, took up where His left off. The project, which was funded by the Carnegie Institute and led by His' student, Franklin Paine Mall, saw doctors amass around 10,000 specimens from cases of miscarriage between 1913 and 1944. Their aim was to materialize the embryo's 'empirical substance, body and form' so that it could be studied and better understood.[47] Mall's endeavour found support from within the medical field – the State Board of Public Health for Maryland even instructed physicians to send specimens in to the collection – and appears to have occurred without noticeable public opposition. Some women may have willingly contributed to the collecting project by giving doctors miscarried foetal remains rather than disposing of them.[48] The Carnegie project constituted a major undertaking by the American medical profession to depict and develop knowledge in the field of embryology. Whereas the research projects led by His and Mall saw embryos taken from wombs homes, and hospitals into the research laboratory, Australian doctors procured specimens within a gift economy for use in the museum and classroom.

## Foetuses preserved in isolation

The Harry Brookes Allen Museum holds dozens of foetuses preserved in isolation – that is, preserved with no maternal material – the majority of which display pathologies. One striking example is a hemisected anencephalic foetus, which has a protrusion of brain tissue over the scalp and into the nasal cavity.[49] The nature of its housing means that it can be viewed from all angles, as an example of a severe developmental disorder. There is no reference to the woman who supported its growth, either visually or in the museum catalogue. Other specimens displaying pathological conditions, such as two foetuses with achondroplasia (a bone growth disorder that causes dwarfism), also focus solely on the condition of the foetus itself.[50] Visually and materially, these specimens entirely exclude any allusion to the female body. This may have occurred simply because the loss of a foetus does not always involve the removal of the uterus or other reproductive organs. In other cases, however, it is likely that the female referent was removed by a male preparator, who decided it was unnecessary for the purposes of display and teaching within the medical sphere.

Anonymized foetal specimens presented in a traditional nineteenth-century manner, suspended within transparent containers of liquid preservative, speak to issues of presence and absence in the museum collection. In particular, they raise questions about the visual and material representation of the women of whom the specimens were once a part. In her study on the display of foetal remains, Emily Porth suggests that female bodies in both human and non-human animal foetal museum displays have been marginalized, made invisible or only included as reproductive beings with a capacity to bear and raise offspring.[51] The presence of foetal specimens that exclude visual and material references to the female body need not be considered as doctors' attempts to ignore or devalue these bodies. Instead, they can be understood in terms of the growing interest in the health of foetuses, babies and children that occurred in early-twentieth-century Australia. Historian Sara Dubow asserts that the visualization of the foetus through technology in the mid-twentieth century 'enabled the identification of a fetus as a "person" separate from the mother, and constructed the fetus as a "citizen" with rights'.[52] But earlier in the twentieth century, well before foetuses began to be granted legal rights, infants went from a state of great vulnerability in society to being of great interest to doctors in Australia.[53]

The speciality of paediatrics developed during this era in which there was widespread public endorsement of measures to encourage a higher birth rate. Australian historian Lisa Featherstone links this pronatalism to concerns over population growth due to a declining white birth rate. Governments and other institutions put in place ante- and post-natal measures to nurture infants and children, and doctors intensified their supervision of mothers during these stages.[54] Doctors' emphasis on improving healthcare for 'vulnerable future citizens' was confined to white babies mainly of the middle and upper classes, which were thought of as potential assets to the nation.[55] Part of this shift saw the foetus transform from a being seen as part of a woman's body to a separate being.[56] As attitudes towards the infant began to change, the medical gaze turned to the foetus, which, in turn, became medicalized and pathologized as an individual body.

To contribute to the broad social aim of increasing the healthy white population, doctors needed to understand pathologies that affected the foetus on the level of each individual body. Retaining and preserving foetal specimens in isolation enabled them to do so. Contemporary articles in the *Australian Medical Journal* and the *Intercolonial Medical Journal of Australasia* detail the sorts of foetal specimens collected and placed into the museum. In July 1892, Harry Brookes Allen reported on a case of a foetus with acephaly and a congenital deformity of the arms and legs. Several years later, in June 1896, Dr W. Atkinson-Wood contributed a long report to the *Intercolonial Medical Journal of Australasia* about a seven-month-old anencephalous foetus, accompanied by photographs of the specimen.⁵⁷ A skiagram – an early type of radiograph, similar to the x-ray – depicting the specimen also featured in the following issue of the journal. The frequency with which doctors noted cases of 'monstrous' foetuses indicates that they engaged with medical questions about the pathologies that severely affected foetal growth and, consequently, could be detrimental to increasing the birth rate.⁵⁸ Foetal specimens in isolation, without reference to the female body, can therefore be interpreted as tools that enabled doctors to visualize a range of foetal pathologies and, by extension, to foster medical dialogue that might work towards treating or minimizing conditions that affect the developing foetus.

The museum collection also includes numerous examples of miscarried foetal specimens that demonstrate different stages of development. These sorts of specimens featured in increasingly frequent discussions and presentations within the medical profession surrounding foetal growth. In August 1892, for instance, Dr G. A. Syme delivered a paper at a meeting of the Medical Society of Victoria on the possible causes and treatments for congenital clubfoot. He brought in two specimens to illustrate the paper – one of a twelve-week-old foetus from Allen's anatomy museum, and the other of a cast recently taken from an eleven-week-old baby with severe congenital clubfoot. Using these specimens, Syme put forward an argument that the identical position of the feet in both specimens meant that 'club-foot is an arrest of development – the permanence of a certain stage in the evolution of the lower limbs'.⁵⁹ There is a specimen in the anatomy museum consisting of a left hand and foot of a foetus, displaying both polydactyly (the occurrence of one or more extra fingers or toes) and congenital club foot.⁶⁰ The combination of Syme's presentation and the museum specimen demonstrates a belief that the preserved, individualized foetus could bring about a greater understanding of this developmental abnormality and, subsequently, lead to preventative treatment. Evidently, the health of the foetus was no longer subsumed under that of the mother, as it had been earlier in the nineteenth century.⁶¹ When considered from this perspective, each foetus retained in isolation on the museum shelves might reflect the new emphasis in the medical sphere on the foetus and baby as individuals with specific medical needs.

Australian anatomists' reasons for collecting foetal specimens in isolation were not confined to the field of biomedicine. It also involved answering questions about perceived racial distinctions between white Europeans and Australia's Indigenous peoples. As O'Sullivan and Jones have discussed, two Aboriginal foetuses of nine- and eighteen-weeks' gestation, collected in 1912 by Australian anthropologists Walter Baldwin Spencer and Herbert Basedow, feature in two published papers of prominent twentieth-century comparative anatomist Frederic Wood-Jones.[62] In the first paper, Wood-Jones tabulates and then compares limb measurements between the Aboriginal specimens and Portuguese and Chinese-Hawaiian foetuses, and in the second he compares the Aboriginal foetuses to a 'normal white foetus'.[63] Wood-Jones was known during his lifetime for his positive outlook on Australia's Indigenous peoples, emphasizing a perceived 'difference rather than inferiority' to the white population. He was simultaneously collecting Aboriginal skulls and body parts to send to the Royal College of Surgeons in London.[64] Neither the specimens nor any documentation that may have accompanied them in the museum have survived, but the diagrams and measurements researchers produced from them ensure their legacy remains.[65]

Despite their small number, these two specimens represent possibly the only Australian Aboriginal foetuses collected during an era when white doctors had 'little room for the *idea* of an Aboriginal mother, let alone the examination of her foetus'.[66] These factors, combined with the limited number of Aboriginal women wanting or being able to receive medical attention from mostly white, male doctors, illustrate a bias towards lower- and middle-class white women within the collection, and the knowledge surrounding foetal development it helped form. The two Aboriginal foetal specimens were collected primarily to benefit medical research, but also represent the physical manifestations of late-nineteenth- and early-twentieth-century ideas of race in Australia.

Specimens in the Melbourne Medical School collection that display the foetus in isolation provide insight into the way doctors formulated ideas within the developing discourse surrounding foetal development and pathology. Predominantly white, male physicians conducted investigations into foetal remains and decided what to include and exclude in the museum space, but the lack of representation of the female body in these specimens does not necessarily signify a belief that they were unimportant. It also reflects the practical reality that the loss of a foetus did not always include the loss of the uterus or other reproductive organs. Instead, these isolated specimens constitute one part of the narrative of growing medicalization of the foetus in late-nineteenth- and early-twentieth-century Australia.

## Foetuses preserved in situ

The claim that foetal displays in museums can devalue the female body may be accurate for some collections, but it poses a challenge for interpreting the collection at the Harry Brookes Allen Museum. The collection contains dozens of specimens that purposefully include the female body as an essential part. As mentioned earlier, almost a quarter of the entries for foetal specimens in the museum catalogue include parts of the female body – most commonly the uterus, fallopian tubes, ovaries or placenta.[67] I do not dispute the observation that the female body is an 'absent referent' in many specimens, nor do I suggest that the inclusion of only the reproductive organs of the female body in the material and visual constitution of the specimens is unproblematic.[68] Rather, in this section I shift the conversation away from assessing the presence or absence of a female referent, to establish instead why doctors collected specimens with a female referent based on the questions about the causes of miscarriage and complications in pregnancy, for which they and prospective mothers desperately sought answers.

Australian medical literature in the late nineteenth and early twentieth centuries reveals a concern for the number of women experiencing miscarriage, and the medical profession's lack of understanding of its cause or methods for its prevention. Doctors who encountered miscarriages before this time did not usually record them, and the reality that many miscarriages would have been unreported or occurred before a woman knew she was pregnant – as remains the case today – makes it difficult to identify the actual rate. That said, the frequency with which Australian women experienced miscarriage in this era made it of pressing concern for doctors and women alike.

Medical case reports written by doctors can present glimpses into women's experiences of complicated pregnancies and miscarriages, rather than only present the perspective of the male doctor in such cases. For example, in 1866, twenty-four-year-old Mrs F was described in a report as a 'remarkably healthy looking person', but out of six pregnancies she had not delivered one living child.[69] When Mrs F became pregnant for a seventh time, she sought medical advice on how she might avoid another miscarriage. She had well-respected Melbourne gynaecologist and obstetrician Dr Richard Tracy visit her in the comfort of her home, which suggests she was an economically secure woman.[70] Tracy encouraged Mrs F to seek a premature induction of labour to heighten the chance of saving the child. She sent for her doctor when she experienced severe rigours and fainting, but the foetus could not be saved. Several months later, Mrs F was again pregnant and, in her words, she 'began to hope … that *this* would be the exceptional case'.[71] Amid the clinical language used by her doctor, Mrs F's case report provides a sense of her humanity, and her anguish at the situation. She describes how during one miscarriage, she 'felt the child die' inside her, and that her situation caused her 'very great uneasiness'.[72] Her hopeful statement illustrates her will and desire to have a baby, despite the obvious distress she had been through in trying so many times before. Although she felt well throughout the first six months of pregnancy, in the eighth month, with little warning, Mrs F miscarried again.

Despite women like Mrs F approaching doctors for advice and assistance with greater regularity as the nineteenth century progressed, Australian doctors at this time were perplexed by women like Mrs F who experienced multiple miscarriages. Tracy was left feeling 'uneasy' and 'very much vexed' at the 'seemingly unaccountable way' in which Mrs F was repeatedly losing pregnancies.[73] He was not alone in his frustration. Several years earlier, in 1858, Dr W. Thomson put forward the theory that 'after one miscarriage … has occurred, the same person is apt to have it occur again *because the womb acquires a habit*'. He did not, however, offer any explanation for how or why this was the case, and even acknowledged that there was 'no earthly explanation' for his conclusion.[74]

Doctors literally took the foetus out of women's grasp, to medicalize the foetal body and miscarriage as concerns that only they knew how to solve. But to do so, they relied on women sharing intimate perceptions of their experiences of pregnancy. Women like twenty-four-year-old Mrs I, who was admitted to the Women's Hospital in 1893 with pain in her abdomen, demonstrate how women's recognition and articulation of symptoms played a crucial role in the formation of a medical understanding of miscarriage and, therefore, contributed to their own better reproductive outcomes. Mrs I told her doctor that she believed she had miscarried because during an episode of profuse bleeding, she 'noticed something like a piece of jelly, which she took for the foetus'.[75] Soon after this discovery, Mrs I was hospitalized for severe pain and exhaustion. She was found to have both a uterine tumour and a thin uterine wall, which her physician, Dr Pinniger, believed had allowed the small, six-week-old foetus to 'escape'.[76] Another medical journal report from 1877 notes that Patient AM stated to her doctor, 'I am sure I am going to have a miscarriage', before she suffered a uterine rupture that led to her death and that of her foetus. In a similar case, Mrs H expressed that 'she felt the child fall dead inside her; after which she did not again feel any motion indicative of its living condition'.[77]

Medical episodes that include the patient's observations about her body and circumstances show that women understood their conditions intimately and expressed themselves to their doctors. In many cases, physicians relied on these perceptions to develop a better understanding and treatments that would enable women to safely deliver the babies they sought to have. While there were no doubt many cases of doctors ignoring women who expressed knowledge about their conditions, these examples provide evidence that some doctors took cues from their patients when diagnosing and treating them.[78] Through the veil of medical authority presented in case reports, women's voices can be detected and woven into the historical narratives surrounding collected foetal remains.

These overlooked voices provide significant context to episodes in which doctors collected specimens from miscarriage cases, as they attempted to better their understanding of the condition's cause, and possibilities for prevention. In many recorded cases in which a doctor detected an expelled or deceased foetus, there is no mention of what became of the remains. It is likely that doctors classified most miscarried embryos and foetuses as medical waste and disposed of them accordingly. In other cases, however, doctors deemed the material remnants of miscarriage worth retaining for what they could reveal about the cause of foetal death. After Mrs F's eighth pregnancy ended in miscarriage, Dr Tracy decided to examine the dead foetus carefully in situ for an explanation of her repeated miscarriages. He noted the presence of a 'gorged and congested' umbilical cord and an unusually large and dense placenta, and described the attached foetus itself as 'remarkably bloated'.[79] These observations led Tracy to believe that the foetus was 'over nourished', and that this was the cause of its unviability.[80] When Mrs F fell pregnant again several months later, Tracy placed her on a strict 'course of depletory measures', which eliminated beer and heavy wine from her diet, and prescribed specially concocted draughts for her to drink instead.[81] Following this intervention, she gave birth to a healthy, living child – a fact Tracy assured the journal's readers was due to his treatment plan.

Whether or not it was an improved diet or another factor that led to this positive outcome, Mrs F's experience illustrates that some doctors responded to women's concerns about their reproductive capabilities by retaining and examining foetal remains. It demonstrates the increasing medicalization of pregnancy and miscarriage and presents this development as one that provided doctors with specimens. This change was not, however, as simple as doctors forcing their way into the lives of pregnant women. Instead, as Mrs F's choice to seek Tracy's medical assurances of preventing miscarriage shows, women's decisions aided doctors in securing their status as experts in the fields of pregnancy and foetal development in the nineteenth century. In her determination to have a baby, Mrs F willingly turned to the medical profession in the hope of preventing further miscarriages; she can hardly be thought of as an unwilling recipient of medical intervention she did not want. While scholars have noted that it took time for the 'consolidation of the medical profession with the middle class', of which Mrs F was likely a part, to shift to the working classes, the case enables one to perceive the beginnings of the shift towards pregnancy and miscarriage as an experience that needed medical intervention rather than one that occurred solely in the domain of women.[82]

Looking outside the museum to depictions of pregnancy, miscarriage and childbirth in the home and clinic that were published in medical journals places the specimens into a new historical narrative that incorporates not only the work of doctors, but also, importantly, the experiences of the women from whom they took specimens. Medical journal reports reveal that doctors used specimens to visualize what occurred in cases of ectopic, or extra-uterine, pregnancy, in an era when it was not possible to see any other way. Rather than remove the foetus from its context, they considered foetal and maternal bodies visually as a whole system, to understand the causes of miscarriage and foetal developmental abnormalities. Analysing case reports that contain physicians' and women's voices concerning pregnancy and miscarriage enables anatomy and pathology museum specimens – like those comprising ruptured fallopian tubes with and without a foetus inside, and foetal remains preserved alongside the placenta or umbilical cord – to gain cultural context that they currently lack.

When considered alongside these accounts, the retention and presentation of foetal remains in situ suggest that medical interest in the body of the mother had not been replaced by interest in the body of the foetus or child. This conclusion is echoed in case books from the Melbourne Women's Hospital during this era, which reveal that doctors were still regularly performing procedures fatal to foetuses without hesitation to save women's lives during childbirth. Practices such as craniotomy or embryotomy, which involved perforating and crushing the foetal skull and removing the body piece by piece, were regularly performed in order to save the woman's life. In one particularly vivid case, in November 1901 Dr W. G. Cuscaden performed a podalic version (a procedure in which the foetus is turned inside the uterus so that one or both feet can move through the cervix), then a craniotomy, in which he 'decapitated and perforated [the] head' of the foetus before extracting its dead body with forceps.[83] In another case of a twenty-one-year-old woman with a breech presentation, Cuscaden 'crushed [the] head [of the foetus] ... and delivered with [a] good deal of traction', and the patient went on to survive and recover from the procedure. The lecture notebooks of Melbourne Medical School student Mary de Garis demonstrate this same prioritization of maternal life over the survival of a foetus. During her studies, de Garis noted that in a situation where there is 'enough enlargement of the head to completely obstruct labour the child's life is of no value' if it meant compromising the life of the mother.[84] Her comment points to the continuing centrality of the mother's body over the foetal body; in this era, without highly effective surgical procedures to aid in childbirth, it was still preferable to perform the 'grisly task' of craniotomy to end the life of the foetus if it meant saving the life of the mother.[85]

It is quite possible that every woman whose body parts or remains of miscarriage ended up on the museum shelves might have had a similar story to Mrs F – one that provides insight and emotionality to enrich our understanding of pregnancy and pregnancy loss in Australian history. Although women's voices are rarely recorded in these case reports, their concerns peek through in some circumstances. By listening carefully for the voices of women like Mrs F, these stories can be included alongside specimens of reproductive organs and foetuses in the anatomy museum. This process gives the specimens greater social and cultural meaning by presenting a more nuanced interpretation that accounts for the experiences of late-nineteenth- and early-twentieth-century women and better acknowledges the foetal specimens that represent, at once, neither a birth nor a death, yet have a continuing existence within the museum walls.

# 5

# War pathology specimens

After almost a century in storage and occasional use by medical professionals and students, a collection of pathological specimens taken from the bodies of Australian soldiers in the First World War went on public display for the first time in 2015. The exhibition included specimens of trench foot, of lungs noticeably disfigured from the effects of mustard gas poisoning, and of a brain with a bullet track wound, showing the damage wrought by projectiles (see Figures 10–12), among others. These examples of medical conditions seen and experienced by Australian soldiers and medical officers on the battlefield were displayed alongside other artefacts pertaining to the work of Australian doctors and dentists during the war. The exhibition, *Compassion and Courage*, opened at the Medical History Museum at the University of Melbourne on 24 April 2015, to coincide with the centenary of the Australian and New Zealand Army Corps (ANZAC) landing at Gallipoli.

My discussion of the collection of war wound specimens from the First World War explores how the lives of specimens intersect with narratives concerning the development of military medicine in Australia, the visual representation of the soldier's body and the display of human remains in museums. Drawing largely on the correspondence of medical officers and those working under the auspices of the Australian War Records Section (AWRS) between 1915 and 1919, this chapter argues that the collection was formed as a result of the collaborative efforts of medical officers who served in the war and medical professionals back home, to build a tradition of military medicine in Australia. The medical profession used the specimens in teaching and research during the interwar period, but the collection has only partly realized its intended purpose, and was not displayed for the first hundred years of its existence.

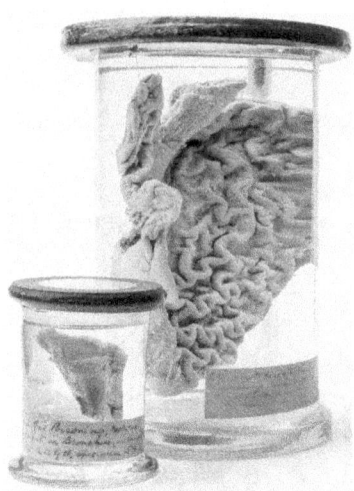

**Figure 10** Bronchus, mustard gas poisoning c. 1914–18; Stomach, mustard gas poisoning c. 1914–18, 531-003784 and 531-003783, Harry Brookes Allen Museum of Anatomy and Pathology, University of Melbourne. Photograph by Gavan Mitchell. (This image may not be copied, reproduced or distributed in any way unless authorized by the Curator, Harry Brookes Allen Museum of Anatomy and Pathology, the University of Melbourne.)

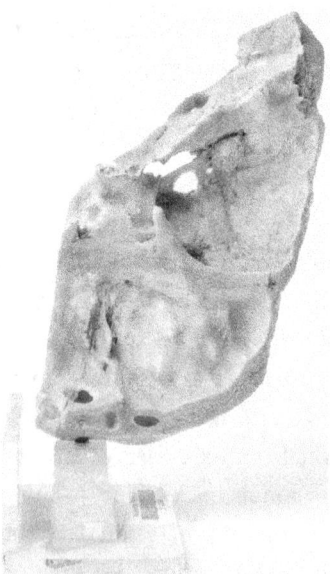

**Figure 11** Sphenoid bone with bullet, 531-003663, Harry Brookes Allen Museum of Anatomy and Pathology, University of Melbourne. Photograph by Gavan Mitchell. (This image may not be copied, reproduced or distributed in any way unless authorized by the Curator, Harry Brookes Allen Museum of Anatomy and Pathology, the University of Melbourne.)

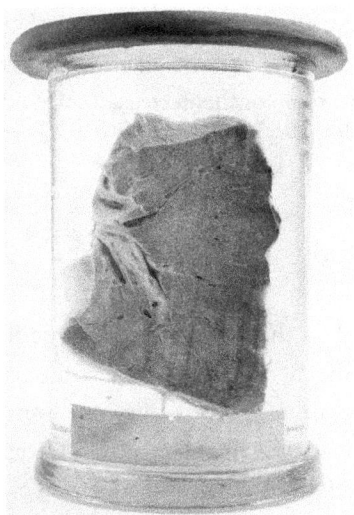

**Figure 12** Lung, poisoning, 531-003617, Harry Brookes Allen Museum of Anatomy and Pathology, University of Melbourne. Photograph by Gavan Mitchell.
(This image may not be copied, reproduced or distributed in any way unless authorized by the Curator, Harry Brookes Allen Museum of Anatomy and Pathology, the University of Melbourne.)

Despite the extensive literature regarding Australia's involvement in the First World War, relatively little attention has been given to the formation and purpose of the war wound specimen collection. Several historians have examined how other types of war relics collected under the AWRS, such as diaries and photographs, constituted a powerful mix of nationalism, historical consciousness and an obligation to the dead.[1] These discussions overlook the war wound collection, which has been labelled a 'gruesome case', without providing further investigation.[2] That said, historian Rosalind Hearder offers an important discussion of the collection's development and legacy, and the *Compassion and Courage* exhibition catalogue features a short yet informative essay which details the conditions in which medical officers procured specimens, the types of injuries they represent, and what might become of the specimens in the future.[3] In his examination of the war pathology collection held at the Royal College of Surgeons (RCS) in London, historian Samuel Alberti also briefly touches on the Australian collection, noting that Australian medical officers originally collected specimens as part of the imperial collecting effort, alongside their British, Canadian, New Zealand and South African contemporaries.[4] Considered alongside collections of war pathology assembled in other nations, including the United Kingdom, France and the United States,[5] this chapter explains the significance of the Australian collection for medical education and shows how debates about the spectatorship of the deceased body – and the soldier's body in particular – have affected its display.

## War specimens and the development of military medicine

Before the First World War, the field of military medicine in Australia barely existed. The curricula at the medical schools in Melbourne, Sydney and Adelaide did not offer courses in military medicine, nor were there any institutions explicitly dedicated to teaching the speciality. The medical profession itself, while growing, was still relatively small and consisted of generalist practitioners, and the state of medical research in Australia was, in the words of historian Peter Hobbins, 'piecemeal [and] part time'.[6] Australia's pledge to fight alongside the forces of the British Empire at the outbreak of the war placed severe strain on the medical profession. Not only would it need to send physicians overseas as medical officers of the Australian Army Medical Corps (AAMC), but it had also to continue to support the healthcare needs of a growing population at home. In response to the increased need for doctors, the Department of Defence requested that the universities 'consider special arrangements to facilitate the graduation of students who might afterwards be attached to the AIF [Australian Imperial Force]'.[7] The universities agreed to shorten their medical courses in the hope that moving students through their education more quickly would help with the issues of demand, and even introduced one-year 'War Emergency courses' in physiotherapy to provide practitioners for the war effort.[8]

At the Melbourne Medical School, however, Harry Brookes Allen expressed his concern that the 'shortage of medical practitioners [in Australia would] become very serious, both for military and for civil purposes'.[9] In the sphere of civilian medicine, Surgeon-General Richard 'Bertie' Fetherston stated in a memorandum to Australian medical professionals that every hospital must be 'prepared to work with a smaller staff than normal'.[10] By early 1916, the Children's Hospital in Melbourne had started employing fifth-year students instead of graduate practitioners, and the Alfred Hospital was also considering this option.[11] The Victorian Medical Women's Society provided support, with a letter to Allen relaying the willingness of the society's members 'to do anything … possible to assist in carrying on medical work in Melbourne'.[12] Although not permitted on the frontline, women served at home and overseas as both doctors and nurses during the war.[13]

Despite these provisions, there was still a shortage of medical officers with adequate training. Fleet-surgeon Algernon Carter Bean expressed desperation for more medics in a letter to Allen in mid-1916, writing that they were 'badly off for surgeons' and that he would be grateful for help 'at this stage with any young medical men'.[14] Such was the scarcity that the Department of Defence requested Allen not admit medical students for their examinations unless they agreed to volunteer for active service. Allen denied this request and repeatedly voiced his opposition to first-, second- and third-year students enlisting before finishing their studies. Statistics reveal that 1,752 men and 24 women medical graduates enlisted Australia-wide – the largest cohort of any Australian university discipline.[15] However, few had extensive training in military medicine to prepare them for the types of injuries and infections they would encounter during their service.

The First World War presented doctors with numerous cases of physical and mental trauma they had never before encountered, such as injuries and illnesses resulting from modern, mechanized trench warfare and explosives, infections like gas gangrene and the effects of so-called 'shell shock'. Not only did medical officers need to learn about these unfamiliar pathologies, but they had to learn quickly in order to treat the wounded soldiers who came to them for assistance.

The skills and techniques that doctors acquired during the war vastly improved the state of military medicine on an international level – the pioneers of modern plastic surgery shaped a new speciality dedicated to treating head and facial trauma, and the introduction of the Thomas splint – for immobilizing fractured limbs – decreased mortality rates from haemorrhage and infection significantly.[16] The war also led to the growth of the medical profession and medical research on a national level in Australia. First, as Dr A. H. Tebbutt wrote in the *Medical Journal of Australia* in 1918, the efforts of medical officers at Gallipoli in particular 'opened the eyes of the War Office to the importance in diagnosis and prevention of disease'.[17] More than that, however, the war's legacy in the field of medicine would continue well into the twentieth century. It led to increased government funding for medical initiatives, including new research institutes and public health measures. These measures, in turn, helped raise the standing of the medical profession among the population by shifting medicine away from the colonial ideal of individual practitioners to a field characterized by collective, utilitarian endeavour.[18]

Those who instigated the collection of war pathology specimens believed that such specimens could play a critical role in developing the field of military medicine in Australia, both during the war and in the years that followed. The purpose of the collection was clear from the beginning: medical officers were to procure pathological specimens to 'ensure that a valuable collection of specimens [would] be available in future years, for purposes of record and teaching in Australian Medical Schools'.[19] Soon after hostilities broke out, the army medical officers of Britain and its dominions began to collect specimens that displayed the disease and injury seen on the battlefield.[20] On 14 June 1915, the Surgeon-General of the British Royal Army Medical Corps (RAMC) circulated a memorandum to medical officers and military hospitals. This memorandum instructed medics to collect examples of the types of wounds produced by projectiles, infections seen in the trenches, fractured bones and injuries of various parts of the body, including the spinal cord, brain, skull and face.[21]

The initial response to the memorandum was slow. In the first eighteen months, the number of Australian specimens received was very small. Not disheartened, as the British had also experienced a slow response, the Australian Army Medical Corps sent out its own explicit instructions in a similar vein to the British.[22] In November 1916, Surgeon-General Neville Reginald Howse wrote: 'It is earnestly requested that all Australian Medical Officers will make every endeavour to collect and forward specimens'.[23] The forwarding site, the RCS in London, became the designated depot for receiving and safeguarding collected pathological material until the war's end.

Australian medical officers heeded instructions to create an 'enduring record ... of the injuries and diseases of warfare' for the purpose of developing the field of military medicine.[24] A report documenting the collection's progress states that between November 1916 and September 1918, 507 specimens made their way to the RCS, with 43 of these sent in August 1918 alone.[25] Collected specimens needed to exhibit the 'causes or effects of disease or wounds occurring in connection with warfare – terrestrial, marine, or aerial – on the tissues of the human body'. This might have included surgical and pathological specimens, as well as casts, microscopic slides, x-ray plates and projectiles or other foreign bodies removed from, or causing, wounds.[26]

Collecting specimens could be a difficult undertaking in peacetime, as established in Chapters 2 and 3. It appears to have been even more challenging in the context of war, but the AWRS laid out guidelines for medical officers on how to prepare and package specimens. These guidelines, written by John R. Drummond, stated that specimens should be removed from a body as soon as possible and preserved in a mixture that contained formalin. Once the specimen was ready to be transferred to London, officers were to wrap each specimen separately and place it into a box filled with sawdust or wood shavings to prevent movement. Hospital pails or petrol tins were recommended for small specimens, and wooden beer barrels sawn in half for larger specimens.[27] Lastly, a tag needed to be affixed to each specimen, stating the hospital from which it was being sent, the name of the sending officer and the disease or subject represented. Letters between the collection's organizers and casualty clearing stations in the field reveal that specimens sometimes arrived forced into containers too small for them, while others had been stained with the red ink of labels or were damaged by the pins with which the labels had been attached.[28] Such correspondence also discloses concern over specimens coming in 'entirely in the rough' that would provide little value to the collection's intended purpose.[29]

For the first two years of the collecting project, the RCS gratefully received all specimens. By the middle of 1918, however, this method of operation was partly replaced with requests for specific types of specimens. For example, a letter from the Third Australian General Hospital on 19 August 1918 requested that Colonel Barber ask his men in the Field Ambulances specifically to obtain 'specimens illustrating the immediate effects of missiles' because, until that point, the collection had been 'practically without them'.[30] The change in instruction suggests that the purpose of the collection was not merely to accumulate as many specimens as possible. Instead, it was to assemble a comprehensive collection of specimens illustrating the precise conditions that would contribute to the growth of military medicine back in Australia. The collection grew as a result of the combined efforts of Australian Army Medical Corps officers in hospitals, clearing stations and field ambulances, generally at first, and then more purposefully over time.

The collaborative nature of the collecting process continued as the specimens began their journey to Australia to become part of anatomy and pathology museums located around the country. Several prominent Australian doctors undertook the task of transferring the specimens from the RCS in London to Australia. They included Lieutenant Colonel Henry Newland, who was a pioneer of plastic surgery techniques during the war before returning to found the Royal Australasian College of Surgeons in 1929; Keith Inglis, who had been stationed in France at the Third Australian General Hospital during the war before assuming his position as pathologist at the Sydney Medical School and Sydney Hospital; and Harry Brookes Allen, who was at this point the Dean of Medicine, as well as Professor of Pathology, at the University of Melbourne.

Prior to their return home, Inglis and Newland worked in London to prepare the collection for transportation. Their task was made difficult when the British doctors overseeing the RCS museum suggested that they were 'entitled to retain for inclusion in the English collection any of [the Australian] specimens that [they] thought fit'.[31]

In a letter to the Australian War Records Office in February 1919, Inglis expressed his great anxiety that the British wanted to keep a large portion of the Australian collection – around eighty individual specimens – for themselves. More than that, Inglis claimed that the specimens in question actually 'constitute[d] the very cream of [the] collection' and were 'probably quite unique' for their precise depictions of war pathologies and excellent preparation.[32] The idea that the British could take specimens from the Australian collection did not sit well with Inglis and Newland, who had put in considerable effort to collect and administer the specimens – Newland alone had contributed 'some hundreds' of specimens to the collection.[33] Inglis wrote to the head of the collection at the RCS, Arthur Keith, to voice his uneasiness over the British retention of such valuable specimens and to press for their return. He noted that the Australian Army Medical Corps had been 'given every assurance' that by sending specimens to the RCS the collection 'would be even more safely guarded than if it remained in their own custody, and would be set aside for subsequent transfer to Australia'.[34] It appears that Keith responded stubbornly, saying that his assistant curator, Cecil Beadles (who later became curator of the RCS collection), had worked 'for the benefit of the English and not the Australian collection' and so wanted to keep specimens that would enhance the former, without concern for the latter.[35] Inglis stated that 'the ultimate fate of the specimens [was] ... a matter of considerable moment' to the Australian medical profession.[36] Despite their efforts, the Australians did not succeed in retaining their full selection of specimens. Just a few months after Inglis' request, Keith wrote to Colonel Millard of the Australian Army Medical Corps, thanking the Corps for its valuable gift of seventy specimens that would fill 'certain blanks which exist[ed] in the Imperial or Central Collection'.[37] The British offered a selection of replacement specimens in return, including examples of pathologies that were poorly represented in the Australian collection.

Regardless of whether or not the specimens lost to the British were indeed the very best of the Australian collection, the sense of pride, attachment and ownership that medical officers felt towards the specimens they had collected during the war is obvious. Inglis explained in his letter to the Australian War Records Office that medical officers knew their cases and the material they collected well. Similar feelings have been noted of medical specimen collecting during the American Civil War (1861–5), with historian Amanda Bevers finding 'physicians formed an intimate connection with their specimens' based not only on sentimentality, but because a physician's identity was tied to each specimen.[38] In the Australian context, not only was a medical officer's name literally attached to a specimen, but they had spent time treating the patient, sometimes performing an autopsy, and had gone to great lengths to preserve, package and send a specimen to the collecting depot. Therefore, without any connection between the medical officers and the 'absolutely unknown' replacement specimens provided by the British, the value of the collection to Australian physicians was diminished.[39] Although Inglis and Newland did not secure the entire Australian collection for transportation, their efforts reveal the sense of national pride and collegiality that accompanied their work.

While the shipment of prepared specimens was en route from London to Australia, Inglis, Dr George Cuscaden – who had served as Principal Medical Officer for Victoria during the war – and Allen met in Melbourne to decide how to divide the collection so that each state would have a selection of specimens.[40] About one-third of the collection went to the University of Sydney, another third to the University of Melbourne and around one hundred specimens to the University of Adelaide, although the specimens would remain 'nominally on loan' from the Department of Defence.[41] There was significant scope for expanding the teaching materials and fields of study at the medical schools in Melbourne, Sydney and Adelaide, as the oldest of these schools was barely fifty years old when the First World War began. Inglis, Allen and Cuscaden put aside the rest of the collection so that it could be distributed to the other states once they opened medical schools that could house and use the specimens.[42] Although the three doctors assigned some states a lesser share in the collection than others, Inglis wrote that they still considered it important that each state have a 'representative and comprehensive collection of specimens'.[43] While these schools had healthy rivalries throughout the late nineteenth and early twentieth centuries, they and the rest of the medical profession had been challenged during the war. The subsequent effort to endow each existing and future medical school with pathological war specimens was built on cooperation and good will. The collection reflects a joint commitment within the Australian medical profession to improve the state of military medicine during the interwar years.

Once each medical school received its collection of specimens, the curators set to work preparing the specimens as pedagogical tools for students learning about war pathology, and the broad field of military medicine. By mid-1919, Inglis had returned to his position in the pathology department at the University of Sydney. The managing committee of the Museum of Normal and Morbid Anatomy at the university invited him to carry out the work of mounting the specimens.[44] Despite his appointment, Inglis lamented in early 1920 that his 'work on the war specimens ... [had] not been progressing at all satisfactorily' due to the fact that he was unable to employ an assistant.[45] Nevertheless, Inglis persisted. He was determined to 'impress the university authorities with the value of [his] work' with the collection, and even paid out of his own pocket to employ an assistant for five months of work.[46] Inglis had been heavily involved in the collecting project and, with assistance not being forthcoming, he took the collection into his personal care so it could be of benefit to the medical school. Similarly, at the University of Melbourne Allen prepared and labelled each specimen to be placed in the anatomy museum he had overseen for several decades. It appears that neither university provided financial support for maintaining the specimens, nor showed interest in integrating them into the medical school curricula. During this era there was still a firm belief in the role of the medical specimen museum as a critical site of education, and Inglis did use the war pathology specimens 'on several occasions' during the 1920s for the instruction of medical officers and nurses.[47] Aside from incidental use, there is little evidence that the specimens became an integral part of teaching at either university, most likely because there was no space in the curriculum dedicated to training students in military medicine.

Although not an integral part of early-twentieth-century Australian medical school curricula, the specimen collection gained some traction in the wider medical profession. The six volumes of the *Australian Medical Journal* from 1916 and 1917 alone contained several dozen articles pertaining to aspects of military medicine, many of which mentioned collected specimens in their discussions. The *Australian Medical Journal* also republished articles in the field from the *British Medical Journal*.[48] While Australia still did not have a strong tradition of laboratory-based science like Britain, the publication of British articles facilitated an exchange of medical information between distant places. Case reports and meeting records published in the *Australian Medical Journal* demonstrate that several medical officers who returned from the First World War transferred their knowledge of the injuries, infections and diseases seen on the battlefield and in collected specimens into improved treatments for the civilian population in Australia.

For instance, at a meeting of the New South Wales branch of the British Medical Association in late 1922, Dr E. Marjory Little read a paper that detailed four types of dysenteric infection. She illustrated her paper with microscopic specimens obtained from troops during the war. Little had been attached to the RAMC as a pathologist in May 1918. Over the next year and a half, she assumed positions at the 25th Stationary Hospital in Rouen and a hospital laboratory in Étaples, before returning to Sydney in January 1920.[49] Back in Australia, she resumed her work as a bacteriologist at the Royal Prince Alfred Hospital and a Demonstrator in Pathology at the University of Sydney. Little's return to the hospital and university may have caused her to consider how pathological conditions she had encountered during the war could manifest in civilian life. After detailing the four types of dysenteric infection seen in the soldier population, and how to diagnose and treat them, Little provided suggestions as to how this research could be used in Australia to provide better treatment to the public.[50] Her research reflects the growing emphasis on population health and mobilization of local resources to respond to large-scale health concerns in the early twentieth century.[51]

At the same meeting of the British Medical Association, the proceedings of which were published in the *Australian Medical Journal* in 1923, Keith Inglis presented on the topic of 'Gas Gangrene in Military and Civil Practice'. He, too, illustrated his remarks with projections and specimens from the museum and hospital collection. After a brief explanation of the wartime experience of gas gangrene (a bacterial infection that affects muscle tissue, commonly seen in wartime cases with open wounds), he drew attention to the fact that cases of the infection in civil life are 'the exact counterpart, both clinically and pathologically' of those in military practice.[52] Based on his experience during the war and his work at Sydney Hospital, Inglis detailed to his colleagues the ways to recognize the infection, some reasons for its occurrence and several methods of treatment. Other doctors in attendance stated that there had been some confusion about how best to treat gas gangrene during the war. They noted '[in]sufficient confidence in the pathological findings' and a lack of specimens from which to learn.[53] By explaining his suggested treatments with specimens from both the war pathology collection and the hospital collection, Inglis was able to bring together military and civilian medicine. Doctors' papers and presentations that incorporated the pathological war specimens demonstrate how the specimens not only contributed to the development of military medicine in Australia, but also informed methods of treatment to benefit the greater population. As Peter MacCallum, Dean of the Faculty of Medicine, noted in 1939, the 'medical care of the remaining nine-tenths of the [non-military] community is not essentially different from that of the Army'.[54]

In 1930, many of the specimens were set on a new course outside the confines of the university setting. In February of that year, Sir Colin McKenzie of the Australian Institute of Anatomy (AIA) in Canberra sent a letter to each university requesting the transfer of war pathology specimens into his institution's possession, where they would be central to the development of knowledge in the 'important field' of military pathology.[55] Queensland University and the University of Western Australia had no hesitation in relinquishing the specimens when asked. At the former, the specimens had been rendered 'practically useless' due to a lack of care, while Western Australia had still not opened a medical school and so deemed the specimens an unnecessary asset.[56] The Sydney Medical School declined the request; Inglis argued that 'more use [could] be made of them [the specimens] from the point of view of the Army Medical Services' if they remained in Sydney.[57] He cited their implementation for instructing medical officers and nurses, and his personal connection to the specimens likely provided informative and vivid lessons for these men and women.

When the University of Melbourne received the AIA's request for war pathology specimens in 1930, the respondent expressed the desire that the university retain and care for its share of the collection.[58] The medical school's anatomy and pathology museum collection went through a period of uncertainty following Allen's death in 1926, but a new handwritten catalogue produced in 1927 suggests the museum still held a prominent position at the medical school. Within this catalogue, 130 war pathology specimens are listed, numbered and accompanied by case notes and other explanatory remarks.[59] It appears that the university recognized the effort that Allen and his successor, MacCallum, had put into preparing, labelling, ordering and cataloguing the war wound specimens and considered the collection of ongoing value to the medical school.

Contrary to his initial sentiment, in 1933 MacCallum decided that not all the specimens were required for teaching purposes and, with the blessing of the Department of Defence, approved their transfer to the AIA.[60] But this did not mark the end of their use at the university. On the eve of the Second World War, MacCallum borrowed some of the specimens from the AIA to illustrate a lecture given to post-graduate students.[61] Of course, the Second World War would see different types of pathologies and new challenges for medical officers, but the collection of First World War specimens played a role in preparing personnel for their upcoming service.

Australian medical officers in the First World War worked diligently to create 'an enduring record ... of the injuries and diseases of warfare' in the form of pathological specimens. In the field and at the Royal College of Surgeons, physicians worked in collaboration to bring home a specimen collection that would develop the tradition of military medicine in Australia. Once the specimens arrived in Australia, however, they had no straightforward application; medical schools did not offer military medicine as a subject, and only on occasion did physicians incorporate the specimens into their research. Without a clear purpose, and following Allen's passing and Inglis' assumption of a different professional position, the specimens largely fell into a state of disuse and, in some cases, disrepair. While the collecting project appears to have provided Australian medical officers and physicians with a sense of unity in their pursuit of a common goal, its intention of creating a continuing tradition of military medicine was not fully realized. That said, the specimens endured throughout the twentieth century and into the twenty-first century.

## Displaying the collection

Soon after the war pathology collection had been transported from London to Melbourne, the Department of Defence sent a letter to the registrars at the Melbourne, Sydney and Adelaide Medical Schools about the possibility of displaying the specimens. The letter stated that it was 'desirable to restrict the viewing of these specimens' to medical students and professionals, much like other specimens within anatomy and pathology museum collections.[62] The curators at each university museum adhered strictly to these instructions and kept the specimens out of the public eye for almost one hundred years. Instead, they have been held in universities around the country, as well as at the AIA, and the National Museum of Australia (NMA), which acquired the specimens following the permanent closure of the AIA in 1984.

Australian anatomy and pathology museum curators' decision not to display the war pathology specimens until the 2015 exhibition at the Medical History Museum at the University of Melbourne contrasts with the treatment of other national war wound specimen collections. Collections in the United Kingdom, the United States and France, for example, have been displayed for reasons of education and commemoration and to present narratives of medical and national progress. What motivated overseas institutions to display collected war pathology specimens? And why was the Australian collection not used in a similar manner?

First, body parts taken from soldiers have often been displayed for commemorative purposes. At the Army Medical Museum (AMM) in suburban Washington, DC (now the National Museum of Health and Medicine, located in Silver Spring, Maryland), for example, thousands of body parts removed from soldiers during the American Civil War have been on continuous display since the early 1860s. Doctors exploited their 'unfettered access to medicalised bodies' to retain more than 4,000 specimens for the collection – a project that played a pivotal role in the creation of a distinctly North American medical science, as well as formed a source of national pride.[63] Historian Shauna Devine states that the Army Medical Museum was laid out as a 'great, systematically arranged object-lesson' for physicians to learn the basic principles of military medicine and for the American public to better appreciate the work of doctors during the Civil War.[64] The museum was also set up to be a place of commemoration, and of mourning. It proved very popular with the public; visitors flocked to see the specimens in numbers so large the museum's opening hours had to be extended.[65]

The fact that most specimens could be linked directly to a soldier's name contributed greatly to their commemorative function. It enabled visitors to establish a strong emotional connection to the specimens they viewed. Some surviving soldiers requested photographs of their body parts in the museum, and bereaved families and friends sometimes visited the preserved limbs of those they lost during the war. In one case, Major General Daniel E. Sickles forwarded his own amputated leg to the museum, and even came to visit the limb each year on the anniversary of its amputation.[66] Not all visitors came to the museum to commemorate the war dead. Scholar Mark B. Feldman suggests that those voyeuristically inclined viewed the museum as a sensationalist tourist attraction that contained body parts reminiscent of the 'Barnumesque freaks' at contemporaneous travelling 'freak shows'.[67] There is, however, no indication of widespread revulsion at the exhibited specimens, nor of the outrage that greeted the opening of popular anatomy museums in Melbourne in the late nineteenth century (see Chapter 3), and it appears that most members of the public who visited the museum did so to learn about doctors' work in treating wounded soldiers during the Civil War. The named body parts retained a certain humanity – they 'occupied the space between science and sentiment' that made possible a powerful connection between the spectator and a humanized object.[68] The strong commemorative pull of the specimens in the Army Medical Museum meant that many visitors could overcome an aversion to viewing dismembered body parts. As a result, named specimens served as poignant reminders of the human cost of the Civil War and the dedicated work of medics to treat the wounded. While the Civil War specimens are from a different era to the First World War collections, their continuous presence as commemorative objects presents a point of contrast to the Australian collection, which has not assumed a similar function.

Specimens taken from soldiers' bodies and displayed in museum contexts also served to demonstrate a narrative of progress within a nation's medical profession and national reconstruction during and after the First World War. During the war, the Val-de-Grâce hospital museum in Paris, said to contain more than 10,000 war pathology specimens, functioned primarily as the teaching collection of the attached training centre for medical officers. A report in the *British Medical Journal* in June 1917 noted that many British surgeons had visited the collection and been impressed with the 'care and completeness' of its documentation and display.[69] Art historian Amy Lyford argues that the Val-de-Grâce also assumed a 'political and an aesthetic role in the state's public relations program to deflect criticism about the huge numbers of casualties being incurred along the western front'.[70] In addition to pathological specimens and bone fragments, the museum contained wax models known as 'moulages' that depicted facial trauma in particular. The moulages were arranged to show a progression of treatment, from a severely disfigured face to the face at different stages of recovery, before a final depiction of the face as reconstructed through surgery. In this state, they could be read as a narrative of recovery and repair rather than of a permanent state of trauma, as is the case for an isolated individual specimen. Lyford contends that the exhibits served as a political articulation of the state's commitment to the collective regeneration and therapy of the nation; the nation's healing would mirror that of the disfigured soldier's body.[71] Large crowds comprising the civilian public visited the exhibition in 1916, eager to see what the state was doing to assist soldiers during the war.[72] The display they viewed at the Val-de-Grâce demonstrates how nations could mobilize pathology specimens to promote specific narratives of the war to the public.

Finally, war pathology specimens have been displayed in museums as part of organized meetings of medical professionals. In this setting, specimens could be read and learnt from, as medical documents and pedagogical tools. Those in charge of the RCS collection, for instance, hoped that the museum 'might become [a centre] round which surgeons from special military hospitals could meet' for conferences about war-related treatments and injuries.[73] Although the British had originally proposed to wait until after the war to display the specimens, the Director General of Medical Services insisted that there was an 'immediate educative value' to be gained by exhibiting the collection as quickly as possible.[74] With about 1,200 specimens on display at the end of the war, that number grew steadily to more than 2,000 in the following years.[75] The exhibition guide details that the display consisted of dissected and prepared wounds, alongside drawings and paintings of wounds and a room displaying protective equipment, such as helmets and gas masks. Prominent British medical journal *The Lancet* declared the exhibition 'of immense scientific value both to the RAMC, to the civil medical profession and to the nation'.[76] As Alberti notes, in an era in which few questioned the importance of medical museums for their educative and research potential, the coming together of specimens with pertinent text and images in this centralized location provided the British medical profession with the opportunity to develop their knowledge in war pathology.[77]

The nature and context of the Australian pathological war collection vary from these overseas collections in several ways that have contributed to its absence from museum display. First, the anonymity of specimens in the Australian pathological war collection limits their potential for commemorative display. Australian medical officers who contributed to the collecting effort labelled specimens only with the name of the sender, or sometimes the hospital from which it was sent, but not the name of the person from whom it was taken. This method of labelling specimens to identify the clinician rather than the casualty was common across the British imperial forces.[78] The original numbering system developed at the RCS in London was muddled during the collection's transfer to Australia and needed to be reconfigured when the collection was divided among the local medical schools and universities. Although it would be theoretically possible for a medical expert to use army medical records and case descriptions accompany specimens to link some with a name, the process of repotting and renumbering the collection led curators at the National Museum of Australia to conclude in 1992 that this process would be extremely difficult.[79] Instead, the specimens more resemble medical records in three dimensions rather than objects to commemorate the loss of soldiers' lives, as in the context of the Army Medical Museum. This anonymity might have allowed each nameless body part to become a symbol of all soldiers who suffered during the war, similar to the way the tomb of the unknown soldier stands in to 'compensate for so many names that have lost their bodies', as scholar Laura Wittman puts it.[80] However, the aims of the Australian War Memorial (AWM) precluded the specimens' assumption of a symbolic function.

Disfigured and deceased soldiers' bodies, of which specimens can be considered a part, occupy a complex position in the narrative of First World War commemoration in Australia. The image of wounded soldiers elicited a variety of public sentiments in Australia during and after the war, including horror, sympathy and fear. In 1915, for example, Private Claud Head wrote to the *Terang Express* that 'the sight … of wounded men … being brought on to [his] ship … sickened [him]'.[81] Earlier that year, *The Age* newspaper reported on the return to Melbourne of a group of wounded soldiers from Gallipoli. The report described the soldiers as 'crippled heroes' and noted that their 'figures [were] pathetic, but they [wore] the aura of imperishable glory'.[82] In 1922, another article in *The Age* expressed that 'it was natural' for a 'limbless soldier … [to] arouse sympathy' in public, and an article entitled 'Our Glorious Cripples: Work of the Artificial Limb Factory' in the *Sydney Mail* noted that the men who visited to be fitted with artificial limbs 'display[ed] remarkable adaptability, the most notable characteristic of the Australian'.[83] These contradictory opinions demonstrate just a few reactions to disfigured Anzacs upon their return home.

This experience was not unique to the Australian context; responses to the wounded soldier created tensions more broadly. As historian Joanna Bourke contends in her influential work *Dismembering the Male: Men's Bodies, Britain and the Great War*, the First World War 'provoked a major crisis' in the way the male body was viewed and understood in Britain.[84] British soldiers died and wounded soldiers re-entered society on a scale not seen before in modern British history; the war dismembered and disfigured hundreds of thousands of men's bodies, and these broken bodies then returned home. In response, the way in which the wounded soldier's body was viewed had to be negotiated. Bourke states that during the war and the immediate post-war years there existed a certain sentimental attitude towards the war wounded, as visible wounds and absent body parts embodied the patriotic sacrifice of the soldier. From the early 1920s, however, a widespread public desire to forget the war and the devastation it had caused overshadowed sympathy towards the wounded British soldier.[85]

Despite numerous similarities, several distinctions manifested between Australian and British reactions to wounded soldiers. Historian Marina Larsson suggests that the diversity of responses to wounded soldiers, whom she terms 'shattered Anzacs', in Australia was, in part, the result of the Australian public and medical profession never having experienced, and not being prepared for, such a large proportion of its soldiers returning with 'shattered health' and 'broken bodies'.[86] Soldiers often shielded their families from the truth about the extent of their injuries, and Australian news reports also downplayed the destruction wrought upon soldiers' bodies during the war so as not to lower morale.[87] For instance, when Claude Dunshea wrote to his sister from a military hospital in France in April 1917, he told her he had 'improved wonderfully' during treatment, but did not mention his facial wounds.[88] Furthermore, the distance between the home front and the war front may have limited Australians' knowledge of the devastating effects of the war. If, as Bourke suggests, 'front-line dismemberment was beyond the imagination' of many civilians even in Britain, where war was much closer to home, one has reason to believe this would also apply to the Australian public.[89] The apparent censorship of the realities of war trauma and the distance between Australia and the war front meant images of an 'idealised disabled Anzac', reminiscent of the 'crippled heroes' described above, became part of the standard imagery in the discourse of wounded Australian soldiers who returned in need of rehabilitation.[90]

The Australian medical profession, like the public, was not adequately prepared for the number of returning wounded soldiers. Whereas Britain had many well-resourced centres for rehabilitating amputee and disfigured soldiers, Australian provisions for rehabilitation were relatively deficient. As early as mid-1916, the *Australian Medical Journal* reported that the 'absence of an organised system of orthopaedic treatment in the Australian Army Medical Service has led and is still leading to a great economic loss'.[91] Wilfrid 'Billy' Kent Hughes also wrote to the journal that he had 'no hesitation in saying that our Australian soldiers, who have lost a leg, are not getting by any means the best artificial limbs to help them along'.[92] In the 1920s, when around 3,000 Australian veterans received a pension for having lost a limb in the war, Australia continued to trail Britain significantly in the fields of orthopaedics, prosthetic limb development and physiotherapy.[93]

In the past fifteen years, scholars have begun to discuss the public and medical responses to soldiers returning with severe forms of bodily mutilation, such as facial disfigurement. In the Australian context, historian Kerry Neale states that the public had been poorly prepared to deal with the return of these soldiers compared to soldiers with other types of wounds.[94] She notes that the Repatriation Department referred to the facially disfigured as 'repulsive' rather than using terms reminiscent of the aforementioned 'glorious cripples', or other heroic descriptions, as was the case for other returning soldiers.[95] Historian of art and visual culture Suzannah Biernoff also emphasizes that a wounded face is not the equivalent of a wounded body. Rather, it 'presents the trauma of mechanised warfare as a loss of identity and humanity' – the 'worst loss of all'.[96] Members of the public had difficulty reconciling this loss of identity and humanity, and their visual anxiety that led to soldiers with facial mutilations rarely being represented visually outside the professional medical context.[97]

Dismembered pathological war wound specimens, including brain material and skin fragments exposed to the effects of gas, ruptured organs, and amputated and infected limbs, are also not the same as a wounded body. They, too, have occupied an uneasy space in the landscape of visual culture concerning the First World War soldier's body, particularly in the context of museum commemoration and display. Whereas the pathology specimens and moulages on display at France's Val-de-Grâce served a political function in demonstrating to the public a narrative of national reconstruction through medical advancement, the timing of the Australian specimens' arrival in the country, after the war had ended, and Australia's comparative distance from the war front did not necessitate a similar use.

Objects of material culture, and the memorials that enshrine them, play a significant part in the development, manipulation and maintenance of community and national identity. Larsson states that the 'image at the heart' of the Anzac experience is that of a 'youthful, able-bodied man before he had been wounded or made immortal through a courageous death'.[98] This image guided the creation of the AWM as a space to commemorate and provide an understanding of Australia's part in the war. Focusing almost entirely on valorizing the mythology of the ordinary male Australian soldier, the exhibitions of the AWM presented a masculine, 'combat-related, soldier's eye view of the war' using objects accumulated under the AWRS, which had been established in 1917.[99]

The AWRS set in motion the acquisition of records for a national collection in three classes: war trophies consisting of enemy armaments, articles of medical and surgical interest, and surgical and pathological museum specimens. While objects in the first and second categories fit into the triumphalist narrative set forth in the AWM, the biomedical specimens did not. With reference to the presentation of bodies in British First World War museum exhibits, historian Jay Winter notes that 'there was an unstated rule of decorum in representation, ruling out ugly or shocking images; when bodies were represented, they were intact'.[100] The same can be said of the exhibitions at the AWM in the early twentieth century. Perhaps sensing a public anxiety over viewing wounded soldiers' bodies, the director of the AWM John Treloar reassured visitors that 'nothing gruesome [would] be shown' in a photographic exhibition held at the museum soon after the war.[101] Similarly, when images of casualty clearing stations appeared in exhibitions, they were presented as places of healing rather than places housing often badly maimed soldiers.[102]

Preserved and potted diseased and damaged body parts offered a profound contrast to this image. They depicted experiences of war that conformed to neither the narrative of First World War commemoration at the AWM nor the imagery of the 'glorious cripples' discussed earlier. In pursuit of a triumphalist narrative of Australia's war effort, the AWM excluded many of the realities that medical officers faced – in particular, the treatment of horrifically disfigured soldiers' bodies and the collection of dismembered pathology specimens. Furthermore, the AWM did not utilize specimens to display medical and national progress during and after the war, as did the French at the Val-de-Grâce. The specimens therefore remained in an ambivalent position, neither commemorative objects nor entities used for political means.

The potted specimens did, however, represent a visual medical record of wartime pathology that was accessible to doctors and medical students who had learnt to overcome their natural aversion to the dead body. Rather than see a brain or skull cap specimen as part of an identifiable individual, physicians are trained to view the specimen as a dehumanized object that can be read and analysed clinically as a medical document. This method enabled doctors to incorporate the largely anonymous specimens in the Australian war wounds collection to their published research. However, the collection did not become a centre for medical research and debate, nor did it form the basis of a large-scale exhibition for medical professionals, as occurred at the RCS in London. The initial decision to split the collection into six parts in 1918 meant it was not localized in the same way as the British collection. With the field of military medicine still in its infancy and a lack of centralized exhibition space, the Australian specimens lacked the applicability needed to become an integral part of medical education and research.

## The collection re-emerges

What to do with 150 bottles containing soldiers' body parts was the question facing the NMA in 1992. The Museum's acting director told the *Sydney Morning Herald* at the time that the war pathology collection had sat on shelves for years as it did not 'fit into any of the themes of the National Museum'.[103] In the mid-1990s, newspaper reports surfaced again, casting the specimens as a 'bizarre war wounds collection', about which little was known 'except that it was hidden in a Canberra storeroom and had never been publicly displayed'.[104] During these years, the National Museum of Australia engaged with a complex web of legal, ethical and social issues to return the specimens to the care of the AWM.

Still technically holding custody over the specimens since their collection during the First World War, the AWM accepted the transfer of the specimens from the NMA into its possession, following which it intended to loan the material to the New South Wales Institute of Forensic Medicine in Sydney. No longer wanting to hold human remains in its collections, the NMA set the transfer in motion in 1993.[105] The collection's movement over the following three years drew the attention of several politicians and became the topic of discussion in parliament in mid-1996. Opposition Arts spokeswoman Carmen Lawrence described the collection as 'fairly grisly' on face value and queried why it had originally been assembled. It was labelled 'bizarre' and 'mysterious' in the media, and members of parliament and the public alike expressed concern about whether or not the specimens had been obtained with consent.[106] Although the transfer saw the specimens placed into storage rather than on public display, the accompanying media reports marked one of their only appearances in the public sphere from their collection until the 2015 exhibition.

* * *

The main instigators of a permanent, national collection of pathological war specimens envisioned a project that would develop a previously non-existent tradition of military medicine in Australia. Collectors like Inglis, Newland and Allen worked in collaboration to ensure that each medical school received a selection of specimens. Until 2015, the collection had not been publicly displayed, in keeping with a national narrative of war commemoration that has historically excluded the visual representation of severely disfigured soldiers and dismembered body parts. The anonymity of the specimens further limited their commemorative potential. As such, the benefits of the collection in the early twentieth century were reserved for medical professionals and students, and further limited due to the distant locations of the specimens. With these factors taken into account, the specimens can best be understood as the prized possessions of the medical officers who worked together to collect and bring the specimens to Australia as a record of wartime achievements in medicine.

The *Compassion and Courage* exhibition provided the public with the opportunity to view the specimens for the first time, and to appreciate some of the realities of military pathology work during the First World War. The exhibition also shifted the limit of the spectatorship of wounded soldiers' bodies in Australia, from one that had previously censored the specimens to one that presented them within a narrative of wartime medicine. While the original collectors' vision did not necessarily come to fruition, their work represented the medical profession's growing sense of professional identity in Australia during a period of great hardship. This is, perhaps, the collection's legacy. By discussing how the lives of the pathology specimens engage with these broader narratives of medical development and First World War commemoration, this chapter incorporates this often-overlooked collection into the history of collected human remains in Australia.

Today, only a small proportion of the original war wounds collection remains in existence. The Harry Brookes Allen Museum continues to hold about a dozen specimens which are accessible to medical students only, while specimens originally sent to Sydney and Adelaide are anecdotally said to have been destroyed at the direction of university staff, but their fate remains unknown.[107] Some specimens have been used in the latter part of the twentieth century. For instance, in the 1990s the New South Wales Institute of Forensic Medicine (now the Department of Forensic Medicine) curated a small selection of specimens for teaching purposes. Professor John Hilton, founding director of the institute between 1991 and 2001, used the specimens to demonstrate the effects of war injuries and disease to students, some of whom may well have subsequently had cause to treat identical wounds or illnesses in either civilian or military settings. Hilton also found the specimens useful in preparing serving personnel prior to their deployment to conflict zones in the late 1990s.[108]

By that time, the largest portion of the original collection had, however, fallen into a poor state. Many specimens had been irreparably damaged through the evaporation of the preservative solution that once encased them. To display specimens that have succumbed to such a fate and to ensure any future application for them, significant specialist conservation work would need to be undertaken.[109]

The public re-emergence of the pathological war wound specimens occurred in a climate with considerably different attitudes towards the collection of human remains compared to that in which it was collected. Not only had attitudes evolved through challenges to medical and scientific authority, but legislation had also been enacted to protect members of the public from having their bodies exploited after death, and being coerced into participating in studies that resulted in the retention of biomedical specimens. The next chapter considers the evolution of attitudes towards collecting human remains in the twentieth and twenty-first centuries, to discuss the implications of these changes for anatomy and pathology museum collections in Australia in the present day.

# 6

# Moving parts: Repatriation and bioethics

When the Melbourne Medical School celebrated its jubilee in 1914, the anatomy and pathology museum stood out as one of its most striking achievements. As part of the celebrations, the medical school invited the city's general practitioners to inspect the museum, and Professor of Anatomy Harry Brookes Allen demonstrated interesting specimens to all those 'anxious to witness' the '"University side" of medical science'.[1] At this time, the museum contained thousands of specimens of anatomy and pathology, including the hydrocephalus skeleton Professor Archibald Watson sent from Adelaide, a specimen showing cystic disease of the kidney, and examples of foetal pathologies described in previous chapters. In addition to this comprehensive array of collected, prepared and ordered specimens, there were over 7,000 body parts awaiting preservation.[2]

By the same year, the museum had also acquired more than 200 crania of Indigenous Australian people, at the direction of the Professor of Anatomy, Richard Berry. The crania were positioned alongside other skeletal remains of Indigenous origin, as examples of what Berry and many of his contemporaries believed to be proof of human variation. *The Age* newspaper reported that the museum's open house and jubilee celebrations were a 'field day' for all involved.[3]

When standing in what is now named the Harry Brookes Allen Museum of Anatomy and Pathology today, one is amid a collection that contains more than 12,000 specimens. As part of the University of Melbourne's yearly open day, visitors are invited to view the museum that is at all other times off-limits to the public without an appointment and the curator's supervision. While handling by students over many decades has reduced some specimens 'to minute fragments and dust', one can still gaze upon the same hydrocephalus skeleton, preserved kidney and foetal specimens that so interested Melbourne's physicians more than a century ago.[4] One can also find the war pathology specimens that arrived at the museum in 1919 to teach medical students about the effects of wartime injury and illness on the human body. Several hundred other specimens have been disposed of in the past half-century due to physical deterioration from inadequate storage, but for the most part the collection has remained largely intact and used, in an echo of the past, for medical education.[5]

There is one prominent difference between the collection of 1914 and the collection today: the absence of Aboriginal and Torres Strait Islander Ancestral Remains. In the wake of new legislation and the Aboriginal-led repatriation movement that began in the 1980s, material of Aboriginal origin has been removed from the collection over time and returned to the custodianship of the Traditional Owners. This movement of specimens reflects how anatomy and pathology collections like the Harry Brookes Allen Museum have been challenged and, in some cases, dismantled over the colonial conditions in which they were assembled. In a far cry from experiencing a field day of celebrations, these museums have been forced to confront the legacies of their predecessors and reconsider the role of their collections in the twenty-first century.

This chapter follows the lives of specimens into the late twentieth and twenty-first centuries, to discuss how they have become moving parts amid evolving attitudes towards the treatment of human remains in Australia. Organized in two parts, it first considers the position of collected specimens within discussions surrounding decolonization in Australia. I discuss how the Aboriginal-led repatriation movement, which began in the 1980s and continues today, has challenged the deep-seated colonial power structures evident in the fields of medicine, science and museums. Debates about moral authority over Ancestral Remains have led to their physical removal from museums, as well as revealed their emotive potential.

In the second half of the chapter, I show that the adoption of bioethics and introduction of new legislation in the mid- to late-twentieth century has affected historic collections of non-Indigenous specimens, and led the medical profession to re-evaluate the deeply entrenched position of collected human remains in medical education and research. Despite changes to the methods by which medical schools procure cadavers and new teaching specimens, historic specimen collections have mostly escaped scrutiny; for the most part, they remain intact and a recognized component of medical education in Australia. Although there has been a perceptible transformation in attitudes towards collected human remains in the twentieth and twenty-first centuries, continuities between past and present practices reflect the unease that has always surrounded interactions between the living and the dead.

## The persistent culture of anatomy

Late-nineteenth- and early-twentieth-century Australian physicians and medical students worked within a culture of anatomy based on the central premise of Western biomedicine: that to become an expert in the field, one must learn about human anatomy directly from the body itself. This principle established their need for cadavers and human specimens, and set in motion much of the collecting activity described in previous chapters. Despite legislation during this era governing professional conduct, such as anatomy acts and licensing regulations, Australian physicians and medical students enjoyed relative autonomy and authority when conducting their post-mortem work. It was easiest for doctors to take bodies and body parts from those without families to claim their bodies after death, or from those whose families lacked the finances or social capital to assert their possession of the corpse. The case of J. T. Wilson, mentioned in Chapter 1, who removed the bones of a man post-mortem, without consulting or even notifying the deceased man's family or friends, typifies the sense of authority that many physicians felt regarding their patients' bodies in this era.

This select group of predominantly white, educated men often flouted the laws dictating the appropriate use of human remains, and the rarity of punishment for those who contravened the relevant Anatomy Act meant that legislation did little to deter physicians from taking and treating bodies unlawfully.[6] The way Adelaide coroner William Ramsay Smith treated unclaimed bodies, known as 'Government corpses', in 1903 – snipping off fingers and toes as part of 'anatomical examinations', and ordering a body to be punctured with a metal stake to investigate the effects of such a weapon on the body – further indicates the culture of impunity in which colonial Australian physicians and their medical students operated.[7]

Physicians like Allen also accepted specimens procured by doctors in their local networks, seemingly without concern over the manner in which the body parts had been taken. Indeed, a skeleton preserved at the University of Adelaide's anatomy museum displaying fibrodysplasia ossificans progressiva demonstrates the problematic circumstances in which many specimens were procured during this era. In 1886, anatomist Archibald Watson reportedly removed the skeleton from a recently deceased patient before replacing 'the bones with whatever he could find on the premises including broomsticks and spade handles ... [and] the undertaker's umbrella' to preserve the semblance of the body's physical form. When crematorium staff discovered Watson's macabre handiwork, a scandal was barely averted.⁸ Nevertheless, an extensive paper about the incident was published the following year, and the specimen was retained for museum display. In this case, the museum's desire for useful and interesting specimens appears to have outweighed concern for the method of their procurement. Without well-defined bioethical principles and strictly enforced legal regulation in this era, Australian physicians exercised their professional authority over the human body, and particularly over vulnerable bodies. They did so to develop anatomical knowledge, to provide pedagogical tools for medical students and to ensure that Australia was relevant in the international medical scene.

Within the culture of anatomy, medical professionals also collected human remains of Indigenous origin as part of a global project to 'understand humanity through a changing kaleidoscope of ideas about the human body, notions of "race", and, increasingly, human origins and prehistory'.⁹ Since European colonization in 1788, the bodily remains of Australia's Indigenous peoples have been collected, displayed and researched upon in local and overseas settings. Between the 1860s and 1920s in particular, debates about human evolution in the wake of Darwin's *On the Origin of Species*, Britain's colonial expansion in Australia and the growing prominence of the discipline of anatomy, led anatomists, anthropologists, scientists and amateur collectors, among others, to collect between 5,000 and 10,000 Aboriginal skulls, skeletal remains and occasionally soft tissues from traditional burial grounds and the dissection table.¹⁰

Believing they were witnessing the extinction of Australia's Indigenous peoples, many colonial collectors accumulated their remains as curious anatomical examples of what they thought would become, in nineteenth-century Sydney-based medical practitioner George Bennett's words, 'memorials of the former races inhabiting the land'.¹¹ The case of William Lanne (also spelt Lanney), who was purported to be the last surviving Tasmanian Aboriginal man, demonstrates this intention clearly. Following Lanne's death in Hobart in 1869, the colonial government received two requests for his body. Before any decision could be made, however, one of the petitioners, William Crowther, took Lanne's skull from the dead house of the Hobart Town General Hospital where he was an honorary medical officer and replaced it with that of a dead white man whose head was lying in the same room.¹² When the other petitioners learnt of this, they asked the hospital's resident surgeon to disinter and mutilate the remainder of the body by cutting off the hands and feet. They did so to discourage Crowther, or any other collectors, from coming back to claim the rest of the body. By the time news of the incident reached shocked Hobart residents, Crowther had sent the skull to the Hunterian Museum in London. Upon its arrival in England, the skull was not subject to scientific study but, instead, was displayed in the museum as a curio of the last Tasmanian Aboriginal man.[13] The methods by which Crowther took Lanne's skull and the rest of the body was disfigured highlight the authority white colonial anatomists assumed over the Aboriginal body, as well as the violence that often underscored such encounters. Collectors sought to possess anatomical specimens of what they believed to be an inferior and 'dying' race, and, as such, the bodies and body parts they collected became material manifestations of colonialism.

Anatomists and practitioners in related fields, such as anthropology, collected Aboriginal remains to incorporate into studies in racial science, and the pseudoscience of phrenology, aimed at quantifying the differences between 'races' by systematically analysing physical variations in collected skeletal remains.[14] Historian Paul Turnbull explains that late-nineteenth- and early-twentieth-century scientists believed the Australian Aboriginal skull provided a glimpse into the 'ground zero' of humanity's past, from which they would be able to understand how 'environmental factors could, over time, significantly modify human bodily structures'.[15] To contribute to studies that explored this conviction, many Aboriginal remains were sent overseas, particularly to Britain, where anatomists and scientists connected with colonial collectors to bolster their collections.[16] At the University of Melbourne, anatomist Richard Berry – who historian Alexandra Roginski aptly labels 'the great surveyor of Melbourne's heads' – set about soliciting the skulls of Indigenous Australians through his networks, to support his conviction that the behavioural characteristics of individuals could be determined by measuring skull size.[17] Berry amassed hundreds of specimens and published several studies from his subsequent research.[18]

Aboriginal remains continued to be collected well into the twentieth century, despite knowledge of the cultural violence, both physical and spiritual, caused by disturbing Aboriginal graves.[19] For example, between the 1920s and 1950s, Gippsland pastoralist George Murray Black stole over 1,600 sets of Aboriginal skeletal remains from traditional burial grounds along the Murray River in Victoria and New South Wales on behalf of the Australian Institute of Anatomy and the University of Melbourne. He would deposit the remains at his field camps along the Murray River and at pumping stations, for representatives of the AIA to pick up.[20] The remains that Black pillaged were part of the Melbourne Medical School anatomy and pathology museum until the 1980s, under the control of non-Indigenous curators.

Thousands of Ancestral Remains have resided in collections under non-Indigenous custodianship for decades, as material evidence of colonial scientific beliefs and power structures that marginalized, victimized and exploited Indigenous people. Their ongoing presence in these collections has sustained and perpetuated the portrayal of Indigenous people that grew within colonial ideology as a static, biologically and culturally inferior 'race' compared to white Europeans. Until the 1980s, and in many cases far beyond, the specimens continued to be controlled by the professional successors of the colonial actors who first collected them. These successors in the fields of medicine, science and the museum industry continued to benefit from ingrained colonial power structures that prioritized white European scientific beliefs and methods over Aboriginal peoples' dignity, and cultural beliefs about kinship as an embodied relationship encompassing people, species and ancestors, and the importance of an ancestor being returned to Country.[21] In many cases, practitioners in the aforementioned fields also continued to enact their dominance through refusing to relinquish claims to authority over Ancestral Remains.

In Australia, this culture of anatomy, and its infiltration into the associated fields of science and the museum industry, endured well into the second half of the twentieth century. Correspondence from within the Melbourne Medical School Department of Pathology reveals that doctors continued to send specimens taken from their patients to the anatomy and pathology museum in the early 1980s.[22] There, medical students and physicians used the specimens for learning and research, just as they had done a century earlier. In the mid-to-late twentieth century, however, two cultural movements disrupted the culture of anatomy; they changed the journeys of specimens held in collections, as well as the people and institutions that held them.

## Moving parts within the context of decolonization

The Aboriginal-led repatriation movement that began in the 1980s provides a lens through which to explore how collected Ancestral Remains have become moving parts as museums have undertaken processes of decolonization in Australia. The movement set Ancestral Remains on new physical, discursive, and emotive journeys, many of which continue to evolve in the present day. Proponents of repatriation placed these materials at the centre of discussions that challenged structures of authority within the fields of medicine, science and the museum industry in three main ways: the repatriation movement not only ensured the physical return of thousands of specimens for reburial on Country,[23] but also contested the foundation of the medical profession that empowered physicians to conduct posthumous work on the bodies of the vulnerable; it challenged the authority of the medical profession to transform collected bodies and body parts into objects for research; and it provoked a reconsideration of the role that museums played in possessing, ordering and interpreting objectified human specimens. Exploring these ideas reveals how the repatriation movement forced practitioners and institutions whose predecessors participated in the collection of Aboriginal remains in the late nineteenth and early twentieth centuries to confront the material and ethical consequences of past collecting and research practices that in many ways continued to shape their work.[24]

The legal action brought by Gunditjmara man Jim Berg against the University of Melbourne in mid-1984 over its holdings of Aboriginal remains – specifically, the Murray Black Collection – presented one of many challenges in Victoria to an institution and set of practitioners who had long claimed authority over human specimens. Since 1972, the Museum of Victoria had been the designated lodging place for Aboriginal remains in Victoria, under the *Archaeological and Aboriginal Relics Preservation Act*.[25] In April 1984, the Act was amended to include the provision that only individuals or institutions with permission from the Secretary for Planning and Environment could possess or control Aboriginal remains.[26] Upon realizing the Department of Anatomy within the Melbourne Medical School held the Murray Black Collection (which had been in its possession since the 1930s) without legal permission, Berg acted in his capacity as an Inspector and Warden under the Act to issue proceedings against the university.[27] Following protracted discussions characterized by the university's reluctance to relinquish the specimens, the University of Melbourne was given until 23 August 1984 to 'deliver up to the Museum of Victoria possession and control' of the Murray Black Collection.[28] By challenging the university's self-perceived authority to control the specimens regardless of the new legislation, Berg's legal action began to shift the position of specimens in debates about who could claim moral authority to decide the future of collected human remains.

Berg's success in having the specimens transferred to the Museum of Victoria presented a threat to the system under which physicians had been working, including their requirement for a supply of body parts for research and teaching purposes. It elicited defensive and uncooperative responses from the Department of Anatomy at the University of Melbourne, as well as from physical anthropologists who also had a vested interest in being able to conduct research using the collection. For instance, the Chairman of the Department of Anatomy, Graeme Ryan, stated in August 1984 that the collection was 'of vast medical interest and importance' within his department.[29] He noted in a letter to the President of the Victorian Branch of the Australian Medical Association (AMA Vic) that the specimens were essential to two ongoing medical research projects – an investigation into middle ear disease and a study of disease caused by *Mycobacterium ulcerans*.[30] In light of these projects, Ryan asked the AMA Vic to 'support [the university's] effort to ensure preservation of the material contained in the collection'.[31] Similarly, physical anthropologists in Australia, who had for decades depended on collections of Aboriginal skeletal remains like the Murray Black Collection, argued that the destruction or reburial of the specimens would lead to an 'irretrievable loss of unique scientific data' and that their work would suffer greatly as a result.[32] British anthropologist Roger Lewin suggested in July 1984 that, as 'Australia's most significant physical anthropology collection', the repatriation of the Murray Black Collection threatened 'to end physical anthropology as a serious science' in Australia.[33] Writing in 1994, anthropologist Denise Donlon stated that there was 'strong research activity' using the specimens from the Murray Black Collection, during the 1970s in particular, until a moratorium on their use was put in place from 1983 until 1986. Interestingly, despite the desire to conduct research with the specimens being a primary argument against repatriation, several scholars have noted that relatively little research using the collection has been published.[34]

Taken together, the comments made by medical and scientific practitioners implied that the collection's research potential outweighed Aboriginal cultural beliefs and the consequent repatriation request; in their views, Aboriginal remains were objects to study, and practitioners who possessed them should have been able to continue to use them in research. The responses also demonstrate the threat that these practitioners believed repatriation posed to their way of working, and their assumed professional authority over the collection. By having the specimens removed from non-Aboriginal control, repatriation prevented late-twentieth-century physicians and scientists from using specimens, initially collected to substantiate claims of Aboriginal inferiority, in ways that perpetuated the harm Black himself had caused by removing the specimens earlier in the century. In doing so, this act challenged the foundations of the cultures of anatomy that mandated close study of human bodies and body parts – in this case, the remains of Aboriginal people that were taken in acts of colonial physical and cultural violence.

Responses to the request for the return of the Murray Black Collection also reveal how repatriation disrupted the processes through which anatomists and scientists transformed body parts into objectified specimens. As discussed in Chapters 2 and 3, the lives of specimens usually followed a journey from the body of a patient to the medical school anatomy and pathology museum, where anatomists and medical students stained, injected and potted them. These processes shifted body parts away from their status as subjective parts of people and fashioned them into divisible, stable, dehumanized objects that functioned as effective pedagogical tools. Although there is evidence that medical students sometimes found it difficult to grapple with the inherent humanity of cadavers and specimens, medical school taught them how to develop a clinical, medical gaze that dehumanized these materials. The ingrained nature of the clinical gaze that created an object out of bodies and body parts differs greatly from the Aboriginal belief that human remains represent personified subjects and should be treated as ancestors.

The disparity between many anatomists' belief that human remains constitute objects and the Aboriginal belief that they represent subjects was manifested through the repatriation movement's challenge to Western European notions of kinship. When presented with the repatriation request, Ryan rejected the notion that the remains had 'any ancestral relationship to the modern Aborigine'. He also cast doubt over the claims-makers' assertion that the university was causing them harm by continuing to hold the specimens he termed 'fossil material'.[35] This attitude articulated dominant Western understandings of kinship based on direct genetic lineage. Ryan was by no means alone in this view; many Western physicians and scientists in this era worked under the assumption that without identifiable descendants for the collected remains, no one could claim the right to make decisions about their treatment or be harmed through their use in research. To them, the remains fell outside social relationships as defined in broadly accepted Western terms; they were not considered the 'remains of people-now-dead' but, instead, objects from an ancient past that had no connection to living people.[36]

However, these attitudes reflected a limited understanding of Aboriginal kinship, based on a shared sense of place and spiritual connectedness, upon which claims-makers based their opposition to the collection and study of their ancestors' remains. From this perspective, there was no distinction between recent burials of known individuals and ancient remains.[37] Instead, based on the concept of a 'continuous culture' in which the past, present and future continually interact with each other, kinship could be based on geography and spiritual connectedness, not DNA or genealogy, and the age of remains did not necessarily diminish the intensity of the ancestral relationship.[38] This concept underpinned the belief that the remains in the Murray Black Collection 'were not specimens, they were Ancestors' who needed to return to Country to be spiritually at rest.[39] The defensive nature of the responses of Western physicians, scientists and museum institutions towards these non-Western notions of kinship demonstrates the threat such claims presented to the culture in which they worked. Repatriation disrupted the processes intrinsic to the Australian cultures of anatomy and science that fashioned body parts into pedagogical objects. It also contested the belief within these cultures that the anonymity of historic collected specimens ensured that no harm could be caused to living people. In doing so, repatriation changed what Aboriginal remains represented within discussions surrounding decolonization, from objects to be studied to ancestors who required burial.

On 22 November 1985, just over a year after the University of Melbourne transferred the Murray Black Collection to the custodianship of the Museum of Victoria, members of Victorian Aboriginal communities carried thirty-eight individual bones from the museum to a prepared site in Kings Domain, Melbourne, for reburial.[40] In the face of defensiveness and protestation from the medical and scientific professions, the passion and determination with which claims-makers pursued their right to moral authority over Ancestral Remains were such that this led to the physical movement of the specimens.

Recollections of the repatriation ceremony that took place in Kings Domain reveal the emotive potential of Ancestral Remains. Citing Aboriginal laws that the 'deceased will not enjoy spiritual rest until they are returned to their ancestral home', claims-making groups have frequently contended that the return of Ancestral Remains taken through often violent means can have a therapeutic effect on communities.[41] It can help to alleviate some of the pain Aboriginal people felt when their ancestors' remains were not in their rightful place. Some of those in attendance at the Kings Domain repatriation ceremony wrote of the happiness and pride they felt when the remains, wrapped in bark, were carried out of the 'cold, musty and gloomy' museum space to make their journey 'to their ancestral home and [be] given the last rites in accordance with tradition'.[42] Repatriation could be a confronting event that opened unhealed wounds and triggered the grief, anger and pain that characterized the complex historical relationships between Indigenous and non-Indigenous peoples, and between the living and the dead, but in this case it also brought participants a profound sense of relief and fulfilment. These sentiments convey the emotions that specimens evoked during repatriation ceremonies and reveal the emotional potential of human remains.[43] They also provide a sense that such events could somewhat contribute to relieving the lasting spiritual and cultural damage caused by the collection of Ancestral Remains in the past.

The repatriation request also challenged the deeply ingrained authority of the Melbourne Medical School's anatomy and pathology museum, and the museum institution more broadly, to possess and control human remains. The nineteenth-century museum was a space in which objects were held, classified and ordered. Curators like Allen at the Melbourne Medical School assumed authority as experts in their field, to take possession of specimens, transform them into knowable objects and then order them in a manner that presented and promoted a particular view of the anatomical world to an exclusive audience. Within the museum space, Ancestral Remains materialized the oppression and dispossession of Aboriginal people at the hands of colonial actors. By continuing to hold the specimens in the late twentieth century, the museum perpetuated the concept of Indigenous inferiority that it had propagated in earlier decades.

The Department of Anatomy's actions following the failed attempt to prevent the specimens' legal removal on medical and scientific grounds show how acutely it felt the threat that repatriation posed to its moral authority over the body. Faced with the prospect of losing control of the collection permanently, Ryan invoked that long-standing authority in an attempt to regain custody through an exemption from the *Archaeological and Aboriginal Relics Preservation Act*. In September 1984, he wrote to the Victorian Secretary for Planning and Environment to promote the department's 'outstanding record of curatorial responsibility in preserving the collection for many years'.[44] Stating that the conditions under which the Museum of Victoria held the collection were 'inferior to those at the university ... thereby exposing the collection to risk of damage', Ryan requested the return of the collection to the university, 'where its long-term preservation [would be] assured'.[45] The request was denied, largely as a result of Aboriginal activism to reclaim moral authority over the future treatment of Ancestral Remains, and this refusal confirmed the breakdown of the museum's power over those remains.

The repatriation of the Murray Black Collection to Aboriginal custodianship sowed the seeds for future cultural changes to the museum institution. It compelled the University of Melbourne, as well as museums in Australia and overseas, to acknowledge the violent colonial conditions under which collectors acquired the remains of Indigenous Australians, and to confront their role as the ongoing beneficiaries of colonial practices and power structures.

Resulting from challenges to its authority and remit, the museum institution began to embrace a set of values and practices, commonly known as the 'new museology'. It started to become more inclusive, more willing to share authority and involve communities, and to shift away from the position it had developed in the nineteenth century as a cultural authority exclusively for the elite.[46] While not solely responsible for these changes, repatriation activism left an indelible legacy on the museum institution, which had exercised its self-appointed moral authority over Ancestral Remains for decades. Through their central role in the repatriation movement, the lives of the specimens taken in late-nineteenth- and early-twentieth-century Australia were bound up in shifting power dynamics within discussions surrounding decolonization in the museum institution in late twentieth-century Australia.

Written responses to the repatriation request regarding the Murray Black Collection betray a sense of defensiveness, increasing desperation to retain the remains, and a steadfast belief that the medical school had the right to continue its ownership of the specimens, as it had done historically. Through their language, the responses show the strength of the threat the repatriation movement posed to the Melbourne Medical School's cultural authority over the remains. They also reveal the strength of Aboriginal peoples' attitudes towards collected Ancestral Remains, and the tenacity of their activism. Through this activism, repatriation caused specimens to become moving parts in debates about decolonization. It disrupted the medical school's long-standing requirement for bodies and body parts, and challenged the clinical gaze of Western biomedicine that created objects in places where Aboriginal people perceived ancestral subjects.[47] It also began to dislodge the anatomy and pathology museum as a space that had not only tangibly possessed Ancestral Remains, but had also used them to create and perpetuate notions of Indigenous inferiority. The discursive journeys that specimens took manifested into their physical movement out of the Harry Brookes Allen Museum, and back into the care of Aboriginal communities. The specimens' physical and discursive movement brought to light their emotive potential as materials that embodied more than 150 years of cultural and physical trauma inflicted upon Australia's Indigenous peoples.

In its early days, repatriation may not have achieved genuine attitudinal and intellectual changes to the fields of medicine, science and the museum industry. As Michael Pickering, the former director of the repatriation program at the National Museum of Australia, states, early cases of repatriation were driven by Indigenous activists, not a philosophical change of mind by institutions that held Aboriginal remains. As such, institutional responses generally consisted of the 'simple removal of the offending remains on the basis of immediate response rather than informed debate'.[48] Over time, however, this confrontation between the powerful culture of anatomy and the powerful convictions of Indigenous people over their ancestors has reshaped the status of Ancestral Remains, to create a deep and lasting impact on specimens, and the relationships between communities, collectors and the collected. Early repatriations, like that of the Murray Black Collection, therefore, laid the foundation for thousands of ancestors, not specimens, to return home to Country.[49]

## Finding provenance

Although repatriation has led to the return and reburial of thousands of Ancestral Remains, as well as change to the meanings attributed to these materials, these efforts still face practical difficulties. Determining the provenance of specimens, which is generally necessary for return to occur, is not always straightforward. As previously discussed, the documentation for human specimens collected in the late nineteenth and early twentieth centuries is generally quite thin. The Murray Black Collection was accompanied by scant records, which did not bode well for identifying provenance that would allow reburial to occur. Black himself noted the physical orientation of the skeletons he exhumed but did not record any other data that would aid in identifying the exact locations of the grave sites.[50] An inventory of the remains dated from between 1942 and 1950 lists each individual specimen, accompanied by dashes and crosses to denote certain physical features. Many listings are undated, and there often appears to be confusion over the sex of the specimen.[51]

To prepare for the specimens' repatriation, in 1985 the university commissioned a scientific analysis of the collection. The resulting report noted that the collection contained the remains of over 1,000 individuals from four different tribal areas in New South Wales and Victoria.[52] Some specimens could be linked to specific areas, but others, like the remains interred at Kings Domain, could only be identified to a state. Despite an inexact provenance, Berg stated that it 'felt wrong' to allow the remains to stay in the museum storeroom indefinitely, and so the decision was made to bury them together.[53]

An inability to identify the provenance of remains has made the return and reburial of hundreds of specimens impossible. In his essay, 'Restless Indigenous Remains', journalist and writer Paul Daley states that the 'identities of pitifully few' Aboriginal remains held in a repository at the National Museum of Australia can be determined.[54] Indeed, of the 725 sets of remains held at the museum in 2014, 434 had no discernible provenance.[55] A further 291 specimens are being held indefinitely at the National Museum of Australia at the request of communities, or because communities either cannot or choose not to accept repatriated remains. On occasion, communities have only been contacted about remains when they are already packed and ready to be returned, and thus do not have funds or appropriate spaces for reburial to occur. In some cases, communities do not accept remains identified as 'belonging' to them if they do not themselves identify the remains as having an appropriate connection to Country, and that community politics can also sometimes preclude return.[56] Without provenance or a community able to accept identifiable remains, they exist in limbo within museums, usually held in separate areas that contain only Aboriginal skeletal material.

The issue of determining provenance is compounded when Ancestral Remains are located and returned from places other than museums. For instance, in 2002, Freemasons Victoria handed over a large collection of crania and arm and leg bones to Museums Victoria. The remains, found to be of both Indigenous and non-Indigenous origin, had been used for 'ceremonies' and had no accompanying documentation that might indicate where or when they were sourced.[57] The physical movement of specimens is impeded without documentation, known provenance or a clear pathway back to communities and Country. Such specimens remain in museum repositories indefinitely – a fact that demonstrates the political and cultural aspirations of repatriation have not always aligned with the practical aspects of returning and reburying remains.

The uncertain future of specimens in repositories continues to inflict ongoing trauma on many Aboriginal people, who believe the remains need to be returned to Country to be properly at rest. Jim Berg found visiting museum repositories of repatriated remains to be a distressing experience. In *Power and the Passion: Our Ancestors Return Home* – a book published to commemorate the twenty-fifth anniversary of the reburial at Kings Domain – he stated that the 'sight of Skeletal Remains of Our Ancestors' in the storeroom at Melbourne Museum gave him 'a chill throughout [his] body, into [his] inner soul'.[58] Similarly, Sarah Morton notes the sentiment of one Ngarrindjeri Elder she interviewed, who expressed that 'the Old People often made their presence [in the museum storeroom] felt and that sitting in the store and talking with them [the ancestors] was sometimes comforting and others upsetting, confronting or frustrating'.[59] The Elder's interaction with the ancestors reveals their continuing ability to have a powerful emotional impact on him, even in death.[60] It also indicates the distress he felt at ancestors' remains sitting in cardboard boxes.

One solution to address the thousands of unprovenanced and unclaimed Ancestral Remains in museums has been to create a National Resting Place in Australia's capital city, Canberra. More than twenty years after it was first proposed, the federal government committed in 2022 to establishing the precinct, which will be known as 'Ngurra' – a word meaning home, or a place of belonging and inclusion. Part memorial, tomb, repository, educational facility and research centre, 'Ngurra' is intended to house remains that cannot be returned to the Traditional Owners, under the management of Indigenous custodians, and to provide a site for private mourning, public memorial and cultural activities.[61] The space would not only alleviate some of the practical issues of storage for museums that indefinitely hold Indigenous remains, but would also ensure that all of these specimens are in one place should new techniques be developed, or research completed, to identify provenance for previously unidentifiable specimens.[62] While many Ancestral Remains have found their spiritual resting place on traditional lands, the process of repatriation is ongoing as more institutions come to terms with their role in perpetuating cultural harm towards Aboriginal people and seek to work closely with communities to ensure their return. As Michael Pickering expresses, repatriation is 'more than just the return of an object, it is the return of authority, the return of responsibility, and the return of an important part of a group's social, religious, and historical identity'.[63]

Ancestral Remains have not only become potent symbols in discussions about decolonization but have also had a dramatic effect on the physical make-up of Australian and overseas collections that have contained such remains. The repatriation movement has set thousands of Aboriginal specimens moving on new courses; collections have been dismantled, and remains have been returned to the Traditional Owners for reburial on traditional lands, or placed in designated repositories under Indigenous management in cases where return has not proven possible. By 2016, Museums Victoria had facilitated the repatriation of 2,269 sets of remains to the Traditional Owners for reburial; at that point, it still held 1,507 sets of remains.[64] The physical journey that specimens have taken, from museum collections to reburial or repositories, has not always been straightforward, but it represents one outcome of their shifting position within the debates about decolonization in the fields of Australian medicine, science and the museum industry.

There is some evidence, albeit limited, of the attitudinal shift towards Ancestral Remains that has resulted from the repatriation movement being applied in the handling of historic collections of non-Indigenous specimens. For example, in 1992, a National Museum of Australia curator invoked some of the lessons about cultural sensitivity learnt from the repatriation of Aboriginal remains when devising the best course of action to remove the war wound collection from the museum. The curator stated in a letter to the director of the museum that they should 'be "upfront" about th[e] collection and ... do what [they had] done with Aboriginal remains'. He suggested they be transparent about the collection, and 'negotiate with descendants about the return of material if so requested'.[65] The specimens' anonymity precluded this possibility, but the curator's reaction to their presence acknowledged the need for sensitivity when dealing with human remains taken in conditions without well-developed ethical and legal safeguards. This incident was, however, unusual, and for the most part, repatriation of Ancestral Remains has not triggered changes to the lives of historic specimens of non-Indigenous origin.

## The Berry Collection

The repatriation movement that began in the 1980s continues to have ongoing implications for institutions that took part in collecting historically. For instance, in 2002, the University of Melbourne was again forced to confront its past collecting practices following a routine audit that led to the 'discovery' in a storeroom within the Department of Anatomy and Cell Biology of around 400 Aboriginal bones and skulls that belonged to the otherwise well-documented Berry Collection.[66] Correspondence reveals that there existed a general belief among senior management at the university, staff at Aboriginal Affairs Victoria and staff at Museums Victoria that all Aboriginal remains had been transferred from the university in the 1980s following litigation over the Murray Black Collection.[67] However, the collection's ongoing existence on campus, without the required legislative consent, was reported to have been an 'open secret' among some retired academics.[68]

In the changed ethical climate of the early twenty-first century, what had for decades been deemed a scientific and medical collection of great significance to the university had become a source of genuine alarm and cause for shame. The university alerted Aboriginal Affairs Victoria to the discovery, apologized for the 'hurt and understandable indignation' felt by Indigenous Australians concerning the collection and requested that all university departments undertake audits to ensure that they did not hold any further Ancestral Remains.[69] In response to the revelation, Aboriginal Affairs Victoria gave the university five days to catalogue, pack and transfer the remains from the Berry Collection to the custody of

Museums Victoria. The university was also asked to bear the significant costs of repatriation.⁷⁰

Although the University of Melbourne apologized and put in place a team of physical anthropologists and museum experts to document and repatriate the remains, it must be recognized that it took more than a decade from initial discussions for the university, as an institution, to take responsibility for the cultural harm the collection had caused. However, the legacy of the Berry collection lay not only in the repatriation of Aboriginal remains. For a further fifteen years, Richard Berry's name adorned a prominent building at the university's Parkville campus. It was only removed in 2017 following a student-led campaign.⁷¹

## Moving parts within a changing bioethical climate

At the same time as repatriation brought attention to the holdings of human remains at the Melbourne Medical School in the 1980s, the advent and widespread adoption of bioethical frameworks, regulation and legislation from the middle of the twentieth century challenged the ways in which the medical profession engaged with the deceased body.

Scholars commonly cite the post-Second World War revelation of the wartime use of human bodies and body parts by the Nazis as a turning point in the history of regulation for the use of human tissue within the cultures of medicine and science.⁷² In light of these revelations, protectionist measures, such as the Nuremberg Code (1947) and the Declaration of Helsinki (1964), were introduced to protect the rights of human subjects in medical research and clinical trials. These codes, commonly known as 'bioethics', reconfigured the way in which physicians and scientists interact with human remains. It is beyond the scope of this book to provide a detailed discussion of how bioethics govern the procurement of human tissue for medical and scientific purposes today, but their advent is significant because as they provide a window onto the shifting meanings and status of historic specimens taken under markedly different legal and ethical norms.

The advance of bioethics in the 1980s saw major changes to the methods of acquiring cadavers and specimens for medical education in Australia. All Australian states and territories have their own Human Tissue Act and Anatomy Act to govern the ethical use of human tissue. Since their introduction, these pieces of legislation have meant medical schools face strict regulations for acquiring human tissue, but it has not been exactly clear how the law would apply to historic collections taken in a different era with different socio-cultural and ethical practices. Following the introduction of the Victorian *Human Tissue Act* (1982), for example, medical schools could no longer rely on equivocal practices or tacit permission when sourcing the bodies and body parts that were still a requisite component of medical education. Instead, they needed to obtain cadavers and specimens from consenting donors, many of whom had signed up to a body donor programme during their life.[73]

In the wake of both repatriation and new laws governing the use of human tissue for educational and research purposes, the historic specimen collections discussed in this book have not experienced significant changes to their physical constitutions. That said, as discussed in Chapter 5, the National Museum of Australia transferred 155 pathological war wound specimens from its holdings to the custodianship of the Australian War Memorial in the mid-1990s because they did not comply with the collection and display policies it developed during this period. Furthermore, there is anecdotal information that staff at the Sydney Medical School disposed of many specimens in the 1960s deemed useless for educating students.[74] Despite these two examples, historic non-Indigenous specimens have, for the most part, stayed staunchly in place – largely unmoved amid the cultural, ethical, legal and technological changes that have happened around them. They remain an integral part of medical education, and there are few signs that they will be removed in the near future.

Perhaps the key reason medical school collections of non-Indigenous remains have remained intact and avoided scrutiny is that they are not on general display and are thus little-known to the public. Without public visibility or pressure, the curators of these collections have not actively avoided a contentious issue; rather, there has simply been no issue with which to be concerned.[75] In relation to anatomy and pathology museums, this statement betrays the medical profession's continuing authority over the collected body within the prevailing culture of anatomy. Medical school anatomy and pathology museums have historically been insular spaces, accessed and controlled by an elite group of medical staff and students. In the late nineteenth and early twentieth centuries, Allen and the collecting network that surrounded the Melbourne Medical School took measures to ensure their activities occurred out of the public eye, and to minimize damage to the relationship between the public and the medical profession when such activities were exposed. These methods of working with specimens continued throughout much of the twentieth century, as medical students and staff used specimens and dissected cadavers away from the public, in accordance with professional norms. Specimens that arrived at the medical school during the late 1970s and early 1980s joined their antecedents in the same spaces, behind the same closed doors, that they had occupied since the late nineteenth century. Without a public profile or public pressure over specimen collections, there was little reason for medical schools to reconsider them, despite being collected originally under conditions that would be deemed unethical by twenty-first-century standards.

Do historic specimen collections have a future as pedagogical tools and institutional assets? Transferring present-day ethical considerations, such as the need for informed consent, to specimens collected in the past is generally not deemed necessary for them to remain in use.[76] At the University of Melbourne, specimens' continuing presence in the Harry Brookes Allen Museum is supported by the reasons for their initial collection: medical education. Biomedical and science students participate in classes that use the museum's specimens. While there is no forthcoming data about University of Melbourne students' attitudes towards classes with the museum specimens, a study conducted in a comparable context in 2012, at the Institute of Pathology at the Friedrich-Alexander-Universität Erlangen-Nürnberg, revealed that students there found historic specimens to be effective learning tools. The study also found little difference between students' preference for working with historic specimens compared to newly acquired specimens.[77] Historic specimens allow medical students and doctors to research the variable nature of diseases across time, and to visualize pathologies that are rare or difficult to acquire in the current medical and bioethical climate. Further, historic specimens have been used in ways never imagined when they were first collected, and this 'promise of future usefulness' has underpinned their retention.[78] While holding human remains indefinitely and without a clearly defined purpose could be deemed unethical, the Melbourne Medical School's decision to include specimens in students' education today adheres closely to the specimens' original purpose and function, within the limits laid out by legislation that governs anatomy schools and the uses of human tissue.

In contrast, some specimens have been set moving on new courses as institutions have chosen to dispose of them or, in some cases, consider returning them to descendants. Disposal of historic specimens has often occurred when the specimens have been damaged beyond repair due to inadequate preservation and storage. A report from 1974 revealed that approximately 20 per cent of the General Pathology Teaching collection at the Harry Brookes Allen Museum required 'urgent remounting', and more than half the specimens needed their preservative fluid changed. The condition of the Special Pathology Teaching collection was even worse. As well as around 50 per cent of specimens requiring attention, the report deemed that 'many existing [were] not worth remounting' at all. Indeed, following this report, the museum disposed of about 600 specimens that had no future potential as pedagogical tools.[79] Once their utility had been lost, the museum decided the best course of action was to move them out of the collection.

Historic specimens have also been removed from collections globally, on ethical grounds related to the conditions in which they were originally acquired. Perhaps the most prominent set of cases occurred in the late 1980s, when it came to light that well-regarded German and Austrian medical and scientific institutions continued to use specimens taken from victims of the Nazis. In particular, the University of Tübingen still used specimens taken from cadavers of executed Soviet and Polish slave labourers to teach medical students, the Neurological Institute in Frankfurt held a collection of brains taken from euthanasia victims, and the Kaiser Wilhelm Institute in Berlin had a large collection of blood samples and other specimens of heterochromia (the condition of having a different colour in each eye) taken from the victims of Nazi experimentation in the 1940s. Following the revelations, these institutions disposed of thousands of specimens in an attempt to distance themselves from their association with such a dark history. This often involved burying or cremating the remains, and melting down the glass slides that had encased specimens. Sometimes an institute conducted a ceremony to accompany the disposal of remains, but in many instances it occurred quickly and quietly, often without comprehensive research into the specimens' provenance.[80] Although the provenance of many non-Indigenous specimens in Australian collections, such as those in the war pathology collection, has garnered criticism, it has not yet reached a level that would see them disposed of. Moreover, simply removing specimens from collections is not an ethically neutral act – disposal is not necessarily preferable to use for teaching or research purposes.[81]

One further reason historic specimens might become displaced from the institutions in which they reside is if they can be accurately identified and returned to descendants who request them. Indeed, physician and anthropologist Philippe Charlier suggests that the 'only precise element permitting any restitution should be the name of the individual'.[82] The case of Charles Byrne, the Irish Giant, for instance, courts controversy because, despite documentation to prove Byrne's name, and his explicit wishes not to be anatomized after death, the Hunterian Museum continued to display his skeleton for more than 200 years (see Chapter 2). While Byrne did not have direct descendants, numerous individuals and groups have lodged restitution requests based on broader categories of 'relatedness' based on shared ancestry, as well as notions of collective identity and shared experience on an individual, local and national scale.[83] These requests have been unsuccessful to date, but they signal the potential for movement to occur in the rare case when the source of a specimen is identifiable. However, as I have shown in earlier chapters, most specimens in the Australian context, as well as those in comparable collections of the era, are not named. Anatomists deliberately anonymized and objectified them as part of the processes that transformed body parts into specimens appropriate for pedagogical use. As such, restitution is not a viable option for most specimens in the Harry Brookes Allen Museum collection, nor has there been a public campaign to demand it.

The material make-up of the Harry Brookes Allen Museum has changed as a result of repatriation activity, and the removal of damaged or otherwise unusable specimens, but rarely due to ethical concerns over specimens' origins, or public pressure to reconsider their role in medical education. The requirement that newly acquired specimens adhere to the stipulations of the Victorian *Human Tissue Act* (1982), while historic specimens collected before this legislation was introduced continue to be a mainstay of medical education at the Melbourne Medical School, demonstrates that the specimens' role in the twenty-first century is far from black and white. Specimens collected between the late nineteenth and mid-twentieth centuries are objects collected under a different set of ethical, cultural and legal norms that have often been grandfathered into today's bioethical climate.

Despite the lack of public scrutiny applied to historic collections of non-Indigenous specimens in Australia, these body parts still have emotive potential. Several exhibitions in recent years containing human body parts have elicited strong reactions from members of the public. For example, in 2018 the exhibition *Real Bodies: The Exhibition* opened its doors in Sydney. It displayed twenty anonymous cadavers posed as dynamic body sculptures, preserved using the 'plastination' technique invented by German anatomist Gunther von Hagens in 1977, and used in his *Body Worlds* exhibitions that have been seen by millions worldwide. For many visitors, the exhibition presented an opportunity to see and learn about the body's internal anatomy. For others, however, questions about how the bodies had been acquired evoked palpable discomfort and even outrage. Indeed, a group of lawyers, academics and human rights activists from the International Coalition to End Organ Transplant Abuse in China launched a petition to pressure the New South Wales government to shut down the exhibition immediately and investigate claims that the displayed bodies and organs had been sourced from executed Chinese prisoners of conscience.[84] The company behind *Real Bodies*, Imagine Exhibitions, maintained that each cadaver was sourced legally, from a person who died of natural causes and showed no sign of physical trauma.[85] Despite these statements, without proof of the bodies' identities or donor consent forms, the coalition of protestors contended that the exhibition most likely did not meet the stipulations of the New South Wales Anatomy Act or Human Tissue Act. The exhibition ran its course without any further issues.

Around the same time as the organizers of *Real Bodies* came under scrutiny, Museums Victoria chose to remove two Viking skulls from display in the travelling exhibition *Vikings: Beyond the Legend*, which was on show at Melbourne Museum between 26 March and 26 August 2018. The decision was made following consultation with Aboriginal community groups, citing cultural sensitivities surrounding the display of human remains, as well as the organization's commitment to placing First Peoples' living cultures, histories and knowledge at the core of its practice.[86] These two exhibitions underline the complexity of responses towards museum displays that include human remains in Australia today. While displays containing the mummified remains of ancient Egyptian and bodies preserved in peat bogs, presented in an educational manner alongside informative interpretation, are generally accepted and even expected in many British museums, the same cannot be said in Australia.[87] Instead, it is rare to see any human remains on display in Australian museums, I would argue largely due to the cultural sensitivities surrounding Ancestral Remains. Further, the two exhibitions introduced above show that while many Australian museums and cultural institutions have their own policies for displaying human remains, these are not consistent across the board.[88]

The repatriation movement set Ancestral Remains on discursive journeys, culminating in their shift in status, from a Western biomedical perspective, from specimens to ancestors. Accompanying this change has been the physical movement of such remains out of museum collections in Australia and overseas, either to be reburied according to traditional customs or to remain in museum repositories under the care of Indigenous custodians. When the passion of repatriation activists collided with the long-standing, powerful culture of anatomy, it was the nature of human remains as body parts that moved people emotionally, and revealed the ongoing cultural violence being enacted through their enduring presence in museum collections.

Although non-Indigenous specimens have remained comparably static in a literal sense, they have shifted considerably in the realms of medical education and research during an era of established bioethics. In the face of these bioethical developments in the late twentieth and early twenty-first centuries, museums, scientists and medical professionals have had to negotiate difficult questions about whether or not they retain specimens that are deemed to have been taken unethically by today's standards. While some museums and research institutes around the world have chosen to dispose of offending specimens, most anatomy and pathology collections in Australia have grandfathered historic specimens into today's bioethical and legal climate. Their unbroken line of use as active pedagogical tools since the nineteenth century, as well as the general inability to identify descendants who could claim possession of them, justifies their retention. Despite rationalizing their ongoing use in this manner, attitudes towards the role of human remains in medical education are constantly evolving.

Following the journeys of collected specimens into the late twentieth and twenty-first centuries brings to light times in which the distortion of human values has led anatomy and its associated fields down dark routes that have proven difficult to confront. It also enables one to appreciate the vast number of medical students and medical professionals who have benefitted from engaging with the collected body during their education and subsequent careers. While contrasts can be readily made between the material constitutions of collections in the late nineteenth and early twentieth centuries and today, through comparing museum catalogues or photographs of museum shelves, this chapter has accounted for some of the evolving attitudes, emotive episodes and shifting power dynamics that led to these changes. This approach reveals the lives of historic specimens to provide a window into the difference between legitimate scientific research, and the appallingly unethical misuse of bodies within the culture of anatomy. As such, collected specimens encourage reflection on the effects of practices undertaken in a past that is not quite yet past.

# Conclusion: Afterlives

This book began with the story of a skeleton set on a journey by sea, rail and road from an Adelaide hospital to the Melbourne Medical School. Packed in a case and mislabelled to maintain its secrecy, the skeleton passed through the hands of a collecting network that valued it simultaneously as an example of the condition hydrocephalus, and as a medical curiosity. For over a century, this skeleton has been a mainstay of the Harry Brookes Allen Museum of Anatomy and Pathology, alongside other specimens used by successive generations of medical students and professionals to further their knowledge of the human body. With little accompanying contextual information about the patient and his condition, however, the specimen's full story had been untold.

This skeleton was one of thousands of human specimens that have had afterlives in museums and institutions around the country and overseas. Despite their presence, often over many decades, these specimens continue to be overlooked in the existing histories of Australian medicine. With the exception of the robust scholarship on the collecting of Indigenous Australian Ancestral Remains, when discussed, collected bodies and body parts used for medical instruction and research in late-nineteenth- and early-twentieth-century Australia have been largely understood as biological objects, and the mechanisms and motivations behind their collection have seldom been investigated. What can we learn from studying these remains? How did they contribute to the development of knowledge and education in Australia? And how can we understand their shifting scientific, social, cultural and political meanings across time and place?

This book has looked beyond the conventional perception of collected specimens through their biological attributes to unearth their rich social and cultural histories. Specimens are dynamic entities whose stories are entangled with the actions and motivations of those who collected them, used them and have been their custodians. Specimens show us what medical professionals and students knew and thought about the human body in the past and reveal how those attitudes have evolved over time and even persist in the present day. Centring specimens as historical subjects rather than viewing them solely as objects brings to life stories of collectors and the collected that deepen our knowledge of how Australian medicine has developed since the late nineteenth century.

Why have the social and cultural lives of specimens remained underexplored in the Australian context? This is partly because engagement with collected specimens is limited; anatomy and pathology museums in Australia are, for the most part, closed to the public, as they have been since they emerged in the nineteenth century. Further, a perception persists that these museums are remnants of the past, rather than active collections that continue to be used in contemporary medical education, and to shape current medical and museum practices. Finally, when specimens are encountered, they are often presented as biological objects, but lack historical context. By exploring the anatomy and pathology museum, this book has transformed what have been entries in acquisition ledgers and jars on museum shelves into historical sources that present a fuller picture of their purpose and meaning.

We have seen that the culture in which human anatomy and pathology specimens were collected in late-nineteenth- and early-twentieth-century Australia was characterized by local tensions and those inherited from Britain between the medical profession and the public about what constituted an appropriate treatment for the deceased human body. They did so based on the tradition established in the Western biomedical world that necessitated learning directly from the body itself. Australian anatomists navigated legislation, administration, isolation and, sometimes, their own internal conflicts to undertake morbid work. At times clinical and objective, work with the dead was also a reflexive exercise that confronted medical practitioners with questions about human dignity and mortality.

Specimen collecting proved fundamental to the development of the Australian medical profession during its nascent years. Procuring and preserving human specimens forged personal and professional ties that overcame physical and intellectual distance. Collected specimens enabled Australian medical professionals to partake in collaborative diagnosis and share findings and breakthroughs on a domestic level. They also formed the basis for publications and presentations that brought Australian medical research to the field at large which, in turn, established the nation as a producer of medical knowledge and enabled it to develop its own traditions of anatomy and pathology. In an era before technology made it possible to view the intact body's interior, doctors used collected specimens to develop their understanding of the body in illness and good health, and to achieve better outcomes for their patients.

More than that, collected specimens assumed a crucial role in Australian medical education. Whether in the classroom or the anatomy and pathology museum itself, learning from specimens informed medical students' understanding of the body in a way that learning only from books could not. Medical students observed preserved parts of the body from every angle, passed them around classrooms and even turned their hands to preparing specimens themselves. That former students sent specimens to the Melbourne Medical School after they entered the medical profession attests to the importance of these materials as tools to teach each new generation of physicians.

As I have shown, work with the collected dead occurred in spaces that were the exclusive domain of the medical profession. At times, though, the terminology and ideas derived from specimens entered the public sphere. The public anatomy museums of nineteenth-century Melbourne contextualized medical information – albeit not always from reputable sources – alongside models of the body, to inform the public about various afflictions and their treatments. While the public readily absorbed these exhibits, other medical collections, such as the war pathology specimens taken from Australian soldiers in the First World War, show us that without appropriate spaces and context within which to exhibit human remains, their potential as educational resources has been limited. That said, taking a social and cultural lens to collected specimens presents an opportunity to recover narratives that have been underrepresented, such as those of patients who sought and received medical assistance.

A richer understanding of how collected human remains have been used in the past raises pertinent questions about their future amid developments in the discourses of bioethics and decolonization in Australia. How should human remains be used in medical education? What should happen to the historic collections held in institutions around Australia and overseas? How can museum exhibits involving human remains be framed and contextualized? Should we collect and display the dead at all?

Like their late-nineteenth- and early-twentieth-century predecessors, Australian medical students today gather around cadavers and display cases holding specimens, to learn about anatomy and pathology. In recent years, however, a greater emphasis on the ethics of using cadavers and changes in methods of medical education have seen a sharp decline in anatomical dissection of cadavers in Australian medical schools. As new technologies, such as virtual dissection tables and 3D modelling, provide suitable – in some cases, superior – alternatives to the cadaver, medical faculties have questioned whether human dissection classes are still necessary. In particular, they wonder if high-tech substitutes used alongside traditional teaching tools, such as articulated skeletons, medical models and radiological film, can render cadavers and specimens as a thing of the past.[1] Medical educators also note the ethical, legal and financial implications of a reliance on human tissue, as well as the negative emotional impact dissection can have on students.[2] At the same time, many medical school staff have leapt to dissection's defence. They argue that students gain unparalleled experience from dissecting cadavers, learning practical surgical skills, developing heuristic techniques, and tactile awareness of the body's tissues, and engaging in an important act of socializing with their peers.[3] While statistics from 2016 show that the majority of Australian medical schools continue to offer anatomical dissection, those that have chosen to move forward with what they deem to be more ethical, effective and pennywise alternatives to the cadaver demonstrate that dissection's historically central role in medical education is subject to change.[4]

Several incidents over the past two decades have also cast a pall over medical professionals' dealings with cadavers and other medical specimens derived from the collected dead. The revelation that 1,000 human organs had been discovered at the Adelaide Women's and Children's Hospital in 2001 quickly became a source of public distress. Just two months earlier, allegations that body parts were being harvested, and bodies were being mistreated at the New South Wales Institute of Forensic Medicine, erupted in the Australian media.[5] These incidents occurred in the wake of disturbing reports from the United Kingdom that hundreds of organs had been retained post-mortem without the knowledge or consent of parents from the Bristol Royal Infirmary and the Alder Hey Children's Hospital in Liverpool.[6] Authorities launched inquiries into operations at both Australian institutions, but the subsequent reports did not find unlawful conduct had occurred under the relevant legislation.[7] The inquiries do reveal, however, the contrasting views of the public and the medical profession surrounding the retention and use of human remains for education and research in the early twenty-first century. Regardless of legality, as can be said of the late nineteenth and early twentieth centuries, there were serious social and ethical concerns the medical profession needed to confront.

\* \* \*

When I came face to face with the culture of anatomy, I was at first overwhelmed to be in such a morbid space. Standing in a dissecting room, wearing a surgical gown and surrounded by sixteen cadaver heads placed on chilled black plastic trays, I felt that I had taken a rather large step away from the historian's customary space among archives and historical records. As I came to terms with this unfamiliar environment, I recalled accounts of late-nineteenth- and early-twentieth-century medical students gathered around dissecting tables at the Melbourne Medical School, ready for their introduction to the study of anatomy and their first glimpse of the body's interior. I was equipped with tales of their dissecting room behaviour, characterized by boisterous antics, but also knew how these medical students reflected on their encounters with the dead, and how they and their professors transformed bodies and body parts into educational tools through which to acquire anatomical knowledge. The 'dissecting room' in which I stood was not, however, occupied by medical students, but by highly trained surgeons taking part in the skills laboratory sessions of the Melbourne Advanced Facial Anatomy Course.[8]

In the sterile laboratory space, I observed as these surgeons – but dissectors for the day – took measures to transform each donated cadaver into a useful educational tool. Working in pairs under expert instruction, they first draped their dissection subjects to frame the face as the area of interest. Then, using a pen, the surgeons placed marks on each cadaver's skin that would guide their scalpels to the correct incision points. I watched as they began to dissect the subjects, incising along the jawline in front of the ear, before pulling back the skin to reveal the anatomical structures inside the lower part of the face. As the surgeons moved from exterior to interior, they were simultaneously encouraged to think about anatomy as a converse process of trying to think from the inside out. In some cases, the structures so clearly presented in diagrams proved difficult to identify in the real, individual specimen. But when they were found, palpable excitement filled the room as the surgeon made a new personal anatomical discovery.

Acutely aware that I had entered an insular space reserved for those who have been trained to work with a medical gaze, I endeavoured to view the cadavers solely as objects of learning. I tried to trick myself into thinking that the subjects were not real, to look past their humanity. But I couldn't do so. Each time I scanned the room or looked at a surgeon's work up close, something reminded me that these were not just dissection subjects but people who had chosen to donate their bodies to science. The feeling never really subsided. I wondered whether the surgeons shared these thoughts or whether they focused their minds exclusively on dissecting. Upon reflection, what became clear was that, despite shifts in ethics, attitudes, legislation and requirements between the late nineteenth and early twentieth centuries and today, the collected body – whether newly procured cadavers or historic specimens – continues to form an essential component of medical education.

At the heart of this book has been a will to explain how and why the living used the collected deceased body to develop medical knowledge in late-nineteenth- and early-twentieth-century Australia. Investigating the Australian experience of collecting human remains offers an important revision to a history typically told from the perspective of prominent centres of knowledge in Britain, Europe and the United States. Positioning collected specimens as materials worthy of historical investigation reveals how they influenced and informed the people who engaged with them. What emerges, however, is that these collecting practices and their legacies do not fit into neat boxes that can be confined to the past. Despite the passage of time, collections are never truly forgotten. People continue to collect specimens and engage with human remains in a variety of contexts, be they in medical education and research, museum exhibitions, or anthropological and historical investigation. As these engagements occur, specimens accumulate new meanings, values and narratives.

Just as this book offers one interpretation of the lives of collected specimens, it presents the opportunity for further exploration of their ongoing, multifaceted afterlives. While the use of the deceased body to develop medical and scientific knowledge has led to remarkable breakthroughs and innovation, we must acknowledge the harm it has caused to individuals and communities in the past, and continues to cause in the present. It is my hope that, through this book, future researchers, medical professionals, medical students, curators and collectors might forge new relationships between the living and the collected dead, equipped with a more comprehensive understanding of the complex encounters that preceded them. We might, perhaps, be guided in this process by the advice given to nineteenth-century Australian medical students, and keep at the forefront of this work the humanity and dignity of those who become subjects in the pursuit of knowledge.

# Notes

## Introduction

1. Archibald Watson to Harry Brookes Allen, 18 July 1907, Sir Harry Brookes Allen Collection, 76/6, Box 1, File 17, University of Melbourne Archives. Archibald Watson to Harry Brookes Allen, 5 August 1907, Sir Harry Brookes Allen Collection, 76/6, Box 1, File 17, University of Melbourne Archives.
2. For insight into the unconventional and, at times, controversial life and career of Archibald Watson, see Jennifer M. T. Carter, *Painting the Islands Vermilion: Archibald Watson and the brig Carl* (Carlton South: Melbourne University Press, 1999).
3. *Australasian Medical Congress, Transactions of the Eighth Session, Held in Melbourne, Victoria, October 1908 (Three Vols)*, Vol. 2 (Melbourne: J. Kemp, Government Printer, 1909), 348.
4. Lisa O'Sullivan and Ross Jones, 'Two Australian Fetuses: Frederic Wood Jones and the Work of an Anatomical Specimen', *Bulletin of the History of Medicine* 89, no. 2 (2015): 258.
5. This approach takes inspiration from Hussey's methodology which examines knowledge construction in one city – the city of London – on a small scale. See Kristin D. Hussey, *Imperial Bodies in London: Empire, Mobility, and the Making of British Medicine, 1880–1914* (Pittsburgh: University of Pittsburgh Press, 2021), 7.
6. Ross L. Jones, *Humanity's Mirror: 150 Years of Anatomy in Melbourne* (South Yarra, VIC: Haddington Press, 2007); Department of Pathology, University of Melbourne, *The Melbourne School of Pathology: Phases and Contrasts* (Parkville: University of Melbourne Department of Pathology, 1962); K. F. Russell, *The Melbourne Medical School, 1862–1962* (Carlton, VIC: Melbourne University Press, 1977); J. A. Young et al., *Centenary Book of the University of Sydney Faculty of Medicine* (Sydney: Sydney University Press, 1984); R. G. Elmslie, 'Early Anatomists of the Adelaide Medical School', *Australian and New Zealand Journal of Surgery* 57, no. 11 (1987): 865–9; Bryan Gandevia, *The Melbourne Medical Students, 1862–1942: Being a Review of Their Numerous Activities, with a Summary of the History of the Medical School and a List of Office-Bearers in the M.S.S.* (Melbourne: Melbourne Medical Students' Society, 1948); Milton J. Lewis, 'Medicine in Colonial Australia, 1788–1900', *Medical Journal of Australia* 201, no. 1 Suppl (2014): S5–10;

R. J. W. Selleck, *The Shop: The University of Melbourne, 1850–1939* (Carlton, VIC: Melbourne University Press, 2003).

7   Donald Simpson, 'English Roots of Medical Education in Australasia: Kenneth F. Russell Memorial Lecture', *Australian and New Zealand Journal of Surgery* 70, no. 12 (2000): 843–50; Donald Simpson, 'The Adelaide Medical School, 1885–1913: A Study of Anglo-Australian Synergies in Medical Education' (PhD thesis, University of Adelaide, 2000); Laurence M. Geary, 'The Scottish-Australian Connection, 1850–1900', in *The History of Medical Education in Britain*, ed. Vivian Nutton and Roy Porter (Atlanta: Rodopi, 1995), 51–75; for scholarship on the development of British medical education, see Vivian Nutton and Roy Porter, eds., *The History of Medical Education in Britain* (Atlanta: Rodopi, 1995); Jonathan Reinarz, *Health Care in Birmingham: The Birmingham Teaching Hospitals 1779–1939* (Woodbridge: Boydell Press, 2009); Keir Waddington, *Medical Education at St. Bartholomew's Hospital* (Suffolk: The Boydell Press, 2003).

8   Helen MacDonald, *Possessing the Dead: The Artful Science of Anatomy* (Carlton, VIC: Melbourne University Press, 2010); Helen MacDonald, *Human Remains: Episodes in Human Dissection* (Carlton: Melbourne University Press, 2005); Helen MacDonald, 'Procuring Corpses: The English Anatomy Inspectorate, 1842–1858', *Medical History* 53, no. 3 (2009): 379–96; Ross L. Jones, 'Cadavers and the Social Dimension of Dissection', in *The Body Divided: Human Beings and Human 'Material' in Modern Medical History*, ed. Sarah Ferber and Sally Wilde (Surrey and Burlington: Ashgate, 2011), 29–52; Paul Turnbull, *Science, Museums and Collecting the Indigenous Dead in Colonial Australia* (Basingstoke: Palgrave Macmillan, 2017).

9   Ruth Richardson, *Death, Dissection, and the Destitute* (London: Routledge, 1987); Elizabeth Hurren, *Dying for Victorian Medicine: English Anatomy and Its Trade in the Dead Poor, c. 1834–1929* (Basingstoke and New York: Palgrave MacMillan, 2012); Elizabeth T. Hurren, *Dissecting the Criminal Corpse: Staging Post-Execution Punishment in Early Modern England* (London: Palgrave Macmillan, 2016); Michael Sappol, *A Traffic of Dead Bodies: Anatomy and Embodied Social Identity in Nineteenth-Century America* (Princeton, NJ: Princeton University Press, 2002); Tinne Claes, *Corpses in Belgian Anatomy, 1860–1914: Nobody's Dead* (Cham: Palgrave Macmillan, 2019); Tatjana Buklijas, 'Cultures of Death and Politics of Corpse Supply', *Bulletin of the History of Medicine* 82, no. 3 (2008): 570–607; Warwick Anderson, *The Cultivation of Whiteness: Science, Health and Racial Destiny in Australia* (Carlton, VIC: Melbourne University Publishing, 2005).

10  Samuel J. M. M. Alberti, *Morbid Curiosities: Medical Museums in Nineteenth-Century Britain* (Oxford: Oxford University Press, 2011); Jonathan Reinarz, 'The Age of Museum Medicine: The Rise and Fall of the Medical Museum at Birmingham's School of Medicine', *Social History of Medicine* 18, no. 3 (2005): 419–37; Erin McLeary, 'Science in a Bottle: The Medical Museum in North America,

1860–1940' (PhD diss., University of Pennsylvania, 2001); see also Elizabeth Hallam, *Anatomy Museum: Death and the Body Displayed* (London: Reaktion Books Ltd., 2016); Hieke Huistra, *The Afterlife of the Leiden Anatomical Collections: Hands On, Hands Off*, The History of Medicine in Context (London: Routledge, 2019); Marieke M. A. Hendriksen, *Elegant Anatomy: The Eighteenth-Century Leiden Anatomical Collections* (Leiden: Brill, 2014); Alison Kraft and Samuel J. M. M. Alberti, '"Equal Though Different": Laboratories, Museums and the Institutional Development of Biology in Late-Victorian Northern England', *Studies in History and Philosophy of Biological & Biomedical Sciences* 34, no. 2 (2003): 203–36.

11 Reinarz, 'The Age of Museum Medicine', 419.
12 McLeary, 'Science in a Bottle'; Reinarz, 'The Age of Museum Medicine', 420; Alberti, *Morbid Curiosities*, 11.
13 Daniela Bleichmar and Peter C. Mancall, eds., *Collecting across Cultures: Material Exchanges in the Early Modern Atlantic World*, Early Modern Americas (Philadelphia: University of Pennsylvania Press, 2011); Lissa Roberts, ed., *Centres and Cycles of Accumulation in and around the Netherlands during the Early Modern Period*, Low Countries Studies on the Circulation of Natural Knowledge: Vol. 2 (Berlin: Lit, 2011); Alison Petch, 'Collecting Immortality: The Field Collectors Who Contributed to the Pitt Rivers Museum, Oxford', *Journal of Museum Ethnography*, 16 (2004): 127–39; Tom Griffiths, *Hunters and Collectors: The Antiquarian Imagination in Australia* (Cambridge: Cambridge University Press, 1996).
14 Tamson Pietsch, *Empire of Scholars: Universities, Networks and the British Academic World, 1850–1939* (Manchester: Manchester University Press, 2013), 6.
15 See Ross L. Jones, *Anatomists of Empire: Race, Evolution and the Discovery of Human Biology in the British World* (Melbourne: Australian Scholarly Publishing, 2020); Turnbull, *Science, Museums and Collecting the Indigenous Dead in Colonial Australia*; Tamson Pietsch, 'Between the Nation and the World: J. T. Wilson and Scientific Networks in the Early Twentieth Century', in *Science and Empire: Knowledge and Networks of Science across the British Empire 1800–1970*, ed. Joseph M. Hodge and Brett M. Bennett (London: Palgrave Macmillan, 2011), 148–50.
16 Tamson Pietsch, 'Wandering Scholars? Academic Mobility and the British World, 1850–1940', *Journal of Historical Geography* 36, no. 4 (2010): 377–87, 381–2; Peter Hoffenburg, '"A Science of Our Own": Nineteenth Century Exhibitions, Australians and the History of Science', in *Science and Empire: Knowledge and Networks of Science across the British Empire, 1800–1970*, ed. Brett M. Bennett and Joseph M. Hodge (London: Palgrave Macmillan UK, 2011), 123; Patricia Morison, *J. T. Wilson and the Fraternity of Duckmaloi* (Netherlands: Rodopi B.B., 1997), 325.
17 Pietsch, 'Between the Nation and the World', 154.
18 For example, see Ian Hodder, *Entangled: An Archaeology of the Relationships between Humans and Things* (Malden, MA: Wiley-Blackwell, 2012); *History from*

*Things: Essays on Material Culture*, ed. Stephen Lubar and David W. Kingery (Washington DC: Smithsonian Institution, 2013); Ewa Domańska, 'The Return to Things', *Archaeologia Polona* 44 (2006): 171–85.

19  Igor Kopytoff, 'The Cultural Biography of Things: Commoditisation as Process', in *The Social Life of Things: Commodities in Cultural Perspective*, ed. Arjun Appadurai (Cambridge: Cambridge University Press, 1986), 64–94; Arjun Appadurai, 'Introduction: Commodities and the Politics of Value', in *The Social Life of Things: Commodities in Cultural Perspective* (Cambridge: Cambridge University Press, 1986), 3–63.

# Chapter 1

1  These descriptions and processes are drawn largely from the second edition of D. J. Cunningham's *Manual of Practical Anatomy*, first published in 1895, and into its sixteenth edition, published in 2017. Daniel John Cunningham, *Manual of Practical Anatomy* (Edinburgh: Y. J. Pentland, 1896).

2  For example, see Christine Quigley, *The Corpse: A History* (Jefferson, NC: McFarland, 1996); Thomas W. Laqueur, *The Work of the Dead: A Cultural History of Mortal Remains* (Princeton, NJ: Princeton University Press, 2018); Richardson, *Death, Dissection, and the Destitute*; D. Gareth Jones, *Speaking for the Dead: Cadavers in Biology and Medicine* (Aldershot: Ashgate, 2000); Fay Bound Alberti, *This Mortal Coil: The Human Body in History and Culture* (Oxford: Oxford University Press, 2016); Stephen C. Kenny, 'The Development of Medical Museums in the Antebellum American South: Slave Bodies in Networks of Anatomical Exchange', *Bulletin of the History of Medicine* 87, no. 1 (2013): 32–62; Ruth Penfold-Mounce, 'Consuming Criminal Corpses: Fascination with the Dead Criminal Body', *Mortality* 15, no. 3 (2010): 250–65; MacDonald, *Human Remains*; MacDonald, *Possessing the Dead*; Jones, 'Cadavers and the Social Dimension of Dissection'; Turnbull, *Science, Museums and Collecting the Indigenous Dead in Colonial Australia*.

3  See Cynthia Klestinec, *Theaters of Anatomy: Students, Teachers, and Traditions of Dissection in Renaissance Venice* (Baltimore: Johns Hopkins University Press, 2011); Katharine Park, 'The Life of the Corpse: Division and Dissection in Late Medieval Europe', *Journal of the History of Medicine and Allied Sciences* 50, no. 1 (1995): 111–32.

4  An Act for Better Preventing the Horrid Crime of Murder 1752, 25 Geo. 2, c. 37.

5  For an account of a public dissection following execution in colonial Van Diemen's Land, see Helen MacDonald, 'A Dissection in Reverse: Mary McLauchlan, Hobart Town, 1830', *Lilith: A Feminist History Journal* 13 (2006): 15. Hurren details the

common demographic for those hanged and dissected. See Hurren, *Dissecting the Criminal Corpse*, 150.

6   *Hobart Town Advertiser*, 3 October 1845, quoted in Helen MacDonald, 'A Dissection in Reverse', 15.

7   Richardson, *Death, Dissection, and the Destitute*, 90. For more on death and burial practices in late-nineteenth- and early-twentieth-century Australia, see Patricia Jalland, *Australian Ways of Death: A Social and Cultural History 1840–1918* (South Melbourne: Oxford University Press, 2002), esp. 51–68. Historians note that continental European countries generally faced less opposition to dissection than their British and North American contemporaries due to religious and cultural differences. See Buklijas, 'Cultures of Death and Politics of Corpse Supply'; Claes, '"By What Right Does the Scalpel Enter the Pauper's Corpse?" Dissections and Consent in Late Nineteenth-Century Belgium', *Social History of Medicine* (2018): 258–77.

8   'Inefficacy of Unnatural Punishments', *The Sydney Gazette and New South Wales Advertiser*, 6 April 1833, 4.

9   Helen MacDonald, '"Humanity's Discards": The New South Wales Anatomy Act 1881', *Mortality* 12, no. 4 (2007): 365–82.

10  There was a marked decrease in the number of executions in Britain when the Judgement of Death Act passed in 1823. See V. A. C. Gatrell, *The Hanging Tree: Execution and the English People 1770–1868* (Oxford: Oxford University Press, 1994); Rosalind Crone, *Violent Victorians: Popular Entertainment in Nineteenth-Century London* (Manchester and New York: Manchester University Press, 2012).

11  For more on Burke and Hare, see Caroline McCracken-Flesher, *The Doctor Dissected: A Cultural Autopsy of the Burke and Hare Murders* (Oxford: Oxford University Press, 2012); Lisa Rosner, *The Anatomy Murders: Being the True and Spectacular History of Edinburgh's Notorious Burke and Hare and of the Man of Science Who Abetted Them in the Commission of Their Most Heinous Crimes* (Philadelphia: University of Pennsylvania Press, 2011).

12  MacDonald, *Possessing the Dead*, 6.

13  'Riot at Aberdeen. Destruction of the Theatre of Anatomy', 7 July 1832, *The Sydney Monitor*, 3.

14  Sappol, *A Traffic of Dead Bodies*, 105–10.

15  'The Late Horrible Murders in Edinburgh, to Obtain Subjects for Dissection', *Sydney Gazette and New South Wales Advertiser*, 12 May 1829, 3; 'Burke's Confession', *The Sydney Monitor*, 27 June 1829, 3; *The Australian*, 30 January 1829, 3.

16  William Roberts, *Mr. Warburton's Anatomy Bill: Thoughts on Its Mischievous Tendency; with Suggestions for an Entirely New One, Founded upon an Available Anti-Septic Process, in an Appeal to Medical Practitioners, Students of Anatomy,*

and the Public at Large, on the Injury to Medical Sciences and the Hindrances to the Decent Interment of Unclaimed Pauper Bodies Now Delivered up for Anatomical 'Examination', Consequent upon the Rejection of Such an Process* (London: J. Ollivier, 1843), 16. Emphasis in original.
17 *An Act for Regulating Schools of Anatomy 1862*, Parliament of Victoria Victoria, CLVI.
18 Ibid.
19 In the twenty-two years after the introduction of the Victorian Anatomy Act, the colonies of Tasmania (1869), New South Wales (1881) and South Australia (1884) also introduced legislation to regulate the trade and treatment of cadavers. For a discussion of the similarities between the British Anatomy Act and colonial Australian acts, see MacDonald, *Possessing the Dead*, 10–12.
20 *The Electoral Act 1863*, Parliament of Victoria, CLXVIII.
21 Richardson, *Death, Dissection, and the Destitute*, 281. Hurren notes that in Britain, even 'few contemporaries doubted that the Anatomy Act exaggerated the experience of being poor'. See Hurren, *Dying for Victorian Medicine*, 6.
22 J. T. Wilson to Registrar, Sydney University, 8 April 1892, G.63, Folder 1, Sydney University Archives.
23 Ibid.
24 Ibid.
25 'More Charges', *The Advertiser*, 5 September 1903, 13.
26 Ibid.
27 Ibid.
28 'Ramsay Smith Case', *The Advertiser*, 23 September 1903, 5. For a detailed discussion of the ambiguities inherent in the wording of the South Australian Anatomy Act, see Helen MacDonald, 'The Anatomy Inspector and the Government Corpse', *History Australia* 6, no. 2 (2009): 40.1. Richardson also discusses how the phrasing of the British Anatomy Act allowed doctors to find loopholes in the law and elude the risk of punishment for transgressions. Richardson, *Death, Dissection, and the Destitute*, esp. 129.
29 'Ramsay Smith Case', 5.
30 MacDonald, 'The Anatomy Inspector and the Government Corpse', 40.6 and 40.7; MacDonald, 'Humanity's Discards', 376.
31 'The Pauper Dead', *The Herald*, 28 January 1895, 1.
32 For a case in which the body of a deceased woman was missing when her friends arrived to claim it, see 'Intercolonial News, Melbourne', *Geelong Advertiser*, 11 February 1886, 3.
33 Richardson, *Death, Dissection, and the Destitute*, 250.
34 Jones, *Humanity's Mirror*, 2.
35 The first building on the site was completed in 1884 and the first building of the 'New' Medical School was erected in 1885. For more on the early stages

of the Melbourne Medical School, see K. F. Russell, *The Melbourne Medical School, 1862–1962* (Carlton: Melbourne University Press, 1977), 28; Selleck, *The Shop*, 84.
36  'Opening a School of Medicine', May 1858, University of Melbourne Registrar UM 419, 93/46, Folder 1, University of Melbourne Archives. For more on the exchange of personnel and philosophy between prestigious schools in Britain and the colonial Australian medical schools, see Donald Simpson, 'The Adelaide Medical School, 1885–1913: A Study of Anglo-Australian Synergies in Medical Education' (PhD thesis, University of Adelaide, 2000).
37  James Paget to Anthony Colling Brownless, quoted in Selleck, *The Shop*, 90.
38  *Speculum*, no. 8, February 1887, 31.
39  *Speculum*, no. 16, January 1889, 1.
40  *Speculum*, no. 62, May 1905, 2.
41  Jones, *Humanity's Mirror*, 90.
42  'Melbourne Benevolent Asylum', *The Argus*, 30 May 1879.
43  Jalland, *Australian Ways of Death*, 203–6; Jones, *Humanity's Mirror*, 12, 90. For the British context, see Hurren, *Dying for Victorian Medicine*, 167.
44  *An Act for Regulating Schools of Anatomy 1862*, Victoria, CLVI.
45  *Speculum*, no. 13, May 1888, 13.
46  'Benevolent Asylum', *The Argus*, 27 May 1870; 'Subjects for Dissection', *The Age*, 27 June 1873. For a history of the Melbourne Benevolent Asylum, see Mary Kehoe, *The Melbourne Benevolent Asylum: Hotham's Premier Building*, The Annals of Hotham, Vol. 1 (North Melbourne: Hotham History Project, 1998).
47  'Subjects for Dissection'.
48  *The Argus*, 30 July 1869, 5.
49  *The Argus*, 13 August 1869, 5.
50  Ibid.
51  Ibid.; Thomas Dickson, 'The Benevolent Asylum and the School of Anatomy', *The Argus*, 10 August 1869, 1.
52  E. L. Zox, 'Subjects for Anatomical Dissection', *The Argus*, 2 July 1873.
53  *Speculum*, no. 13, May 1888, 13.
54  'Spicula', *Speculum*, no. 30, August 1894, 30.
55  'The Medical Students Grievance', *The Age*, 6 April 1889, 4.
56  'The Dissecting Room', *Speculum*, no. 11, October 1887, 12.
57  Selleck, *The Shop*, 267–83.
58  'The Pauper Dead', *The Herald*, 28 June 1895, 1; 'Gathering Bodies for Medical Students', *The Bendigo Advertiser*, 6 January 1893, 4.
59  'The School of Medicine', *The Herald*, 18 July 1864, 3.
60  'The Pathological Department', *Speculum*, no. 9 (May 1887): 11.
61  *Speculum*, no. 40, May 1898, 4.
62  The Medical History Museum at the University of Melbourne holds several student notebooks that provide insight into the content of lectures and demonstrations. For

example, see 'Student Notebook of A. McDonald', MHM 02011, Medical History Museum, University of Melbourne and 'Notebook of Mary Clementina De Garis', MHM 02027, Medical History Museum, University of Melbourne.

63 Thomas Neville Bonner, *Becoming a Physician: Medical Education in Britain, France, Germany, and the United States, 1750–1945* (Baltimore, MD: Johns Hopkins University Press, 2000), 61. See also John Harley Warner and James M. Edmonson, *Dissection: Photographs of a Rite of Passage in American Medicine, 1880–1930* (New York: Blast Books, 2009).

64 Rachel N. Ponce, '"They Increase in Beauty and Elegance": Transforming Cadavers and the Epistemology of Dissection in Early Nineteenth-Century American Medical Education', *Journal of the History of Medicine and Allied Sciences* 68, no. 3 (2013): 331–76, 357.

65 'The Pathological Department', 11.

66 Ibid.

67 Ponce, 'They Increase in Beauty and Elegance', 357.

68 For example, see 'Two arrested in Melbourne', *The Advertiser*, 19 April 1926, 17; 'Craving for Cocaine', *Geraldton Guardian*, 5 January 1924, 3; 'Vulgar Medical Students', *The Advertiser*, 18 May 1911, 11; 'Indignation Meeting of Medical Students', *The Argus*, 13 May 1881, 6.

69 'Visit of University Students – Strange Proceedings', *The Argus*, 20 August 1888, 8.

70 Ibid.

71 'The Students and Hamlet', *The Argus*, 1 May 1889, 7.

72 Ibid.

73 Albert Smith, 'Physiology of the London Medical Student', *Punch, or the London Charivari* 1 (1841): 154.

74 Charles Dickens, *The Pickwick Papers*, quoted in Waddington, 'Mayhem and Medical Students', 48. See also A. W. Bates, 'Indecent and Demoralising Representations: Public Anatomy Museums in Mid-Victorian England', *Medical History* 52 (2008): 1–22, 21.

75 Waddington, 'Mayhem and Medical Students', 48–9. For more on the moral concerns over growing urbanism in nineteenth-century London, see Andrew Smith, *Victorian Demons: Medicine, Masculinity and the Gothic at the Fin-de-Siècle* (Manchester: Manchester University Press, 2004), 73–6; Andrew Mearns, *The Bitter Cry of Outcast London* (Boston, MA: Cupples, Upham, 1883).

76 'Bodies for Dissection: Professor Berry interviewed', *The Argus*, 15 March 1907, 21.

77 Richard J. A. Berry, *Chance and Circumstance* (unpublished autobiography, University of Melbourne, Brownless Biomedical Library, 1954), 110. For further discussion on student behaviour at the Melbourne Medical School, see Jones, 'Cadavers and the Social Dimension of Dissection', esp. 40–6.

78 Joseph Cunning, 'Correspondence', *Speculum*, no. 126 (August 1914).

79  Scalpel, 'The Dissector's Vade-mecum', *Speculum*, no. 21 (June 1890): 68 and 60.
80  Lorenzo Servitje, 'Birthed from the Clinic': The Degenerate Medical Students of Edward Berdoe's St. Bernard's', *Critical Survey* 27, no. 2 (2015): 21–35.
81  Hurren, *Dying for Victorian Medicine*, 85. Several articles in *Speculum* suggest that smoking in the dissecting room was common. For an example, see 'On Dit', *Speculum*, no. 65 (May 1906): 24.
82  Sappol, *A Traffic of Dead Bodies*, 81.
83  Kelly, 'Irish Medical Student Culture and the Performance of Masculinity, c. 1880–1930', 39–57. For more on the history of medical students, see also Eugenia Pacitti, 'Dissecting the Student Experience at Australian Medical Schools, 1884–1912', *Social History of Medicine* 34, no. 1 (2021): 467–88; Waddington, 'Mayhem and Medical Students'; Waddington, 'Death at St Bernard's: Anti-Vivisection, Medicine and the Gothic', *Journal of Victorian Culture* 18, no. 2 (2013): 246–62.
84  'Editorial', *Speculum*, no. 1 (July 1884): 6.
85  'Medical Students' Society', *Speculum*, no. 2 (December 1884): 5.
86  *Speculum*, no. 60, July 1904, 85; 'Minutes from 8 May', Minutes 1880–1888, Medical Students' Society, 1978.0129, University of Melbourne Archives.
87  Hunter, Two Introductory Lectures, quoted in Richardson, Death, Dissection, and the Destitute, 31.
88  Several Melbourne Medical School faculty members, most notably Harry Brookes Allen, were also enthusiastic writers who regularly contributed poetry and prose to *Speculum*.
89  Alberti, *This Mortal Coil*, 109.
90  Femur, 'A Night in the Dissecting Room', *Speculum*, no. 18 (August 1889): 47.
91  Ibid.
92  Cadavers sometimes posed a risk of contagion to those undertaking dissections. See Ponce, 'They Increase in Beauty and Elegance', 338; Burrell and Gill, 'The Liverpool Cholera Epidemic of 1832 and Anatomical Dissection – Medical Mistrust and Civil Unrest', 495; Hurren, *Dissecting the Criminal Corpse*, 260.
93  Chris Willis, 'A House for the Dead: Victorian Mausolea and Graveyard Gothic', *Victorian Gothic: Leeds Centre for Working Papers in Victorian Studies* 6 (2003): 159; Andrew Mangham, 'Buried Alive: The Gothic Awakening of Taphephobia', *The Journal of Literature and Science* 3, no. 1 (2010): 10–22.
94  G. Leonetti et al., 'Evidence of Pin Implantation as a Means of Verifying Death during the Great Plague of Marseilles (1722)', *Journal of Forensic Sciences* 42, no. 4 (1997): 745; Elena Del Río Parra, '"He Has No Pulse": Typologies of the Fear of Being Buried Alive in Preindustrial Spain', *South Atlantic Review* 76, no. 3 (2011): 129–50.
95  *Kyneton Observer*, 16 January 1866, 2.

96  Rothwell Adam, 'Ideals in the Pursuit of Medicine', *Speculum*, no. 47 (September 1900): 28; P. Ward Farmer, 'Our Duties and Responsibilities', *Speculum*, no. 41 (July 1898): 55–8.
97  Patriarch, 'The Student and his Responsibilities', *Speculum*, no. 51 (December 1901): 87.
98  Shane McCorristine, *The Spectral Arctic: A History of Dreams and Ghosts in Polar Exploration* (London: UCL Press, 2018), 46.
99  Femur, 'A Night in the Dissecting Room', 48.
100 'The Wail of the Wraith', *Speculum*, no. 72 (September 1908): 71.
101 Ibid. Lithotomy is the removal of kidney, bladder, or gallbladder stones.
102 Ibid.
103 G. A. Syme, 'Lecture on Medical Ethics', *Speculum*, no. 66 (August 1906): 48.
104 'The Wail of the Wraith', 72. The omentum is a thin sheet of fatty tissue that connects and protects internal abdominal structures.
105 Byron J. Good, *Medicine, Rationality, and Experience: An Anthropological Perspective* (Cambridge: Cambridge University Press, 1994), 73.
106 Ruth Richardson and Brian Hurwitz, 'Celebrating New Year in Bart's Dissecting Room', *Clinical Anatomy* 9, no. 6 (1996): 408–13, 408.
107 'The Wail of the Wraith', 71.
108 Syme, 'Lecture on Medical Ethics', 47.
109 Farmer, 'Our Duties and Responsibilities', 55, 58.
110 Ibid., 58.
111 'Ourselves', *Speculum*, no. 56 (May 1903): 1.
112 Ibid.
113 Jones, *Humanity's Mirror*, xv. Gandevia also discusses the origins of the phrase. See Gandevia, *The Melbourne Medical Students, 1862–1942*, 40.

# Chapter 2

1  Findlen, *Possessing Nature*, 155.
2  'The Prospects of the Year', *Speculum*, no. 5 (April 1886): 3. In 1886, the museum had around 3,000 specimens. Today, it holds approximately 12,000 specimens. See 'Harry Brookes Allen Museum of Anatomy and Pathology', https://harrybrookesallenmuseum.mdhs.unimelb.edu.au/about-the-museum/history.
3  Griffiths, *Hunters and Collectors*; Paul Turnbull, 'Anthropological collecting and colonial violence in colonial Queensland: A response to "the blood and bone"', *Journal of Australian Colonial History* 17 (2015): 133–58; Bleichmar and Mancall, eds., *Collecting across Cultures*; Lissa Roberts, ed., *Centres and Cycles of Accumulation in and around the Netherlands during the Early Modern Period*

(Berlin: Lit, 2011); Glenn Penny, *Objects of Culture: Ethnology and Ethnographic Museums in Imperial Germany* (Chapel Hill, NC: University of North Carolina Press, 2002).

4   For a discussion on the development of preservation methods for natural history specimens, see Christopher M. Parsons and Kathleen S. Murphy, 'Ecosystems under Sail: Specimen Transport in the Eighteenth-Century French and British Atlantics', *Early American Studies: An Interdisciplinary Journal* 10, no. 3 (2012): 503–39.

5   Griffiths, *Hunters and Collectors*, 17.

6   'Australian Indigenous Plants', *The Argus*, 28 April 1876, 6. See also Sara Maroske, '"A Taste for Botanic Science": Ferdinand Mueller's Female Collectors and the History of Australian Botany', *Muelleria* 32 (2014): 72–91; A. M. Lucas, 'Specimens and the Currency of Honour: The Museum Trade of Ferdinand von Mueller', *Historical Records of Australian Science* 24, no. 1 (n.d.): 15–39.

7   Parsons and Murphy, 'Ecosystems under Sail', 510. See also Anne Coote, '"Pray Write Me a List of Species … That Will Pay Me Best": The Business and Culture of Natural History Collecting in Mid-Nineteenth Century New South Wales', *History Australia* 11, no. 2 (2014): 80–100.

8   See, for example: Brett M. Bennett and Joseph M. Hodge, eds., *Science and Empire: Knowledge and Networks of Science across the British Empire, 1800–1970* (London: Palgrave Macmillan UK, 2011); Alan Lester, 'Imperial Circuits and Networks: Geographies of the British Empire: Imperial Circuits and Networks', *History Compass* 4, no. 1 (2006): 124–41; Petch, 'Collecting Immortality', 127–39; Carl Bridge and Kent Fedorowich, 'Mapping the British World', *The Journal of Imperial and Commonwealth History* 31, no. 2 (2003): 1–15; Michael Jones, 'From Catalogues to Contextual Networks: Reconfiguring Collection Documentation in Museums', *Archives and Records* 39, no. 1 (2018): 4–20.

9   See Jones, *Anatomists of Empire*, esp. 69; Lester, 'Imperial Circuits and Networks'.

10  Kopytoff, 'The Cultural Biography of Things', 66.

11  Harry Brookes Allen, 'Letter to the Editor', 1 October 1886, Sir Harry Brookes Allen Collection, 63/3, Box 1, Folder 1, University of Melbourne Archives.

12  Ibid.

13  Ibid.

14  'People We Know', *Melbourne Punch* 2278, vol. CIX, 23 October 1908, 612. Allen also served as Dean of the Faculty of Medicine from 1886 to 1890 and again from 1896 to 1924. He led several public health projects towards the end of his career, particularly in public sanitation. Allen died in 1926, following ill health and several strokes.

15  During Allen's tenure, the anatomy and pathology museum amassed thousands of specimens. For many specimens, the donor's name and location are not

recorded. For the purpose of this chapter, I have only included named or locatable contributors derived from Allen's extant correspondence.

16 Archibald Watson to Harry Brookes Allen, 18 July 1907, Sir Harry Brookes Allen Collection, 76/6, Box 1, File 17, University of Melbourne Archives.
17 See Petch, 'Collecting Immortality', 127; Maroske, 'A Taste for Botanic Science'.
18 Alberti, *Morbid Curiosities*, 6.
19 Thomas Shearman Ralph to the Chairman of the Committee of the Pathological Museum, 28 May 1860, University of Melbourne Registrar, Registrar's Correspondence, 93/46, Folder 1 (1857–1870), University of Melbourne Archives.
20 Alberti, *Morbid Curiosities*, 109.
21 Norman Dowling to Harry Brookes Allen, 24 April 1905, Sir Harry Brookes Allen Collection, 76/6, Box 3, Folder 7, University of Melbourne Archives.
22 Walter Fowler to Harry Brookes Allen, 14 March 1904, Sir Harry Brookes Allen Collection, 76/6, Box 1, Folder 1, University of Melbourne Archives; J. Ferguson to Harry Brookes Allen, 23 March 1903, Sir Harry Brookes Allen Collection, 76/6, Box 1, Folder 1, University of Melbourne Archives.
23 J. T. Wilson to Thomas Anderson Stuart, 20 June 1890, Letter Book, G.63, Series 1, University of Sydney Archives.
24 Ibid.
25 Mackenzie notes that the introduction of rail and shipping infrastructure was 'vital in the physical accumulation of collections'. See John M. MacKenzie, *Museums and Empire: Natural History, Human Cultures and Colonial Identities* (Manchester: Manchester University Press, 2009), 9.
26 Harry Brookes Allen to the Chairman of the Finance Committee of the University of Melbourne, 24 September 1888, University of Melbourne Registrar, UM 419/1993.0046, Folder 4, University of Melbourne Archives.
27 Ibid.
28 Charles Smith to Harry Brookes Allen, 1 January 1900, Sir Harry Brookes Allen Collection, 76/6, Box 1, Folder 1, University of Melbourne Archives.
29 W. B. Beattie-Smith to Harry Brookes Allen, 8 June 1887, Sir Harry Brookes Allen Collection, 76/6, Box 1, Folder 1, University of Melbourne Archives; Walter Fowler to Harry Brookes Allen, 17 March 1904, Sir Harry Brookes Allen Collection, 76/6, Box 1, Folder 1, University of Melbourne Archives.
30 Archibald Watson to Harry Brookes Allen, 18 July 1907, MHM 00911, Medical History Museum, University of Melbourne.
31 Ibid.
32 Despite little evidence for anatomy and pathology specimens existing on the open market, in the early to mid-twentieth century there was an overt trade in skulls, and particularly Aboriginal skulls. See Paul Daley, 'Restless Indigenous Remains', *Meanjin* 73, no. 1 (2014).

33  While it may be accurate to state that there was little public engagement in developing the anatomy and pathology collection under Allen's tenure, from the early to mid-twentieth century, amateur collectors and members of the public took part in stealing Australian Aboriginal skulls from burial grounds for museum collections. For example, see Turnbull, *Science, Museums and Collecting the Indigenous Dead in Colonial Australia*.
34  'Battle of the Brains', *The Argus*, 6 August 1864, 5.
35  'The Case of Harrison', *The Argus*, 19 July 1864, 7.
36  'The Post Mortem Examination on the Bodies of Harrison, Woods and Carver', *The Age*, 5 August 1864, 5.
37  'Examination of Harrison's Brain', *Mount Alexander Mail*, 6 August 1864, 3.
38  'A Doctor's Difference', *Melbourne Punch*, 11 August 1864. Emphasis in original.
39  'The Pathological Museum', *The Argus*, 12 June 1905, 6.
40  'The Congress Exhibition and Museum', *The Age*, 22 October 1908, 8; 'Intercolonial Medical Congress: Second Day's Sitting', *The Argus*, 9 January 1889, 5.
41  'Albert Park Tragedy: Man's Dismembered Body', *The Argus*, 21 September 1906, 5.
42  'Albert-Park Tragedy: Pathological Examinations, Murder Theory Strengthened', *The Argus*, 22 September 1906, 15. The suspicion that it was a medical student behind the murder and dismemberment of the body is reminiscent of the Whitechapel Murders committed in 1888. Many members of the public believed the murderer, 'Jack the Ripper', was a disturbed medical student looking for human specimens. See 'The Whitechapel Murders', *South Australian Weekly Chronicle*, 17 November 1888, 7; Waddington, 'Mayhem and Medical Students', 50; Judith R. Walkowitz, *City of Dreadful Delight: Narratives of Sexual Danger in Late-Victorian London* (London: Virago, 1992), 191–228.
43  'Albert Park Sensation: Dragging the Lagoon', *The Age*, 22 September 1906, 13.
44  Roberts, 'Accumulation and Management in Global Historical Perspective', 238.
45  B. Stewart Cohen to Harry Brookes Allen, 27 December 1898, Sir Harry Brookes Allen Collection, 76/6, Box 1, Folder 1, University of Melbourne Archives.
46  'Editorial', *Speculum*, no. 6 (June 1886): 1–2.
47  Kelly to the Lecturer in Obstetrics, 15 September 1901, Sir Harry Brookes Allen Collection, 76/6, Box 1, Folder 8, University of Melbourne Archives.
48  Louis Ashworth to Harry Brookes Allen, 23 July 1896, Sir Harry Brookes Allen Collection, 76/6, Box 1, Folder 8, University of Melbourne Archives.
49  Walter Fowler to Harry Brookes Allen, 14 November 1904, Sir Harry Brookes Allen Collection, 76/6, Box 1, Folder 1, University of Melbourne Archives.
50  Alberti, *Morbid Curiosities*, 23.
51  J. R. H. Willis to Harry Brookes Allen, 15 May 1904, Sir Harry Brookes Allen Collection, 76/6, Box 1, Folder 1, University of Melbourne Archives.

52 Norman Dowling to Harry Brookes Allen, 24 April 1905, Sir Harry Brookes Allen Collection, 76/6, Box 3, Folder 7, University of Melbourne Archives.
53 Ibid.
54 Ibid.
55 Frank R. Legge to Harry Brookes Allen, 7 July 1905, Sir Harry Brookes Allen Collection, 76/6, Box 1, Folder 3, University of Melbourne Archives.
56 Ibid.
57 Letter to Harry Brookes Allen, 2 May 1902, Sir Harry Brookes Allen Collection, 76/6, Box 3, Folder 7, University of Melbourne Archives.
58 *Medical Journal of Australia* (10 April 1926): 416.
59 Knoeff, 'The Visitor's View: Early Modern Tourism and the Polyvalence of Anatomical Exhibits', 173.
60 Gandevia, *The Melbourne Medical Students, 1862–1942*, 19.
61 'Statement on the skeleton of Charles Byrne from the Board of Trustees of the Hunterian Museum', *Royal College of Surgeons of England*, accessed 24 January 2023.
62 Edward Holder to Harry Brookes Allen, 26 December 1910, Sir Harry Brookes Allen Collection, 76/6, Box 1, Folder 1, University of Melbourne Archives; Letter to Allen, undated, Sir Harry Brookes Allen Collection, 76/6, Box 4, Folder 22, University of Melbourne Archives.
63 Numerous letters between the Mother Rectress of St Vincent's Hospital and Allen demonstrate Allen's input into the hospital. See 76/6, Sir Harry Brookes Allen Collection, Box 1, Folder 1, University of Melbourne Archives.
64 Pierre Bourdieu, 'The Forms of Capital', in *Handbook of Theory and Research for the Sociology of Education*, ed. John G. Richardson (New York, NY: Greenwood Press, 1986), 248.
65 Mark C. Lidwill to Harry Brookes Allen, 25 October 1903, Sir Harry Brookes Allen Collection, 76/6, Box 1, Folder 4, University of Melbourne Archives.
66 Mark C. Lidwill to Harry Brookes Allen, 21 August 1904, Sir Harry Brookes Allen Collection, 76/6, Box 1, Folder 4, University of Melbourne Archives.
67 John Ramsay to Harry Brookes Allen, 27 December 1901, Sir Harry Brookes Allen Collection, 76/6, Box 1, Folder 17, University of Melbourne Archives.
68 Jones, *Anatomists of Empire*, 106.
69 Pietsch, *Empire of Scholars*, 113, 41–4.
70 Letter to Harry Brookes Allen, 30 June 1903, Sir Harry Brookes Allen Collection, 76/6, Box 1, Folder 17, University of Melbourne Archives. Allen received a small sum for his work as curator, on top of his regular salary as Professor of Anatomy.
71 Alberti, *Morbid Curiosities*, 80.
72 Wendy Moore, *The Knife Man* (London: Bantam, 2005), 432.

73  Alberti, *Morbid Curiosities*, 87; Eva Åhrén, 'Making Space for Specimens: The Museums of the Karolinska Institute, Stockholm', in *Medical Museums: Past, Present, Future*, ed. Samuel J. M. M. Alberti and Elizabeth Hallam (London: The Royal College of Surgeons of England, 2013), 106; Sappol, *A Traffic of Dead Bodies*, 144.
74  Coote, 'Pray Write Me a List of Species … That Will Pay Me Best', 84.
75  Griffiths, *Hunters and Collectors*, 2.
76  Appadurai, 'Introduction: Commodities and the Politics of Value', 4.

# Chapter 3

1  Reinarz, 'The Age of Museum Medicine', 419.
2  Alberti, *Morbid Curiosities*; Hallam, *Anatomy Museum*; Alberti and Hallam, *Medical Museums: Past, Present, Future*; Reinarz, 'The Age of Museum Medicine'.
3  Huistra, *The Afterlife of the Leiden Anatomical Collections*, 97.
4  McLeary, 'Science in a Bottle'.
5  Kraft and Alberti, 'Equal Though Different', 203.
6  Jones, *Humanity's Mirror*, 71.
7  Alberti, *Morbid Curiosities*, 4, 14, 20.
8  'Opening a Medical School', May 1858, University of Melbourne Registrar, UM 419, 93/46, Folder 1, University of Melbourne Archives; 'Medical School Building, 1907, Bates, Smart, McCutcheon Job 136', Bates, Smart, McCutcheon, 1968.0013, University of Melbourne Archives.
9  Reinarz, 'The Age of Museum Medicine', 162.
10 James Robertson, 'Inaugural Lecture', *Speculum*, no. 27 (March 1892): 157. Robertson had a long relationship with the Melbourne Medical School. He took great interest in its founding and was the first lecturer in the 'theory and practice of medicine'. He was also a member of the University Council, and a founding member of the Medical Society of Victoria.
11 'The Dissecting Room', *Speculum*, no. 11 (October 1887): 12.
12 S. A. Smith, 'A Course of Lectures on Anatomy in its Application to Art', G.63 Accession 116 and 194, Range 14–24, Box no. 2, Folder 14, Sydney University Archives. For more on classical bodies and their relationship to art and anatomy, see Michael Squire, *The Art of the Body: Antiquity and Its Legacy* (New York: Oxford University Press, 2011).
13 Lorraine Daston and Peter Galison, 'The Image of Objectivity', *Representations* 40, no. 40 (1992): 84 and 85. Daston and Galison acknowledge that in the late nineteenth century, some anatomical illustrators began to portray individual bodies, rather than composites: see 95.

14 M. M. Bakhtin, *Rabelais and His World*, trans. Hélène Iswolsky (Bloomington, IN: Indiana University Press, 1984), 25–6.

15 Marieke M. A. Hendriksen, 'Casting Life, Casting Death: Connections between Early Modern Anatomical Corrosive Preparations and Artistic Materials and Techniques', *Notes Rec* 73, no. 3 (2019): 369–97, esp. 379–80. See also Christophe Degueurce, 'The Celebrated Écorchés of Honoré Fragonard, Part 1: The Classical Techniques of Preparation of Dry Anatomical Specimens in the 18th Century', trans. Philip Adds, *Clinical Anatomy* 23, no. 3 (2010): 249–57.

16 J. T. Duncan, 'On the Use of Formalin as a Preservative Fluid', *The Journal of Comparative Medicine and Veterinary Archives* 17, vol. 5 (1896): 383–5; W. McAdam Eccles, 'Formic Aldehyde as a Rapid Hardening Reagent for Animal Tissues', *British Medical Journal*, 26 May 1894, 1124. In the mid-1860s, the University of Melbourne asked for, and was denied, the opportunity to purchase duty-free methylated spirits for use in the museum and dissecting room. Inspector General to Redmond Barry, 2 October 1867, University of Melbourne Registrar UM 419, 93/46, Registrar's Correspondence (1857–70), 370–418, Folder 1, University of Melbourne Archives.

17 Moore, *The Knife Man*, esp. 82. On Towne, see Samuel Alberti, 'Wax Bodies: Art and Anatomy in Victorian Medical Museums', *Museum History Journal* 2, no. 1 (2009): 7–36. On Frederick Ruysch, see Dániel Margócsy, 'Advertising Cadavers in the Republic of Letters: Anatomical Publications in the Early Modern Netherlands', *The British Journal for the History of Science* 42, no. 2 (2009): 187–210.

18 See 'Minutes', 18 September 1890, Reports of the Faculty of Medicine Vol. 1, 1885–1899, Series 142, University of Adelaide Archives; 'Minutes', 17 September 1886, Reports of the Faculty of Medicine Vol. 1, 1885–1899, Series 142, University of Adelaide Archives. The British General Medical Council did not formally recognize the medical course on offer at the University of Adelaide until 1894, almost ten years after it was introduced.

19 Well-known manuals included: Thomas Pole, *The Anatomical Instructor; or an Illustration of the Modern and Most Approved Methods of Preparing and Preserving Different Parts of the Human Body and of Quadrupeds by Injection, Corrosion, Maceration, Distention, Articulation, Modelling, &c* (London: Couchman & Fry, 1790); Robert Hooper, *The Anatomist's Vade-Mecum: Containing a Concise and Accurate Description of the Structure, Situation, and Use of Every Part of the Human Body* (London: Sold by Bell, Oxford-Street, London, 1797); Frederick John Knox, *The Anatomist's Instructor, and Museum Companion: Being Practical Directions for the Formation and Subsequent Management of Anatomical Museums* (Edinburgh: Adam and Charles Black, 1836).

20 'Lardaceous Liver', 76/6, Unit 7, Sir Harry Brookes Allen Collection, University of Melbourne.

21  Ibid.
22  The above quotations in this paragraph are taken from Harry Brookes Allen to Vice-Chancellor and Members of the Council of the University of Melbourne, 20 June 1914, Sir Harry Brookes Allen Collection, 76/6, Box 1, Folder 15, University of Melbourne Archives.
23  'Report of the Medical School Committee', 18 August 1887, Reports of the Faculty of Medicine 1883–1885, Series 142, University of Adelaide Archives.
24  'Practical Histological Pathology – 1892', Sir Harry Brookes Allen Collection, 1990.0009, Unit 51, University of Melbourne Archives.
25  Ibid.
26  *Calendar of the University of Sydney for the Year 1889* (Sydney: Gibbs, Shallard and Co., 1889), 272, accessed 4 February 2023, http://calendararchive.usyd.edu.au/Calendar/1889/1889.pdf; 'Minutes', 21 April 1886, Reports of the Faculty of Medicine Vol. 1, 1885–1899, Series 142, University of Adelaide Archives.
27  Alberti, *Morbid Curiosities*, 117.
28  Huistra, *The Afterlife of the Leiden Anatomical Collections*, 23, 38.
29  Alberti, *Morbid Curiosities*, 122–4. Historian Elizabeth Hallam also discusses the difficulties associated with specimen preparation in the British context. See Hallam, *Anatomy Museum*, 187–8.
30  Catalogue of Specimens in Melbourne Hospital Pathology Museum c. 1870, Sir Harry Brookes Allen Collection, 76/6, Unit 7, Folder 5, University of Melbourne Archives.
31  Ibid.
32  J. Ramsay to Harry Brookes Allen, 27 December 1901, Sir Harry Brookes Allen Collection, 76/6, Unit 3, Folder 17, University of Melbourne Archives; Walter Fowler to Harry Brookes Allen, 7 July 1904, Sir Harry Brookes Allen Collection, 76/6, Unit 3, Folder 17, University of Melbourne Archives.
33  'The Present State of the Medical School', *Speculum*, no. 1 (July 1884): 5.
34  'Special Pathology 1905', Department of Pathology 1876–1976, 1990.0009, Unit 74, University of Melbourne Archives.
35  Alberti, *Morbid Curiosities*, 6.
36  Hallam, *Anatomy Museum*, 14.
37  Ibid., 19–20.
38  Penny, *Objects of Culture*, 2; Krzysztof Pomian, *Collectors and Curiosities: Paris and Venice 1500–1800* (Cambridge: Polity Press, 1990), 45. On Cabinets of Curiosities, see Christine Davenne, *Cabinets of Wonder* (New York: Harry N. Abrams, 2012).
39  Steven Conn, *Museums and American Intellectual Life, 1876–1926* (Chicago, IL: The University of Chicago Press, 1998), 8.
40  Alberti, *Morbid Curiosities*, 8, 126.

41 Elizabeth Stephens, *Anatomy as Spectacle: Public Exhibitions of the Body from 1700 to the Present* (Liverpool: Liverpool University Press, 2011), 22.
42 Reinarz points out that these methods and ideals emerged during the Enlightenment. See Jonathan Reinarz, 'Learning To Use Their Senses: Visitors to Voluntary Hospitals in Eighteenth-Century England', *Journal for Eighteenth-Century Studies* 35, no. 4 (2012): 515.
43 Susan C. Lawrence, 'Educating the Senses: Students, Teachers and Medical Rhetoric in Eighteenth-Century London', in *Medicine and the Five Senses*, ed. W. F. Bynum and Roy Porter (Cambridge: Cambridge University Press, 1993), 155.
44 Reformer, 'Lectures and Demonstrations', *Speculum*, no. 16 (January 1889): 15.
45 'People we know', 612.
46 Reformer, 'Lectures and Demonstrations', 15.
47 Ibid., 14.
48 Hallam, *Anatomy Museum*, 11. British surgeon and anatomist Charles Bell (1774–1842) considered the hand and eye to be analogous in terms of their importance to any surgeon's training. See Charles Bell, *The Hand: Its Mechanism and Vital Endowments as Evincing Design*, 3rd ed., Bridgewater Treatises 4 (London: William Pickering, 1834), 329.
49 *Calendar of the University of Sydney for the Year 1889*.
50 *The Melbourne School of Pathology*, 87.
51 Faculty of Medicine Miscellaneous Medical Publications, Series 57, Box 1, University of Adelaide Archives; *Calendar of the University of Sydney for the Year 1889*.
52 Russell, *The Melbourne Medical School, 1862–1962*, 140.
53 'Minutes', 18 March 1909, Faculty of Medicine Minutes, Vol. 3, Box 1, Series 137, University of Adelaide Archives.
54 Ponce, 'They Increase in Beauty and Elegance', 352.
55 'Residents' Quarters at the Melbourne Hospital', *Speculum*, no. 22 (September 1890): 97.
56 'Medical School Building, 1907, Bates, Smart, McCutcheon Job 136', Bates, Smart, McCutcheon, 1968.0013, University of Melbourne Archives.
57 'The University of Melbourne', *The Argus*, 3 March 1894, 11.
58 'Residents' Quarters at the Melbourne Hospital', *Speculum*, no. 22 (September 1890): 97.
59 'Report of the Medical Students' Society', *Speculum*, no. 6 (June 1886): 14.
60 For discussion on wax anatomical models, see Joan B. Landes, 'Wax Fibers, Wax Bodies, and Moving Figure: Artifice and Nature in Eighteenth-Century Anatomy', in *Ephemeral Bodies: Wax Sculpture and the Human Figure*, ed. Roberta Panzanelli (Los Angeles, CA: Getty Research Institute, 2008), 41–65; Carin Berkowitz, 'The Beauty of Anatomy: Visual Displays and Surgical Education

in Early-Nineteenth-Century London', *Bulletin of the History of Medicine* 85, no. 2 (2011): 248–78; Renato G. Mazzolini, 'Plastic Anatomies and Artificial Distinctions', in *Models: The Third Dimension of Science*, ed. Nick Hopwood and Soraya de Chadarevian (Stanford, CA: Stanford University Press, 2004), 43–70.

61  Thomas Schnalke, 'Dissected Limbs and the Integral Body: On Anatomical Wax Models and Medical Moulages', *Interdisciplinary Science Reviews* 29, no. 3 (2004): 314, 315. Samuel Alberti also claims that models could be based on up to 200 dissections, and take up to twenty months to complete: see Alberti, 'Wax Bodies', 20.

62  Uta Kornmeier, 'Almost Alive: The Spectacle of Verisimilitude in Madame Tussaud's Waxworks', in *Ephemeral Bodiesx*, 67–81, 80.

63  Robertson, 'Inaugural Lecture', 157. For more on the work of Louis Auzoux, see Anna Maerker, 'Between Profession and Performance: Displays of Anatomical Models in London, 1831–32', *Histoire, Médecine et Santé* 5, no. 2 (2014): 47–59.

64  Berry, *Chance and Circumstance*, 109–10.

65  Jones, *Humanity's Mirror*, 74.

66  'A Medical Medley', *Speculum*, no. 67 (December 1906): 121.

67  An article in *Speculum* noted there were 'several noteworthy anatomical peculiarities' from the dissecting room in the museum upon Berry's arrival. See 'Anatomical Peculiarities', *Speculum*, no. 7 (August 1886): 20; *Speculum*, no. 68, May 1907, 50–9.

68  Hallam, *Anatomy Museum*, 162.

69  Charles Smith to Harry Brookes Allen, 1 January 1900, Sir Harry Brookes Allen Collection, 76/6, Box 1, Folder 17, University of Melbourne Archives.

70  Archibald Watson to Harry Brookes Allen, 18 July 1907, Sir Harry Brookes Allen Collection, 76/6, Box 1, Folder 17, University of Melbourne Archives.

71  For example, see 'A Two-Headed Monster (Pleuropagus)', *British Medical Journal* 2, no. 1825 (December 1895): 1568–9; 'Pregnancy in a Double Monster', *British Medical Journal* 2, no. 1447 (September 1888): 676; Francis Bolster, 'An Anencephalous Monster', *British Medical Journal* 1, no. 1900 (May 1897): 1346–7; De Vere Condon, 'Double Monster: Thoracopagus: Single Heart', *British Medical Journal* 1, no. 2042 (February 1900): 380.

72  'A Case of Dicephalic Monstrosity Delivered without Medical Aid [to a Full-blooded Aborigine]', *Medical Journal of Australia* 35 (April 1948): 531–2; T. Wilson Roddie, 'Case of Uniumbilical-Dibrachidicephalic Monster', *British Medical Journal* 1, no. 4966 (March 1956): 552.

73  Tony Bennett, *The Birth of the Museum: History, Theory, Politics* (London: Routledge, 1995), 7. Emphasis in original.

74  Russell, *The Melbourne Medical School, 1862–1962*, 130.

75 Reinarz, 'The Age of Museum Medicine', 422. Alberti states that Hunter's museum in Glasgow was open for one hour per day for 'strangers'. Alberti, *Morbid Curiosities*, 171. Huistra has discussed in detail the way that stories provided in museum catalogues and by tour guides at the Leiden University collection made museum preparations accessible for a lay audience. Huistra, *The Afterlife of the Leiden Anatomical Collections*, 95–8.

76 Nadja Durbach, *Spectacle of Deformity: Freak Shows and Modern British Culture* (Berkeley: University of California Press, 2010); Sadiah Qureshi, *Peoples on Parade: Exhibitions, Empire, and Anthropology in Nineteenth-Century Britain* (Chicago and London: The University of Chicago Press, 2011); Stephens, *Anatomy as Spectacle*.

77 Bennett, *The Birth of the Museum*, 60–1.

78 Durbach, *Spectacle of Deformity*, 39–41.

79 *Catalogue of Messrs. Baume & Kreitmayer's Grand Anatomical Museum* (Melbourne: Shaw, Harnett & Co., 1861), iv.

80 Bennett, *The Birth of the Museum*, 8.

81 Bates, 'Indecent and Demoralising Representations', 1–2. For example, see Richard D. Altick, *The Shows of London* (Cambridge, MA: Belknap Press, 1978), 339; Roy Porter and Lesley Hall, *The Facts of Life: The Creation of Sexual Knowledge in Britain, 1650–1950* (New Haven, CT: Yale University Press, 1995), 138.

82 Michael Mason, *The Making of Victorian Sexuality* (Oxford: Oxford University Press, 1995), 190.

83 Mimi Colligan, 'Anatomical Wax Museums in Melbourne 1861–1887', *Australian Cultural History* 13, no. 1 (1994): 53.

84 Stephens, *Anatomy as Spectacle*; Bates, 'Indecent and Demoralising Representations'.

85 *Catalogue of Messrs. Baume & Kreitmayer's Grand Anatomical Museum*, iv.

86 On the anatomical Venus, see Joanna Ebenstein, *The Anatomical Venus* (London: Thames and Hudson, 2016).

87 'Anatomical Museum', *The Bendigo Advertiser*, 7 September 1861, 2.

88 'The Anatomical Museum', *The Examiner*, 11 March 1862, 3.

89 Bennett, *The Birth of the Museum*, 8.

90 'Criminal Prosecution for Libel: Jordan v. Syme', *The Age*, 10 September 1869, 3. For a full account of the case against Jordan, see E. Graeme Robertson, 'Melbourne's Public Anatomical and Anthropological Museums and the Jordans', *Medical Journal of Australia*, 4 February 1956, 164–80. The exhibition catalogue is on page 167 of Robertson's article.

91 'The Pathology of Filth', *The Age*, 9 September 1869, 3.

92 Ibid.

93 'End of the Anthropological Museum', *Leader*, 18 September 1869, 17.

94 Bates, 'Indecent and Demoralising Representations', 13–16.

95  Ibid., 2.
96  P. J. Martyr, *Paradise of Quacks: An Alternative History of Medicine in Australia* (Paddington: Macleay Press, 2002), 63; Eric Maple, *Magic, Medicine & Quackery* (London: Hale, 1968), Chapter 6.
97  'The Medical Profession in Australia', 20 March 1893, *Daily Telegraph*, quoted in Martyr, *Paradise of Quacks*, 7. The Victorian Census of 1891 records 110 irregular practitioners compared to 777 regular practitioners: Martyr, *Paradise of Quacks*, 188–9.
98  'Editorial', *Speculum*, no. 5, April 1886, 1. The student who wrote this piece estimated there were up to 100 quacks in Victoria in the mid-1880s.
99  Syme, 'Medical Ethics', 47.
100 Martyr, *Paradise of Quacks*, 9; Qureshi, *Peoples on Parade*, 5.
101 Shapin provides a fascinating discussion of the difficulties historians face when reconstructing the work of technicians and support personnel. See Steven Shapin, 'The Invisible Technician', *American Scientist*, 77 (1989): 554–63.
102 'People we know', 612.

# Chapter 4

1  531-000671, Harry Brookes Allen Museum of Anatomy and Pathology Catalogue. The specimen is hemisected – or cut in half – to demonstrate the foetus' abnormal presentation.
2  Lynn M. Morgan, *Icons of Life: A Cultural History of Human Embryos* (Berkeley, CA: University of California Press, 2009); Shannon Withycombe, *Lost: Miscarriage in Nineteenth-Century America*, Critical Issues in Health and Medicine (New Brunswick, NJ: Rutgers University Press, 2019; Linda Layne, *Motherhood Lost: A Feminist Account of Pregnancy Loss in America* (New York, NY: Routledge, 2003). Catherine Kevin, '"I Did Not Lose My Baby … My Baby Just Died": Twenty-First-Century Discourses of Miscarriage in Political and Historical Context', *South Atlantic Quarterly* 110, no. 4 (2011): 849–65, 849.
3  Morgan, *Icons of Life*, 15.
4  All quotes from the case of Mrs NL are taken from Cosby W. Morgan, 'Case of Triple Birth with Monstrosity', *Australian Medical Journal* (October 1868): 292–3.
5  Alfred Austin Lendon, 'Case of Ovarian Pregnancy', *Australian Medical Journal* (May 1912): 494–5.
6  Dr Pinniger, 'Hospital Records', *Australian Medical Journal* (November 1893): 583.
7  'Registration of Stillbirths', *Australian Medical Journal* (May 1914): 1544.
8  'Reviews', *Australian Medical Journal* (January 1857): 53, 57. It is important to note that many women in colonial Australia would not have sought medical

attention at any stage of pregnancy, let alone to confirm it as fact. For a discussion of the shifting language of pregnancy, see Barbara Duden, *Disembodying Women: Perspectives on Pregnancy and the Unborn* (Cambridge, MA: Harvard University Press, 1993), 80–95.

9 Judith Walzer Leavitt, 'The Growth of Medical Authority: Technology and Morals in Turn-of-the-Century Obstetrics', *Medical Anthropology Quarterly* 1, no. 3 (1987): 230–55.

10 Janet McCalman, *Sex and Suffering: Women's Health and a Women's Hospital* (Carlton: Melbourne University Press, 1998), 15.

11 See Jacqueline H. Wolf, *Cesarean Section: An American History of Risk, Technology, and Consequence* (Baltimore, MD: Johns Hopkins University Press, 2018), 52.

12 R. H. J. Fetherston, 'Notes of a Case of Labour', *Australian Medical Journal* (December 1893): 611–2.

13 Ibid.

14 Wolf, *Cesarean Section*, 3; Lisa Featherstone, 'The Kindest Cut? The Caesarean Section as Turning Point, Australia 1880–1900', in *Motherhood: Power and Oppression*, ed. Marie Porter, Patricia Short and Andrea O'Reilly (Toronto: Women's Press, 2005), 25–40; McCalman, *Sex and Suffering*.

15 E. J. A. Haynes, 'Abdominal Extra-uterine Formation of Eight Months Duration – Operation', *Australasian Medical Gazette* (October 1892): 369–72.

16 McCalman, *Sex and Suffering*, 59, 64.

17 'Editorial', 1–2. Records from the Adelaide Medical School reveal a similar state of affairs; even in the 1890s, the school lacked funding to purchase basic tools for obstetric training. See the entry for 16 June 1892 in Reports of the Faculty of Medicine Vol. 1, 1885–1899, Series 142, University of Adelaide Archives.

18 A. Fledgling, 'My First " Locum Tenancy"', *Speculum*, no. 12 (February 1888): 19.

19 'Editorial', 1–2.

20 Wolf, *Cesarean Section*, 19. See also Judith Walzer Leavitt, '"Science" Enters the Birthing Room: Obstetrics in America since the Eighteenth Century', *The Journal of American History* 70, no. 2 (1983): 285–94.

21 For attitudes towards midwives in colonial Victoria, see Madonna Grehan, '"From the Sphere of Sarah Gampism": The Professionalisation of Nursing and Midwifery in the Colony of Victoria', *Nursing Inquiry* 11, no. 3 (2004): 192–201; see also Bronte Gould, "The Professional Midwife: Adelaide's Destitute Asylum and Midwifery in South Australia, 1880–1900', *Journal of the Historical Society of South Australia* 42 (2014): 5–16; Nita K. Purcal, 'The Politics of Midwifery Education and Training in New South Wales during the Last Decades of the 19th Century', *Women and Birth* 21, no. 1 (2008): 21–5.

22 Fetherston, 'Notes of a Case of Labour', 611.

23 See 'Fallopius', 'Midwifery: An Easy Way to Practice', *Australian Medical Journal* (June 1878): 178–9; J. W. Dunbar Hooper, 'Some Observations on Midwifery

Private Practice', *Intercolonial Medical Journal of Australasia* (January 1896): 526; Charles Smith, 'Etiology of Puerperal Fever', *Australian Medical Journal* (15 August 1887): 381.

24  Kathleen Fahy, 'An Australian History of the Subordination of Midwifery', *Women and Birth* 20, no. 1 (2007): 25–9, 27; Glenda Strachan, 'Present at the Birth: Midwives, "Handywomen" and Neighbours in Rural New South Wales, 1850–1900', *Labour History* 81 (2001): 13–28, 13–14.

25  Fahy, 'An Australian History of the Subordination of Midwivery', 27. Strachan states that 'there is no doubt that practising midwives who had received no formal training were regarded as valuable members' of rural communities. See Strachan, 'Present at the Birth', 17. Lyn Finch and Jon Stratton, 'The Australian Working Class and the Practice of Abortion 1880–1939', *Journal of Australian Studies* 12, no. 23 (1988): 52.

26  John Elmes, 'Notes of a Case of Extra-uterine Foetation', *Australian Medical Journal* (September 1880): 389.

27  Alphabetical Record of Burials – Old Melbourne Cemetery, 1866–1917, VPRS 9583, P0001, A Index.

28  See Graeme M. Griffin and Des Tobin, *In the Midst of Life … : The Australian Response to Death*, 2nd ed. (Carlton: Melbourne University Press, 1997), 116–17.

29  Shannon Withycombe, 'Slipped Away: Pregnancy Loss in Nineteenth-Century America', (PhD diss., University of Wisconsin, 2010), 150–1.

30  Barbara Duden, 'The Foetus on the "Farther Shore": Toward a History of the Unborn', in *Fetal Subjects, Feminist Positions*, ed. Lynn M. Morgan and Meredith W. Michaels (Philadelphia, PA: University of Pennsylvania Press, 1999), 18. See also Withycombe, *Lost*, 53–5; Lisa Featherstone, 'Becoming a Baby? The Foetus in Late Nineteenth-Century Australia' *Australian Feminist Studies*, 23, no. 58 (2008): 451–65, 453.

31  Withycombe, *Lost*, 31 and 44. See also Catherine Kevin, 'Maternal Responsibility and Traceable Loss: Medicine and Miscarriage in Twentieth-Century Australia', *Women's History Review* 26, no. 6 (2017): 851.

32  Of course, women experienced, and continue to experience, a wide spectrum of emotions towards pregnancy and miscarriage in the twentieth and twenty-first centuries. See Leslie J. Reagan, 'From Hazard to Blessing to Tragedy: Representations of Miscarriage in Twentieth-Century America', *Feminist Studies* 29, no. 2 (2003): 357–78.

33  Withycombe, *Lost*; Judith A. Allen, *Sex & Secrets: Crimes Involving Australian Women Since 1880* (Melbourne: Oxford University Press, 1990), 27.

34  For examples that do not indicate how or if the doctor asked for the family's approval to retain specimens, see Charles Smith to Harry Brookes Allen, 1 January 1900, Sir Harry Brookes Allen Collection, 76/6, Box 1, University of Melbourne Archives; 'Exhibits', *Intercolonial Medical Journal of Australasia* (September 1897): 626.

35 Withycombe, *Lost*, 134.
36 James Pearson Irvine, 'Second Impregnation at the Fourth Month of Utero-Gestation', *Cincinnati Lancet and Observer* 20, no. 4 (April 1859): 262–3, quoted in Withycombe, 'Slipped Away', 180.
37 Withycombe, 'Slipped Away', 178.
38 Morgan discusses the scheme in detail. See Morgan, *Icons of Life*, 125–31. For more on the work and legacy of John Rock, see Loretta McLaughlin, *The Pill, John Rock, and the Church: The Biography of a Revolution* (New York: Little, Brown and Company, 1982), esp. Chapter 4.
39 David Jermyn, 'Notes on the Delivery of an Acephalous Foetus', *Australian Medical Journal* (September 1881): 409.
40 John Maund, 'Case of Extra-Uterine Pregnancy. Death from Peritonitis, Three Years after Conception', *Australian Medical Journal* (July 1857): 181–2.
41 Ibid.
42 Ibid.
43 Morgan, *Icons of Life*, 70.
44 516–100425; 516–100104, Harry Brookes Allen Museum of Anatomy and Pathology Catalogue.
45 Nick Hopwood, 'Producing Development: The Anatomy of Human Embryos and the Norms of Wilhelm His', *Bulletin of the History of Medicine* 74, no. 1 (2000): 29–79, 38.
46 Emily Porth, 'When Women Birthed Mooncalves and Moles: The Display of Fetal Remains and the Invisibility of Females in Museums', *Humanimalia: A Journal of Human/Animal Interface Studies* 4, no. 1 (2012): 1–44, 16.
47 Morgan, *Icons of Life*, 90. Many of the collected embryos were made into slides that could be viewed under a microscope. To give a sense of the scale of this operation, a single four-inch-long specimen could be cut with a microtome into around 250 individual slides. For more on the use of microtome sectioning, see Nick Hopwood, '"Giving Body" to Embryos: Modeling, Mechanism, and the Microtome in Late Nineteenth-Century Anatomy', *Isis* 90, no. 3 (1999): 462–96.
48 Ibid., 33, 82.
49 531–000671, Harry Brookes Allen Museum of Anatomy and Pathology Catalogue.
50 531–003238 and 531–003348, Harry Brookes Allen Museum of Anatomy and Pathology Catalogue.
51 Porth, 'When Women Birthed Mooncalves and Moles', 25.
52 Sara Dubow, *Ourselves Unborn: A History of the Fetus in Modern America* (New York: Oxford University Press, 2010), 6.
53 Lisa Featherstone, '"The Value of the Victorian Infant": Whiteness and the Emergence of Paediatrics in Late Colonial Australia', in *Historicising Whiteness: Transnational Perspectives on the Construction of an Identity* (Historicising Whiteness Conference, Melbourne: RMIT Publishing, 2007), 445–53.

54  Featherstone, 'Becoming a Baby?', 445–53.
55  Janet Lynne Golden, *Babies Made Us Modern: How Infants Brought America into the Twentieth Century* (New York: Cambridge University Press, 2018), 8.
56  Featherstone, 'Becoming a Baby?', 452.
57  W. Atkinson-Wood, 'Anencephalous Foetus (with Photographs)', *Intercolonial Medical Journal of Australasia* (June 1896): 342–4.
58  For example, see 'Pathological Specimens', *Australian Medical Journal* (September 1884): 400; W. Butler Walsh, 'Short Notes on Over One Thousand Consecutive Midwifery Cases', *Intercolonial Medical Journal of Australasia* (December 1901): 565; 'Pediatric Society', *Australian Medical Journal* (May 1912): 472; S. J. Thomas, 'Report of a Case of Double Monster', *Australian Medical Journal* (July 1856): 202–4; Morgan, 'Case of Triple Birth with Monstrosity', 291–4.
59  G. A. Syme, 'Thoughts about Club-Foot', *Australian Medical Journal* (August 1892): 354–5.
60  531-005296, Harry Brookes Allen Museum of Anatomy and Pathology Catalogue.
61  Featherstone, 'The Value of the Victorian Infant', 445.
62  See O'Sullivan and Jones, 'Two Australian Fetuses' for a full discussion of these specimens.
63  Wood-Jones, 'The External Characters of an Australian Foetus', 549; Wood-Jones, 'The External Characters of a Second Australian Foetus', 301.
64  O'Sullivan and Jones, 'Two Australian Fetuses', 247; Anderson, *The Cultivation of Whiteness*, 207.
65  O'Sullivan and Jones, 'Two Australian Fetuses', 253.
66  Featherstone, 'Becoming a Baby?', 253. Emphasis in original.
67  While the placenta might be thought of as just as much a part of the foetal body as the female body, I have chosen to follow the museum catalogue, which includes placental remains alongside foetuses, and as such present such remains as foetuses preserved in situ.
68  Porth, 'When Women Birthed Mooncalves and Moles', 5.
69  R. T. Tracy, 'Case of Repeated Death of the Foetus, and Consequent Miscarriage before the Full Period of Utero-gestation', *Australian Medical Journal* (October 1856): 258.
70  Strachan notes that wealth was not the only determining factor in whether or not a doctor was present at a birth; some wealthy families did not have a doctor present, while some working-class families chose to have a doctor in attendance. Strachan, 'Present at the Birth', 23. Tracy was a member of the original committee for the *Australian Medical Journal* and also instrumental in establishing the Melbourne Lying-in Hospital and Infirmary for Diseases of Women and Children (later the Royal Women's Hospital). See McCalman, *Sex and Suffering*, 3–14.
71  R. T. Tracy, 'Case of Repeated Death of the Foetus'.
72  Ibid.

73  Ibid.
74  W. Thomson, 'Etiology of Placenta Praevia', *Australian Medical Journal* (January 1858): 4. Emphasis in original.
75  Pinniger, 'Hospital Records'.
76  Ibid.
77  Dr Fulton, 'Case of a Rupture of the Uterus', *Australian Medical Journal* (May 1877): 169; Richard T. Tracy, 'Clinical Midwifery', *Australian Medical Journal* (April 1863): 111–2.
78  See Featherstone, 'The Kindest Cut?', 35.
79  Tracy, 'Case of Repeated Death of the Foetus', 258.
80  Ibid.
81  Ibid.
82  Finch and Stratton, 'The Australian Working Class and the Practice of Abortion 1880–1939', 52. See also Golden, *Babies Made Us Modern*, 21.
83  Women's Hospital Labour Ward Case Book, 1901, VPRS 17385/P/0001, Unit 000007, Public Records Office of Victoria. For a discussion of medical debates over the use of craniotomy in the late nineteenth century, see Leavitt, 'The Growth of Medical Authority', 235–40.
84  Mary de Garis, 'Lecture Notes', Lecture XXI, 22 April 1903, MHM 02027, Medical History Museum, University of Melbourne.
85  Wolf, *Cesarean Section*, 36.

# Chapter 5

1  Anne-Marie Condé, 'Imagining a Collection: Creating Australia's Records of War', *ReCollections: Journal of the National Museum of Australia* 2, no. 1 (2007); William M. Taylor, 'War Remains: Contributions of the Imperial War Graves Commission and the Australian War Records Section to Material and National Cultures of Conflict and Commemoration', *National Identities* 17, no. 2 (2015): 217–40.
2  Taylor, 'War Remains', 232.
3  Rosalind Hearder, 'Battlefield Legacies: The Australian Collection of WW1 Pathological Specimens', *Australian Military Medicine* 8, no. 3 (1999): 24–8; Robin A. Cooke, 'Forgotten Bodies: Pathology Specimens from the Trenches', in *Compassion and Courage: Australian Doctors and Dentists in the Great War*, ed. Jacqueline Healy (Melbourne: Medical History Museum, University of Melbourne, 2015), 80–92. See also Ryan Jefferies, 'War Wounds', in *Compassion and Courage*, ed. Healy, 130.
4  Most of the British collection was destroyed when the Royal College of Surgeons building at Lincolns Inn Fields was bombed during the Blitz in 1941. See Samuel J. M. M. Alberti, 'The "Regiment of Skeletons": A First World War Medical Collection', *Social History of Medicine* 28, no. 1 (2015): 108–33, 133.

5   German authorities also collected specimens, which they held in collections in Munich, Vienna and Berlin, for laboratory-based research into wartime afflictions. In particular, the Kaiser-Wilhelm Institute in Berlin (since taken over by the Max Planck Society) held over 6,000 specimens of war pathology. See Prüll Cay-Rudiger, 'Pathology at War 1914–1918: Germany and Britain in Comparison', in *Medicine and Modern Warfare*, ed. Roger Cooter, Mark Harrison and Steve Sturdy (Atlanta, GA: Rodopi, 1999), 131–61.
6   Peter Hobbins, '"Outside the Institute There Is a Desert": The Tenuous Trajectories of Medical Research in Interwar Australia', *Medical History* 54 (2010): 2.
7   Letter from the Deans of the Faculties of Medicine to the Adjutant General of the Department of Defence, 23 December 1915, Sir Harry Brookes Allen Collection, 76/6, Box 3, Folder 1, University of Melbourne Archives.
8   Ibid.; Young et al., *Centenary Book of the University of Sydney Faculty of Medicine*, 3; Joan McMeeken, 'From Massage to Physiotherapy: The Emergence of a Profession', in *The First World War, the Universities and the Professions in Australia 1914–1939*, ed. Kate Darian-Smith and James Waghorne (Carlton: Melbourne University Press, 2019), 80.
9   Harry Brookes Allen to T. Trumble (Secretary for the Department of Defence), 23 October 1915, Sir Harry Brookes Allen Collection, 76/6, Box 3, Folder 1, University of Melbourne Archives.
10  R. H. Fetherston, 'Memorandum to the Medical Profession of Australia', 1916, AWM023048.17 F419M, Australian War Memorial.
11  Harry Brookes Allen to T. Trumble (Secretary for the Department of Defence), 16 March 1916, Sir Harry Brookes Allen Collection, 76/6, Box 3, Folder 1, University of Melbourne Archives.
12  Rachel H. Gross to Harry Brookes Allen, undated letter, Sir Harry Brookes Allen Collection, 1976.0006, Unit 1, Folder 1, University of Melbourne Archives.
13  Jan Bassett, *Guns and Brooches: Australian Army nursing from the Boer War to the Gulf War* (Melbourne: Oxford University Press, 1992); Heather Sheard and Ruth Lee, *Women to the Front* (Sydney: Random House Australia, 2019); Ruth L. Lee, *Woman War Doctor: The Life of Mary De Garis* (Melbourne: Australian Scholarly Publishing, 2014).
14  Algernon Carter Bean to Harry Brookes Allen, 26 September 1916, Sir Harry Brookes Allen Collection, 1976.0006, Unit 1, Folder 1, University of Melbourne Archives.
15  James Waghorne, 'Growth and Specialisation: The Medical Profession in Interwar Australia', in *The First World War, the Universities and the Professions in Australia 1914–1939*, ed. Kate Darian-Smith and James Waghorne (Carlton: Melbourne University Press, 2019), 32.
16  For more on facial trauma during the First World War, including its treatment and ways it affected returning soldiers, see Kerry Neale, '"Without the Faces of

Men": Facially Disfigured Great War Soldiers of Britain and the Dominions', (PhD diss., (University of New South Wales, 2015); Lindsey Fitzharris, *The Facemaker: One Surgeon's Battle to Mend the Disfigured Soldiers of World War I* (London: Penguin UK, 2022); Samuel J. M. M. Alberti, ed., *War, Art, and Surgery. The Work of Henry Tonks and Julia Midgeley* (London: The Royal College of Surgeons of England, 2015); Francesca Kubicki, 'Recreated Faces: Facial Disfigurement, Plastic Surgery, Photography and the Great War', *Photography and Culture* 2, no. 2 (2009): 183–94; Sandy Callister, '"Broken Gargoyles": The Photographic Representation of Severely Wounded New Zealand Soldiers', *Social History of Medicine* 20, no. 1 (April 2007): 111–30. For more on the use of the Thomas splint, see R. Hamilton Russell, 'Fractures of the Lower Extremity', *Medical Journal of Australia*, 2, no. 7 (12 August 1916): 107–12; John Kirkup, 'Fracture Care of Friend and Foe during World War I', *ANZ Journal of Surgery* 73, no. 6 (2003): 453–9.

17  A. H. Tebbutt, 'Pathology in War-Time', *Medical Journal of Australia* 1, no. 21 (May 1918): 433.

18  See Waghorne, 'Growth and Specialisation', 29–30; James Gillespie, 'Medical Markets and Australian Medical Politics, 1920–45', *Labour History* 54 (1988): 30–46; T. S. Pensabene, *The Rise of the Medical Practitioner in Victoria* (Canberra: Australian National University, 1980), 159–77.

19  Neville Reginald Howse to Officer Commanding the No. 3 Australian Auxiliary Hospital, 14 November 1916, AWM 25 737/21, Australian War Memorial.

20  M. W. Russell (Surgeon-General, for Director-General, Army Medical Service) to the General Officer, Commanding in Chief, Mediterranean Expeditionary Forces, 14 June 1915, AWM 25 737/21, Australian War Memorial.

21  M. W. Russell (Surgeon-General for Director-General, Army Medical Service), 13 December 1915, AWM 023048.17 F419M, Australian War Memorial. For a detailed analysis of the British response, see Alberti, 'The "Regiment of Skeletons"'.

22  M. W. Russell to British War Office, 13 December 1915, AWM 16 4364/45/11, Australian War Memorial.

23  Neville Reginald Howse to Officer Commanding the No. 3 Australian Auxiliary Hospital, 14 November 1916, AWM 25 737/21, Australian War Memorial.

24  J. R. Drummond, 'Australian Collection of Surgical and Pathological Specimens Illustrating the Effects of Modern Warfare on the Human Body and on Animals', 6 September 1918, AWM 25 737/6, Australian War Memorial.

25  Ibid.

26  Ibid.

27  J. R. Drummond, 'Preparation of Moist Specimens', 17 September 1918, AWM 25 737/6, Australian War Memorial.

28  J. R. Drummond to S. O. Cowen, 4 September 1918, AWM 16 4364/45/11, Australian War Memorial; Henry Newland to Officer in Charge No. 3 Australian

Casualty Clearing Station, 19 July 1918, AWM 25 737/21; J. R. Drummond to No. 1 Australian Casualty Clearing Station, 8 October 1918, AWM 16 4364/45/11.
29  Letter to Keith Inglis, 1 October 1918, AWM 25 737/15, Australian War Memorial.
30  Third Australian General Hospital to Colonel Barber, 19 August 1918, AWM 16 4364/45/11, Australian War Memorial.
31  Keith Inglis to Curator, Pathological Museum, Australian War Records, 4 February 1919, AWM 25 737/21, Australian War Memorial.
32  Ibid.
33  Director of Medical Services to the Deputy-Adjutant General of the AIF, 8 August 1918, AWM 25 737/21, Australian War Memorial.
34  Keith Inglis to Curator, Pathological Museum, Australian War Records, 4 February 1919, AWM 25 737/21, Australian War Memorial.
35  Ibid.
36  Ibid.
37  Keith Inglis to R. J. Millard, 21 August 1919, AWM 25 737/17, Australian War Memorial.
38  Amanda Bevers, 'To Bind Up the Nation's Wounds: The Army Medical Museum and the Development of American Medical Science, 1862–1913', (PhD diss., University of California San Diego, 2015), 211.
39  Keith Inglis to Curator, Pathological Museum, Australian War Records, 4 February 1919, AWM 25 737/21, Australian War Memorial.
40  Keith Inglis to Warden and Registrar of the University of Sydney, June 1919, AWM 25 737/21, Australian War Memorial.
41  Secretary of the Department of Defence to Registrar, University of Melbourne, 24 December 1918, AWM 16 4364/45/11, Australian War Memorial.
42  'Preliminary Suggestion as to the Division by Sir Harry Allen Subject to Consideration by the Committee', AWM 25 737/21, Australian War Memorial.
43  Keith Inglis to Warden and Registrar of the University of Sydney, June 1919, AWM 25 737/21, Australian War Memorial.
44  Letter to Keith Inglis, 17 July 1919, AWM 25 737/21, Australian War Memorial.
45  Keith Inglis to W. Lindsay, 25 February 1920, AWM 25 737/21, Australian War Memorial.
46  Ibid.
47  'Question of Transfer of Pathological War Specimens from the Universities in All States to the Australian Institute of Anatomy', 11 February 1930, NAA A1928 695/11, National Archives of Australia.
48  For examples of Australian-based cases, see E. T. C. Milligan, 'Medical Experiences in the War Zone', *Medical Journal of Australia* 1, no. 10 (10 March 1917), 201–3; C. MacLaurin, 'War Surgery at the Front', *Medical Journal of Australia* 1, no. 20 (24 March 1917): 241–3; Roland R. Wettenhall, 'Dermatology on Active Service

with the RAMC', *Medical Journal of Australia* 1, no. 10 (3 March 1917), 181–2. For examples of British-based cases that were republished in the journal, see 'Abstracts from Current Medical Literature: Symptoms and Complications of Gunshot Wounds of the Solid Abdominal Viscera', *Medical Journal of Australia* 2, no. 6 (12 August 1916): 122; 'Pathological Conditions at the Dardanelles', *Medical Journal of Australia* 2, no. 10 (2 September 1916): 190–1; 'War Nephritis', *Medical Journal of Australia* 2, no. 20 (11 November 1916): 416.

49 Little wished to enlist in the Australian Army Medical Corps, but as it did not admit female medical officers, she made her own way to England. There she was appointed captain in the RAMC in 1918. Women were not fully enlisted in the RAMC, hence the term 'attached'.

50 E. Marjory Little, 'Dysentery: Bacillary and Amoebic', *Medical Journal of Australia* 1, no. 1 (January 1923): 1–4.

51 Hobbins, 'Outside the Institute There Is a Desert', 3.

52 Keith Inglis, 'Gas Gangrene in Military and Civil Practice', *Medical Journal of Australia* 1, no. 1 (January 1923): 7.

53 *Medical Journal of Australia* (January 1923): 22–3.

54 'War Wounds', lecture delivered by Professor P. MacCallum, 1939, Sir Peter MacCallum Collection, 1975.0042, Box 6, University of Melbourne Archives.

55 Secretary of the Department of Defence to Director-General of Health, 31 July 1930, NAA A1928 695/11, National Archives of Australia.

56 'Question of Transfer of Pathological War Specimens from the Universities in all States to the Australian Institute of Anatomy'.

57 Ibid.

58 Ibid.

59 'Museum Catalogue 1927', Department of Pathology Collection, 1990.0009, Unit 52, University of Melbourne Archives. The war pathology specimens are listed between pages 259 and 301.

60 University of Melbourne Registrar to Secretary, Department of Defence, 26 October 1933, 1999.0014, Unit 500, Box 1952/273, University of Melbourne Archives; Secretary, Department of Defence to Registrar, University of Melbourne, 9 November 1933, 1999.0014, Unit 500, Box 1952/273, University of Melbourne Archives.

61 MacCallum, 'War Wounds'.

62 Secretary of the Department of Defence to Registrar, University of Melbourne, 24 December 1918, AWM 16 4364/45/11, Australian War Memorial. The same letter was sent to the University of Adelaide and the University of Sydney.

63 Shauna Devine, *Learning from the Wounded: The Civil War and the Rise of American Medical Science* (Chapel Hill, NC: The University of North Carolina Press, 2014); Bevers, 'To Bind Up the Nation's Wounds'. See also Lenore Barbian,

Paul Sledzik and Jeffrey Reznick, 'Remains of War', *Museum History Journal* 5, no. 1 (2012): 7–28; L. T. Barbian, P. S. Sledzik and A. M. Nelson, 'Case Studies in Pathology from the National Museum of Health and Medicine, Armed Forces Institute of Pathology', *Annals of Diagnostic Pathology* 4, no. 3 (2000): 170–3; Michael Rhode, 'An Army Museum or a National Collection? Shifting Interests and Fortunes at the National Museum of Health and Medicine', in *Medical Museums: Past, Present, Future*, ed. Samuel J. M. M. Alberti and Elizabeth Hallam (London: Royal College of Surgeons, 2013), 186–99.

64   Devine, *Learning from the Wounded*, 22.
65   Bevers, 'To Bind Up the Nation's Wounds', 153; Devine, *Learning from the Wounded*, 180; Mark B. Feldman, 'Remembering a Convulsive War: Whitman's Memoranda during the War and the Therapeutics of Display', *Walt Whitman Quarterly Review* 23, no. 1 (2005): 18.
66   Tim Clarke, 'Sickles' Leg and the Army Medical Museum', *Military Medicine* 179, no. 9 (2014): 1051. For discussion of the range of responses to soldiers' encounters with their lost body parts, see Lindsay Tuggle, 'The Afterlives of Specimens: Walt Whitman and the Army Medical Museum', *Walt Whitman Quarterly Review* 32, no. 1–2 (2014): 1–35; Devine, *Learning from the Wounded*, 197.
67   Feldman, 'Remembering a Convulsive War', 18.
68   Tuggle, 'The Afterlives of Specimens', 2.
69   'The French Army Medical Museum', *British Medical Journal* 1, no. 2946 (16 June 1917): 820.
70   Amy Lyford, *Surrealist Masculinities: Gender Anxiety and the Aesthetics of Post-World War I Reconstruction in France* (Berkeley, CA: University of California Press, 2007), 48.
71   Ibid., esp. 47–62. Lyford juxtaposes the work of French surrealist artists and authors with the exhibition at Val-de-Grâce. She contends that the surrealists, such as André Breton and Louis Aragon, who frequented the museum mobilized similar imagery of trauma, dismemberment, and fragmentation to critique the official post-war rhetoric of trauma. See also Amy Lyford, 'The Aesthetics of Dismemberment: Surrealism and the Musée du Val-de-Grâce in 1917', *Cultural Critique* 46 (2000): 45–79.
72   Lyford, *Surrealist Masculinities*, 47–8.
73   *A Guide to the Exhibition of the Army Medical Collection of War Specimens: Opened October 11th, 1917* (London: Taylor & Francis, 1917), 26.
74   Ibid., 4.
75   Alberti, 'The "Regiment of Skeletons"', 116.
76   'A National Collection of War Specimens', *The Lancet* 194, no. 5003 (19 July 1919): 120.
77   Alberti, 'The "Regiment of Skeletons"', esp. 111.

78  Ibid., 115–16.
79  Guy Hansen to Ian McShane, 25 June 1992, NMA 89/37, Box 7/249, National Museum of Australia.
80  Laura Wittman, *The Tomb of the Unknown Soldier, Modern Mourning, and the Reinvention of the Mystical Body* (Toronto: University of Toronto Press, 2011), 56.
81  Claud Head, 'Soldier's Letters', *Terang Express*, 3 December 1915.
82  'Melbourne, Wednesday, 11 August 1915', *The Age*, 11 August 1915, 8.
83  'The Lot of the Limbless Soldier: An Unbroken Spirit', *The Age*, 14 August 1922; 'Our Glorious Cripples: Work of the Artificial Limb Factory', *Sydney Mail*, 11 September 1918.
84  Joanna Bourke, *Dismembering the Male: Men's Bodies, Britain and the Great War* (Chicago, IL: The University of Chicago Press, 1996), 13.
85  Bourke, *Dismembering the Male*, 31–70, esp. 59, 70.
86  See Marina Larsson, *Shattered Anzacs: Living with the Scars of War* (Kensington: UNSW Press, 2009); Marina Larsson, 'Restoring the Spirit: The Rehabilitation of Disabled Soldiers in Australia after the Great War', *Health and History* 6, no. 2 (2004): 45–59, 5.
87  Larsson, *Shattered Anzacs*, 41–4, 50–1; Neale, 'Without the Faces of Men'.
88  Letter from Claude Dunshea to his sister, 16 April 1917, quoted in Neale, 'Without the Faces of Men', 160.
89  Bourke, *Dismembering the Male*, 34.
90  Larsson, 'Restoring the Spirit', 50.
91  'The Wastage from Incompleteness', *Medical Journal of Australia* 2, no. 4 (22 July 1916): 59.
92  W. Kent Hughes, 'The Healing of the Maimed', *Medical Journal of Australia* 2, no. 1 (1 July 1916): 17–18.
93  For a discussion of the Australian response to returning soldiers who had lost limbs, see Joanna Bourke, 'The Battle of the Limbs: Amputation, Artificial Limbs and the Great War in Australia', *Australian Historical Studies* 29, no. 110 (1998): 52–8.
94  Neale, 'Without the Faces of Men', 244–54.
95  Ibid.
96  Biernoff, 'The Rhetoric of Disfigurement in First World War Britain', 669.
97  Ibid., 666–8; Callister, 'Broken Gargoyles'; Kubicki, 'Recreated Faces'.
98  Larsson, *Shattered Anzacs*, 22.
99  Condé, 'Imagining a Collection'.
100 Jay Winter, 'Museums and the Representation of War', *Museum and Society* 10, no. 3 (2012): 154.
101 John Treloar, cited in Michael McKernan, *Here Is Their Spirit: A History of the Australian War Memorial 1917–1990* (St. Lucia, Queensland: University of

Queensland Press in association with the Australian War Memorial, 1991), 69. Similarly, in the Canadian context, founder of the Canadian War Records Office Max Aitken indicated that photographers should 'cover up the Canadians' before taking images of their bodies. Max Aitken, quoted in Jeff Keshen, *Propaganda and Censorship during Canada's Great War* (Edmonton: University of Alberta Press, 1996), 36.

102 Craig Melrose, 'The Australian War Memorial and the "Culture Wars": The Representation of Triumph and Sacrifice in Inter-War Commemoration', *ACH: The Journal of the History of Culture in Australia* 26 (2007): 211–32, 211.

103 Catherine Armitage, 'Organ Collection Poses Problem for Museum', *Sydney Morning Herald*, 22 August 1992.

104 Matthew Franklin, 'Bizarre War Wounds Collection', *Courier Mail*, 27 June 1996, 12; 'Body Bits Unveiled', *Herald Sun*, 31 August 1995.

105 S. N. Gower to Margaret Coaldrake, 30 April 1996, NMA 89/37, Box 7/249, National Museum of Australia; 'Council Meeting', 5 February 1993, NMA 89/37, Box 7/249, National Museum of Australia.

106 Franklin, 'Bizarre War Wounds Collection', 12; for discussion of the collection in parliament, see Commonwealth of Australia, 1996, *Parliamentary Debates: House of Representatives: Official Hansard*, 22 August 1996, Question no. 455, 3660, accessed 2 April 2023, http://parlinfo.aph.gov.au/parlInfo/search/display/display. w3p;adv=yes;orderBy=customrank;page=0;query=%22war%20wound%22%20 Date%3A01%2F01%2F1996%20%3E%3E%2001%2F01%2F1997;rec=0;resCount= Default.

107 See Cooke, 'Forgotten Bodies', 91.

108 Personal correspondence with Professor John Hilton, 24 January 2017.

109 'Wet Specimen Survey – undertaken on 16/12/1997', NMA 89/37 7:249, National Museum of Australia.

# Chapter 6

1 'Melbourne Medical School Jubilee Celebrations: Demonstrations and Lecturettes', *The Age*, 2 May 1914, 20.

2 Harry Brookes Allen to the Vice-Chancellor and Members of the Council of the University of Melbourne, 20 June 1914, Sir Harry Brookes Allen Collection, 1976.0006, Unit 1, Folder 8, University of Melbourne Archives.

3 'Melbourne Medical School Jubilee Celebrations', 20.

4 *The Melbourne School of Pathology*, 42.

5 'Museum Programme, 1974', Department of Pathology 1876–1976, 1990.0009, Box 36, University of Melbourne Archives.

6   MacDonald, *Possessing the Dead*; Richardson, *Death, Dissection, and the Destitute*.
7   MacDonald, 'The Anatomy Inspector and the Government Corpse', 41–2. MacDonald notes that the coroner's constable arrived to tidy up the post-mortem room after William Ramsay Smith had been at work, only to find that fingers, toes and internal organs had been removed as part of the coroner's 'anatomical examinations' – acts that blurred the line between a post-mortem and a dissection. See MacDonald, 42.
8   'Professor's Strange Behaviour', *The News*, 31 July 1940, 5. For details of the case in question, see Alfred Austin Lendon, 'Myositis Ossificans', *Transactions of the Intercolonial Medical Congress of Australasia, first session, held in Adelaide, South Australia, August – September 1887* (Adelaide: Webb, Vardon and Pritchard, 1887), 109–21. For more on the episode, see P. W. Allen, 'Adelaide's Blackbirding Pathologist', *Annals of Diagnostic Pathology* 2, no. 3 (1998): 211.
9   Redman, *Bone Rooms*, 3.
10  Alexandra Roginski, *The Hanged Man and the Body Thief: Finding Lives in a Museum Mystery* (Clayton: Monash University Publishing, 2015), 32; Ross Jones, 'Medical Schools and Aboriginal Bodies', in Shannon Faulkhead and Jim Berg, eds., *Power and the Passion: Our Ancestors Return Home* (Melbourne: Koorie Heritage Trust Inc, 2010), 50–5. Although the majority of collected Aboriginal remains are skeletal, on occasion soft tissues have been preserved. Turnbull also notes that before the 1860s, there was 'sporadic and opportunistic' collecting of Aboriginal remains: Turnbull, *Science, Museums and Collecting the Indigenous Dead in Colonial Australia*, 80, 96.
11  George Bennett, *Wanderings in New South Wales … Being the Journal of a Naturalist*, Vol. 1 (London: Richard Bentley, 1834), 69. Quoted in Paul Turnbull, 'British Anatomists, Phrenologists and the Construction of the Aboriginal Race, c. 1790–1830', *History Compass* 5, no. 1 (2007): 43.
12  The colonial government received two requests for Lanne's body: one from the Fellows of the Tasmanian Royal Society, and one from William Crowther on behalf of the Hunterian Museum in London, and its curator, William Flower. For a detailed account and discussion of the episode, see Helen MacDonald, 'A Scandalous Act: Regulating Anatomy in a British Settler Colony, Tasmania 1869', *Social History of Medicine* 20, no. 1 (2007): 39–56.
13  Ibid., 41; Stefan Petrow, 'The Last Man: The Mutilation of William Lanne in 1869 and Its Aftermath', *Aboriginal History Journal* 21 (2011): 108–10.
14  Cressida Fforde, *Collecting the Dead: Archaeology and the Reburial Issue* (London: Duckworth, 2004); Samuel J. Redman, *Bone Rooms: From Scientific Racism to Human Prehistory in Museums* (Cambridge, MA: Harvard University Press, 2016). For a history of phrenology in Australia and Aotearoa New Zealand, see Alexandra Roginski, *Science and Power in the Nineteenth-Century Tasman World: Popular*

*Phrenology in Australia and Aotearoa New Zealand* (Cambridge; New York, NY: Cambridge University Press, 2023).

15 Turnbull, *Science, Museums and Collecting the Indigenous Dead in Colonial Australia*, 71. Turnbull's book provides an excellent discussion of the context surrounding the collection of Indigenous remains in Australian history.

16 Ibid., 12.

17 Roginski, *The Hanged Man and the Body Thief*, 69.

18 R. J. A. Berry, *Transactions of the Royal Society of Victoria. Volume V. Part 1, Dioptrographic Tracings in Four Normae of Fifty-Two Tasmanian Crania* (Melbourne: Published for the Royal Society by Stillwell & Co, 1909); R. J. A. Berry, *Transactions of the Royal Society of Victoria. Volume VI, Dioptrographic Tracings in Three Normae of Ninety Australian Aboriginal Crania* (Melbourne: Published for the Royal Society by Stillwell & Co, 1914). Several historians have discussed Richard Berry's research and collecting activity, particularly with reference to his work in the field of eugenics. See Ross L. Jones, 'The Master Potter and the Rejected Pots: Eugenic Legislation in Victoria, 1918–1939', *Australian Historical Studies* 29, no. 113 (1999): 319–42; K. F. Russell, 'Richard James Arthur Berry, 1867–1962', in *Festschrift for Kenneth Fitzpatrick Russell: Proceedings of a Symposium Arranged by the Section of Medical History, A.M.A. (Victorian Branch), 25 February 1977*, ed. Geoffrey Kenny and Harold Atwood (Carlton, Victoria: Queensberry Hill Press, 1978), 25–45.

19 Paul Turnbull, 'Outlawed Subjects', *Eighteenth-Century Life* 22, no. 1 (February 1998): 169; Johan Galtung, 'Cultural Violence', *Journal of Peace Research* 27, no. 3 (1990): 291–305.

20 George Murray Black to Acting Director of the Australian Institute of Anatomy, 1 December 1937, Institute of Anatomy Specimens Section 2, A1928 695/11, National Archives of Australia. For discussion of the acquisition of this collection, see Faulkhead and Berg, *Power and the Passion*; Rob McWilliams, 'Resting Places: A History of Australian Indigenous Ancestral Remains at Museum Victoria', 2016, https://museumsvictoria.com.au/media/4273/resting_places__history_of_ancestral_remains_25_aug_2016.docx (accessed 3 February 2023).

21 For an analysis of the meanings of relatedness and personhood for Aboriginal Australian people, see Katie Glaskin, 'Anatomies of Relatedness: Considering Personhood in Aboriginal Australia', *American Anthropologist* 114, no. 2 (2012): 297–308. Faulkhead and Berg also provide a succinct discussion of these concepts in relation to repatriation: see *Power and the Passion*, xix–xx.

22 For example, see Campbell Duncan to G. S. Christie, 27 May 1979, Department of Pathology 1876–1976, 1990.0009, Box 36, University of Melbourne Archives; C. R. Green to D. G. Lytton, 9 July 1981, Box 36, 1990.0009, Department of Pathology 1876–1976, University of Melbourne Archives. According to Dr John

Buntine, who was a senior demonstrator in the Melbourne Medical School Department of Anatomy in the early 1960s, specimens often 'simply turned up' at the museum. Personal correspondence with Dr John Buntine, 29 November 2018.

23 Drawing on a range of Aboriginal stories, songs and song-poems, ethnographer Deborah Bird Rose provides an insightful examination of the meanings of Country for Aboriginal people. In brief, she states that 'Country ... is a nourishing terrain. Country is a place that gives and receives life. Not just imagined or represented, it is lived in and lived with ... People speak to country, sing to country, visit country, worry about country, feel sorry for country, and long for country. People say that country knows, hears, smells, takes notice, takes care, is sorry or happy ... country is a living entity with a yesterday, today, and tomorrow, with a consciousness, and a will toward life. Because of this richness, country is home, and peace; nourishment for body, mind, and spirit; heart's ease.' Capitalization appears as in original. See Deborah Bird Rose, *Nourishing Terrains: Australian Aboriginal Views of Landscape and Wilderness* (Canberra: Australian Heritage Commission, 1996), 7.

24 Repatriation in Australia is part of a wider movement in which Indigenous peoples in colonized places, such as North America and New Zealand/Aotearoa, among others, have reclaimed their authority over their ancestors' remains, as well as cultural artefacts. See Megan J. Highet, 'Body Snatching & Grave Robbing: Bodies for Science', *History and Anthropology* 16, no. 4 (2005): 415–40; Ryan M. Seidemann, 'NAGPRA at 20: What Have the States Done to Expand Human Remains Protections?', *Museum Anthropology* 33, no. 2 (2010): 199–209; Te Herekiekie Herewini, 'The Museum of New Zealand Te Papa Tongarewa (Te Papa) and the Repatriation of Kōiwi Tangata (Māori and Moriori Skeletal Remains) and Toi Moko (Mummified Māori Tattooed Heads)', *International Journal of Cultural Property* 15, no. 4 (2008): 405–6. For more on the Australian context, see Cressida Fforde, C. Timothy McKeown, Honor Keeler eds., *The Routledge Companion to Indigenous Repatriation* (London: Routledge, 2020).

25 The Museum of Victoria is now called Museums Victoria and incorporates Melbourne Museum, the Immigration Museum and Scienceworks Museum, all of which are in Melbourne, Victoria. Indigenous remains are held in a specially designated storeroom at Melbourne Museum.

26 *Archaeological and Aboriginal Relics Preservation Act (Amendment), 1984*, Parliament of Victoria. See Section 26B for the applicable wording.

27 The Victorian *Archaeological and Aboriginal Relics Preservation Act* allowed institutions other than the Museum of Victoria to hold Indigenous artefacts and remains only with permission from the Secretary for Planning and Environment. The University of Melbourne had not been granted this permission. See Faulkhead and Berg, *Power and the Passion*, 6.

28 Ronald Merkel, 'The Archaeological and Aboriginal Relics Preservation Act 1972 – Aboriginal Skeletal Remains', Repatriation Files, Harry Brookes Allen Museum of Anatomy and Pathology.

29  Graeme Ryan to Clyde Scaife (President, Australian Medical Association Victoria Branch), 3 August 1984, Repatriation Files, Harry Brookes Allen Museum of Anatomy and Pathology.
30  Ibid.
31  Ibid.
32  Steven Webb, 'The Aboriginal Community Liaison Program', 8, MS 2515, Australian Institute of Aboriginal and Torres Strait Islander Studies. See also Denise Donlon, 'Aboriginal Skeletal Collections and Research in Physical Anthropology: An Historical Perspective', *Australian Archaeology* 39 (1994): 73–82.
33  Roger Lewin, 'Extinction Threatens Australian Anthropology', *Council for Museum Anthropology* Newsletter 9, no. 3 (1985): 7.
34  Donlon, 'Aboriginal Skeletal Collections and Research in Physical Anthropology', 74; Lynette Russell, 'Reflections on Murray Black's Writings', in Faulkhead and Berg, *Power and the Passion*, 60; Jones, 'Medical Schools and Aboriginal Bodies', 50–5.
35  Graeme Ryan to Evan Walker, 6 September 1984, Repatriation Files, Harry Brookes Allen Museum of Anatomy and Pathology. Many museums formed policies that forced claims-makers to present a genuine connection to Ancestral Remains before repatriation would be considered. See Sarah Morton, 'The Legacies of the Repatriation of Human Remains from the Royal College of Surgeons of England' (PhD thesis, University of Oxford, 2018), 68.
36  Jones and Whitaker, 'The Contested Realm of Displaying Dead Bodies', 652.
37  Griffiths, *Hunters and Collectors*, 96.
38  Faulkhead and Berg, *Power and the Passion*, xx. See also Smith, 'The Repatriation of Human Remains – Problem or Opportunity?', 407.
39  Russell, 'Reflections on Murray Black's Writings', 60; Faulkhead and Berg, *Power and the Passion*, xix.
40  Faulkhead and Berg, *Power and the Passion*, 35.
41  Ibid., xix.
42  Ibid., 43 and xix. Faulkhead and Berg's volume contains a discussion, and several personal accounts of the ceremony at Kings Domain that illustrate the emotional and therapeutic aspects of repatriation; see at 34–8. See also Henry Atkinson, 'The Meanings and Values of Repatriation', in *The Long Way Home: The Meanings and Values of Repatriation*, ed. Paul Turnbull and Michael Pickering (New York and Oxford: Berghahn Books, 2010), 15–19.
43  For more on bones as contested objects that can embody a multitude of meanings and provocations in a variety of contexts, see Cara Krmpotich, Joost Fontein, and John Harries, 'The Substance of Bones: The Emotive Materiality and Affective Presence of Human Remains', *Journal of Material Culture* 15, no. 4 (2010): 371–84; Joost Fontein, 'Between Tortured Bodies and Resurfacing Bones: The Politics of the Dead in Zimbabwe', *Journal of Material Culture* 15, no. 4 (2010): 423–48; Cara Krmpotich, 'Remembering and Repatriation: The Production of Kinship, Memory and Respect', *Journal of Material Culture* 15, no. 2 (2010): 157–79.

44 Graeme Ryan to Evan Walker, 20 September 1984, Repatriation Files, Harry Brookes Allen Museum of Anatomy and Pathology.
45 Ibid.
46 For analysis of the values, practices and effects of the 'new museology', see Vikki McCall and Clive Gray, 'Museums and the "New Museology": Theory, Practice and Organisational Change', *Museum Management and Curatorship* 29, no. 1 (2014): 19–35; Peter Vergo, *The New Museology* (London: Reaktion Books, 1989); Eilean Hooper-Greenhill, *Museums and the Shaping of Knowledge* (London: Routledge, 1992); Bennett, *The Birth of the Museum*. Jenkins, *Contesting Human Remains in Museum Collections*; Joshua M. Gorman, 'Universalism and the New Museology: Impacts on the Ethics of Authority and Ownership', *Museums Management and Curatorship* 26, no. 2 (2011): 149–62; Tiffany Jenkins, '"Who Are We to Decide?" Internal Challenges to Cultural Authority in the Contestation over Human Remains in British Museums', *Cultural Sociology* 6, no. 4 (2012): 455–70.
47 Krmpotich, Fontein and Harries, 'The Substance of Bones', 374, 380.
48 Pickering, 'Where Are the Stories?' 80. See also Jordi Rivera Prince, 'Can the Repatriation of the Murray Black Collection Be Considered an Apology? Colonial Institutional Culpability in the Indigenous Australian Fight for Decolonization', *In Situ* 4, no. 1 (2015): 11–13.
49 For a discussion of further repatriations facilitated through Museums Victoria, see McWilliams, 'Resting Places'.
50 'Murray Black Collection 1942–1950', Folder 1, Repatriation Files, Harry Brookes Allen Museum of Anatomy and Pathology.
51 Ibid. Historian Ross L. Jones also notes the poor state of documentation pertaining to the Murray Black Collection: see Jones, 'Medical Schools and Aboriginal Bodies', 52.
52 Faulkhead and Berg, *Power and the Passion*, 60. In the 1980s, the university spent over $220,000 engaging physical anthropologists and museum specialists to analyse, document and prepare the collection for return and reburial. 'Management and Repatriation of 350–80 Ancestral Remains', Folder 1, Repatriation Files, Harry Brookes Allen Museum of Anatomy and Pathology.
53 Faulkhead and Berg, *Power and the Passion*, 35.
54 Daley, 'Restless Indigenous Remains'.
55 Ibid.
56 For examples of cases in which communities could not or chose not to accept remains, see Morton, 'The Legacies of the Repatriation of Human Remains', 180–91, 212.
57 McWilliams, 'Resting Places', 16.
58 Faulkhead and Berg, *Power and the Passion*, 7.
59 Morton, 'The Legacies of the Repatriation of Human Remains', 111.

60 For a deeper understanding of Aboriginal beliefs regarding ancestors and kinship, see Glaskin, 'Anatomies of Relatedness'; Rose, *Nourishing Terrains*, 71.
61 Heidi Norman and Anne Maree Payne, 'Nowhere Else but Home: A National Resting Place for Indigenous Australian Ancestral Remains', *The Museum Journal* 65, no. 4 (October 2022): 817–34; Daley, 'Restless Indigenous Remains'. See also Advisory Committee for Indigenous Repatriation, *National Resting Place Consultation Report 2014* (Canberra: Attorney-General's Office, 2014).
62 The recent identification and return to country of the skull of Aboriginal man Jim Crow, culminating from Alexandra Roginski's research, provides one example of the ongoing possibilities for repatriation of specimens that remain in museum repositories. See Roginski, *The Hanged Man and the Body Thief*.
63 Michael Pickering, '"The Big Picture": The Repatriation of Australian Indigenous Sacred Objects', *Museum Management and Curatorship* 30, no. 5 (2015): 440.
64 McWilliams, 'Resting Places', 1.
65 Richard Baker to Kaye Dal Bon, 30 April 1992, Australian Institute of Anatomy Collection No. 1 – Anatomical (wet specimens) Collection, 89/37, National Museum of Australia.
66 For a discussion of the Berry Collection, see Jones, 'Medical Schools and Aboriginal Bodies', in Faulkhead and Berg, *Power and the Passion*, 50–5.
67 Karen Milward (Acting Executive Director of Aboriginal Affairs Victoria) to Antony Goodwin (Head of the Department of Anatomy and Cell Biology), 12 September 2002, Repatriation Files, Harry Brookes Allen Museum of Anatomy and Pathology; Deputy Vice-Chancellor of the University of Melbourne to Daine Alcorn (Head of the Department of Cell Anatomy and Cell Biology), 27 January 1997, Repatriation Files, Harry Brookes Allen Museum of Anatomy and Pathology; Graham C. Morris (Museum Victoria) to John Poynter (Assistant Vice-Chancellor Cultural Affairs, University of Melbourne), 22 January 1997, Repatriation Files, Harry Brookes Allen Museum of Anatomy and Pathology.
68 'Human remains found in uni storeroom', *The Age*, 16 February 2003, accessed 22 February 2023, https://www.theage.com.au/national/human-remains-found-in-uni-storeroom-20030216-gdv8he.html.
69 Ibid. For more on the university's response, see McWilliams, 'Resting Places', 15.
70 The university projected it would cost over $200,000 to hire several physical anthropologists to conduct identification work on the collection, a collection manager to oversee the project, and to facilitate the collection's return to the Traditional Owners. See 'Management and Repatriation of 350–80 Ancestral Remains', Repatriation Files, Harry Brookes Allen Museum of Anatomy and Pathology.
71 For commentary on the student-led campaign to remove Richard Berry's name from a prominent building at the University of Melbourne's main Parkville campus,

see Marika Dobbin, 'Melbourne University Bows to Pressure, Removes Racist Professor's Name from Campus', *The Age*, 21 March 2017.

72 George J. Annas and Michael A. Grodin, eds., *The Nazi Doctors and the Nuremberg Code: Human Rights in Human Experimentation* (New York: Oxford University Press, 1992); Arthur Caplan, ed., *When Medicine Went Mad: Bioethics and the Holocaust* (Totowa, N. J.: Humana Press, 1992).

73 Australian universities that have body donor programmes include the University of Melbourne, University of Sydney, University of Queensland, University of Western Australia, University of Adelaide, Griffith University, University of Newcastle, University of Wollongong, Australian National University, Macquarie University, University of New England, James Cook University and Queensland University of Technology. The acquisition of cadavers through body donor programmes has grown alongside the rise of donor, or gift, culture in biomedicine.

74 Hearder, 'Battlefield Legacies', 25.

75 Michael Pickering, 'Policy and Research Issues Affecting Human Remains in Australian Museum Collections', in *Human Remains and Museum Practice*, ed. Jack Lohman and Katherine Goodnow (New York, NY: Berghahn Books, 2006), 43.

76 Philip Eichhorn et al., 'Restoration of an Academic Historical Gross Pathology Collection – Refreshed Impact on Current Teaching?' *Virchows Archiv* 473, no. 2 (2018): 219–28, 223; D. G. Jones, R. Gear and K. A. Galvin, 'Stored Human Tissue: An Ethical Perspective on the Fate of Anonymous, Archival Material', *Journal of Medical Ethics* 29, no. 6 (2003): 343–7; Philippe Charlier, 'Naming the Body (or the Bones): Human Remains, Anthropological/Medical Collections, Religious Beliefs, and Restitution', *Clinical Anatomy* 27, no. 3 (2014).

77 Eichhorn et al., 'Restoration of an Academic Historical Gross Pathology Collection', 223–4.

78 Huistra, *The Afterlife of the Leiden Anatomical Collections*, 162.

79 'Museum Programme', Department of Pathology 1876–1976, 1990.0009, Box 36, University of Melbourne Archives.

80 Weindling uses the term 'cleansing' to describe the actions of institutions that have disposed of specimens procured by the Nazis, to point out the fraught nature of simply removing specimens to erase contentious issues of the past. See Paul Weindling, '"Cleansing" Anatomical Collections: The Politics of Removing Specimens from German Anatomical and Medical Collections 1988–92', *Annals of Anatomy* 194, no. 3 (2012): 237–42. See also Paul Weindling, 'From Scientific Object to Commemorated Victim: The Children of the *Spiegelgrund*', *History and Philosophy of the Life Sciences* 35, no. 3 (2013): 415–30; Rüdiger Schultka and Michael Viebig, 'The Fate of the Bodies of Executed Persons in the Anatomical Institute of Halle between 1933 and 1945', *Annals of Anatomy – Anatomischer Anzeiger*, Special Issue: Anatomy in the Third Reich, 194, no. 3 (2012): 274–80.

81 Jones, Gear and Galvin, 'Stored Human Tissue', 344.
82 Charlier, 'Naming the Body (or the Bones)', 291–5, 295.
83 Part of the Hunterian Museum's steadfast defence of its decision to keep Byrne's skeleton in the collection is that it, like many museums, does not have a policy for the return of human remains of non-Indigenous origin. Nash notes that interest groups have pleaded with local Irish communities and the broader Irish diaspora to support their requests to have Byrne's remains buried according to his wishes. See Catherine Nash, 'Making Kinship with Human Remains: Repatriation, Biomedicine and the Many Relations of Charles Byrne', *Environment and Planning D: Society and Space* 36, no. 5 (2018): 872.
84 'Open letter signed by lawyers, academics and ethicists urges the Australian Government to close "Real Bodies: The Exhibition"', *International Coalition to End Transplant Abuse in China*, accessed 26 February 2023, https://endtransplantabuse.org/open-letter-urges-for-real-bodies-the-exhibition-to-be-closed-down/.
85 Frances Mao, '"Real bodies" exhibition causes controversy in Australia', *BBC News*, 26 April 2018.
86 'Why has Museums Victoria decided not to display human remains in Vikings: Beyond the Legend?', *Museums Victoria*, accessed 9 February 2023, https://museumsvictoria.com.au/article/museums-victorias-position-on-displaying-human-remains/
87 Samuel J. M. M. Alberti, Piotr Bienkowski, Malcolm J. Chapman and Rose Drew, 'Should we display the dead?' *Museum and Society* 7, no. 3 (2009): 133–49, 143.
88 For more on the development of policies surrounding the display of human remains in Australia, see Pickering, 'Policy and Research Issues Affecting Human Remains in Australian Museum Collections', 43.

# Conclusion

1 Lisa M. Parker, 'Anatomical Dissection: Why Are We Cutting It Out? Dissection in Undergraduate Teaching', *ANZ Journal of Surgery* 72, no. 12 (2002): 910–2; Salil B. Patel et al., 'Is Dissection the Only Way to Learn Anatomy? Thoughts from Students at a Non-Dissecting Based Medical School', *Perspectives on Medical Education* 4, no. 5 (2015): 259–60; Hope Ellen Bouwer, Krisztina Valter and Alexandra Louise Webb, 'Current Integration of Dissection in Medical Education in Australia and New Zealand: Challenges and Successes', *Anatomical Sciences Education* 9, no. 2 (2016): 168.
2 For perceptive discussions of the legality and ethics of body donation and use of cadavers in medical school education, see Erin F. Hutchinson et al., 'The Law, Ethics and Body Donation: A Tale of Two Bequeathal Programs', *Anatomical*

*Sciences Education*, 2019, 3; Ilan Caplan and Matthew DeCamp, 'Of Discomfort and Disagreement: Unclaimed Bodies in Anatomy Laboratories at United States Medical Schools', *Anatomical Sciences Education* 12, no. 4 (2019): 360–9; Thomas H. Champney et al., 'BODIES R US: Ethical Views on the Commercialization of the Dead in Medical Education and Research', *Anatomical Sciences Education* 12, no. 3 (2019): 317–25. For insight into the emotional impact dissection can have on twenty-first-century medical school students, see Michelle D. Skinner, 'Foundations for a Lifetime: A Qualitative Inquiry into the Recollection, Reconstruction and Meaning-Making Process of Cadaver Dissection' (PhD thesis, University of Utah, 2013), 3–6.

3 Parker, 'Anatomical Dissection', 911; John E. Farey, Jonathan C. Sandeford and Greg D. Evans-McKendry, 'Medical Students Call for National Standards in Anatomical Education', *ANZ Journal of Surgery* 84, no. 11 (2014): 813; Horst-Werner Korf et al., 'The Dissection Course – Necessary and Indispensable for Teaching Anatomy to Medical Students', *Annals of Anatomy* 190, no. 1 (2008): 18; Bouwer, Valter and Webb, 'Current Integration of Dissection in Medical Education in Australia and New Zealand', 162.

4 Ibid., 163.

5 For a small sample of the media coverage, see 'Morgue Chief Removed Over "Sickening" Tests', *Sydney Morning Herald*, 19 March 2001, 3; 'Inquiry into Morgue Experiments', *Daily Telegraph*, 19 March 2001; 'Allegations over Morgue', *Australian Financial Review*, 19 March 2001, 8; 'Morgue in Trouble', *Sydney Morning Herald*, 20 March 2001, 12; 'Morgue's Staff may be Charged', *The Australian*, 20 March 2001; 'Autopsy Body Parts Probe', *Herald Sun*, 20 March 2001, 14.

6 See Secretary of State for Health, *Learning from Bristol: The Report of the Public Inquiry into Children's Heart Surgery at the Bristol Royal Infirmary 1984–1995* (Norwich: HMSO, 2001); Department of Health and Michael Redfern, *The Royal Liverpool Children's Inquiry: Report* (Norwich: Stationery Office, 2001).

7 On the Adelaide case, see Solicitor-General's Office and Bradley Maxwell Selway, *Report into the Retention of Body Parts after Post-Mortems* (Adelaide: Department of Human Services, 2001). On the Sydney case, see New South Wales Department of Health and Bret Walker, *Inquiry into Matters Arising from the Post-Mortem and Anatomical Examination Practices of the Institute of Forensic Medicine: Report* (North Sydney: NSW Department of Health, 2001).

8 I am sincerely grateful to Dr Bryan Mendelson for allowing me to attend the Melbourne Advanced Facial Anatomy Course (MAFAC), and to Jilda Cosentino and Vicki Steggall for facilitating my observation of the dissection component of the course. For information about the course, see 'Melbourne Advanced Facial Anatomy Course', *MAFAC*, accessed 3 February 2023, https://mafac.com.au/history/

# Bibliography

## Primary sources

### Archives and museums

Australian Institute of Aboriginal and Torres Strait Islander Studies, Canberra, Australia
MS 2515, The Aboriginal Community Liaison Program
Australian War Memorial, Canberra, Australia
AWM 16, Australian War Records Section registry of files and registry of file titles, 1914–1918 War
AWM 25, Written Records, 1914–1918 War
Harry Brookes Allen Museum of Anatomy and Pathology, University of Melbourne, Melbourne, Australia
Museum catalogue
Repatriation Files, not accessioned
Medical History Museum, University of Melbourne, Melbourne, Australia
MHM 00911, Archibald Watson to Harry Brookes Allen, 18 July 1907
MHM 02011, Student Notebook of A. McDonald
MHM 02027, Notebook of Mary Clementina De Garis
National Archives of Australia
CA 17, Department of Health, Central Office
Series A1928 Correspondence files, multiple number series (first series)
National Museum of Australia, Canberra, Australia
NMA 89/37, Box 7/249, Conservation Files, Australian Institute of Anatomy Collection
Public Records Office of Victoria, Melbourne, Australia
VPRS 9583/P0003/G Index, Alphabetical Record of Burials – Old Melbourne Cemetery, 1866–1917
VPRS 17385/P/0001, Labour Ward Case Book, Midwifery Department
University of Adelaide Archives, Adelaide, Australia
Series 137, Faculty of Medicine Minutes
Series 142, Reports of the Faculty of Medicine Vol. 1, 1885–1899
University of Melbourne Archives, Melbourne, Australia
1963.0003, Sir Harry Brookes Allen Collection
1968.0013, Bates, Smart, McCutcheon Pty. Ltd.
1990.0014, University of Melbourne, Office of the Registrar
1976.0006, Sir Harry Brookes Allen Collection

1990.0009, University of Melbourne Department of Pathology 1876–1924
1993.0046, University of Melbourne Medical School Correspondence
University of Sydney Archives, Sydney, Australia
G.63, Department of Anatomy
872, University of Sydney Calendar

## Medical journals

*Australian Medical Journal* (1856–95; supersedes *Intercolonial Medical Journal of Australasia*, 1910–4)
*Australia and New Zealand Journal of Surgery*
*British Journal of Neurosurgery*
*British Medical Journal*
*Cincinnati Lancet and Observer*
*Intercolonial Medical Journal of Australasia* (supersedes *Intercolonial Quarterly Journal of Medicine and Surgery*, 1896–1909)
*Journal of Anatomy*
*The Lancet*
*Medical Journal of Australia* (supersedes *Australian Medical Journal*, 1914–present)
*Medical Record*
*Pediatric Neurosurgery*
*Record of Medical Science*
*Speculum*

## Periodicals

*The Advertiser*
*The Age*
*The Argus*
*The Australian*
*The Australian Financial Review*
*BBC News*
*The Bendigo Advertiser*
*The Courier*
*Courier Mail*
*Daily Telegraph*
*The Examiner*
*Geelong Advertiser*
*Geraldton Guardian*
*The Herald*
*Herald Sun*

*Hobart Town Advertiser*
*Kyneton Observer*
*Leader*
*Melbourne Punch*
*Mount Alexander Mail*
*The News*
*New York Post*
*New York Times*
*South Australian Weekly Chronicle*
*The Sydney Gazette and New South Wales Advertiser*
*The Sydney Monitor*
*The Sydney Morning Herald*
*Terang Express*
*Washington Post*

## Medical publications and treatises

*Australasian Medical Congress, transactions of the eighth session, held in Melbourne, Victoria, October 1908 (three vols)*, Vol. 2. Melbourne: J. Kemp, Government Printer, 1909.

Bell, Charles. *The Hand: Its Mechanism and Vital Endowments as Evincing Design*, 3rd ed., Bridgewater Treatises; 4. London: William Pickering, 1834.

Bennett, George. *Wanderings in New South Wales ... Being the Journal of a Naturalist*, Vol. 1. London: Richard Bentley, 1834.

Berry, R. J. A. *Transactions of the Royal Society of Victoria. Volume V. Part 1, Dioptrographic Tracings in Four Normae of Fifty-Two Tasmanian Crania*. Melbourne: Published for the Royal Society by Stillwell & Co., 1909.

Berry, R. J. A. *Transactions of the Royal Society of Victoria. Volume VI, Dioptrographic Tracings in Three Normae of Ninety Australian Aboriginal Crania*. Melbourne: Published for the Royal Society by Stillwell & Co., 1914.

Cunningham, Daniel John. *Manual of Practical Anatomy*. Edinburgh and London: Y. J. Pentland, 1896.

Hooper, Robert. *The Anatomist's Vade-Mecum: Containing a Concise and Accurate Description of the Structure, Situation, and Use of Every Part of the Human Body*. London: Sold by Bell, Oxford-Street, London, 1797.

Hunter, William. *Two Introductory Lectures, Delivered by Dr. William Hunter, to His Last Course of Anatomical Lectures, at His Theatre in Windmill-Street*. London: Trustees of J. Johnson, 1784.

Knox, Frederick John. *The Anatomist's Instructor, and Museums Companion: Being Practical Directions for the Formation and Subsequent Management of Anatomical Museums*. Edinburgh: Adam and Charles Black, 1836.

Mearns, Andrew. *The Bitter Cry of Outcast London*. Boston: Cupples, Upham, 1883.

Pole, Thomas. *The Anatomical Instructor; or an Illustration of the Modern and Most Approved Methods of Preparing and Preserving Different Parts of the Human Body and of Quadrupeds by Injection, Corrosion, Maceration, Distention, Articulation, Modelling, &c.* London: Couchman & Fry, 1790.

Roberts, William. *Mr. Warburton's Anatomy Bill: Thoughts on Its Mischievous Tendency; with Suggestions for an Entirely New One, Founded upon an Available Anti-Septic Process, in an Appeal to Medical Practitioners, Students of Anatomy, and the Public at Large, on the Injury to Medical Sciences and the Hindrances to the Decent Interment of Unclaimed Pauper Bodies Now Delivered Up for Anatomical 'Examination', Consequent upon the Rejection of Such an Process.* London: J. Ollivier, 1843.

*Transactions of the Intercolonial Medical Congress of Australasia, First Session, Held in Adelaide, South Australia, August–September 1887.* Adelaide: Vardon and Pritchard, 1888.

Wood-Jones, Frederic. 'The External Characters of a Second Australian Foetus'. *Journal of Anatomy* 72, no. 2 (January 1938): 301–4.

Wood-Jones, Frederic. 'The External Characters of an Australian Foetus'. *Journal of Anatomy* 67, no. 4 (July 1933): 549–54.

## Memoir

Berry, Richard J. A. *Chance and Circumstance.* Unpublished autobiography. University of Melbourne, Brownless Biomedical Library, 1954.

## Museum catalogues

*A Guide to the Exhibition of the Army Medical Collection of War Specimens: Opened October 11th, 1917.* London: Taylor & Francis, 1917.

*Catalogue of Messrs. Baume & Kreitmayer's Grand Anatomical Museum.* Melbourne: Shaw, Harnett & Co., 1861.

## Novels

Dickens, Charles. *The Pickwick Papers.* Oxford: Oxford University Press, 1988.

Shelley, Mary. *Frankenstein.* London: Penguin Classics, 2003.

Stevenson, Robert Louis. *The Body Snatcher and Other Tales.* Mineola: Dover Publications Inc., 2003.

## Legal acts and parliamentary proceedings

*An Act for Better Preventing the Horrid Crime of Murder 1752.* 25 Geo. 2, c. 37.

*An Act for Regulating Schools of Anatomy 1862*, CLVI (Vic). Parliament of Victoria: CLVI.

*Archaeological and Aboriginal Relics Preservation Act (Amendment), 1984* (Vic). Parliament of Victoria.
Commonwealth of Australia, House of Representatives, 1996. *Parliamentary Debates*, 22 August 1996, Question no. 455, 3660.
*Human Tissue Act 1982* (Vic). Parliament of Victoria.
*The Electoral Act 1863,* CLXVIII (Vic). Parliament Victoria: CLXVIII.

## Websites

International Coalition to End Transplant Abuse in China. 'Open Letter Signed by Lawyers, Academics and Ethicists Urges the Australian Government to Close "Real Bodies: The Exhibition"'. https://endtransplantabuse.org/open-letter-urges-for-real-bodies-the-exhibition-to-be-closed-down (accessed 26 February 2023).
MAFAC. 'Melbourne Advanced Facial Anatomy Course'. https://mafac.com.au/history/ (accessed 3 February 2023).

## Other

Advisory Committee for Indigenous Repatriation. *National Resting Place Consultation Report 2014.* Canberra: Attorney-General's Office, 2014.
Department of Health and Michael Redfern. *The Royal Liverpool Children's Inquiry: Report.* Norwich: Stationery Office, 2001.
New South Wales Department of Health and Bret Walker. *Inquiry into Matters Arising from the Post-Mortem and Anatomical Examination Practices of the Institute of Forensic Medicine: Report.* North Sydney: NSW Department of Health, 2001.
Personal correspondence with Dr John Buntine, 2017.
Personal correspondence with Professor John Hilton, January 2017.
Secretary of State for Health. *Learning from Bristol: The Report of the Public Inquiry into Children's Heart Surgery at the Bristol Royal Infirmary 1984–1995.* Norwich: HMSO, 2001.
Solicitor-General's Office and Bradley Maxwell Selway. *Report into the Retention of Body Parts after Post-Mortems.* Adelaide: Department of Human Services, 2001.

# Secondary sources

Åhrén, Eva. 'Making Space for Specimens: The Museums of the Karolinska Institute, Stockholm'. In *Medical Museums: Past, Present, Future,* edited by Samuel J. M. M. Alberti and Elizabeth Hallam, 102–15. London: The Royal College of Surgeons of England, 2013.

Alberti, Fay Bound. 'Bodies, Hearts, and Minds: Why Emotions Matter to Historians of Science and Medicine'. *Isis* 100, no. 4 (2009): 798–810.
Alberti, Fay Bound. *This Mortal Coil: The Human Body in History and Culture*. Oxford and New York: Oxford University Press, 2016.
Alberti, Samuel J. M. M. *Morbid Curiosities: Medical Museums in Nineteenth-Century Britain*. Oxford: Oxford University Press, 2011.
Alberti, Samuel J. M. M. 'The "Regiment of Skeletons": A First World War Medical Collection'. *Social History of Medicine* 28, no. 1 (2015): 108–33.
Alberti, Samuel J. M. M. 'Wax Bodies: Art and Anatomy in Victorian Medical Museums'. *Museum History Journal* 2, no. 1 (2009): 7–36.
Alberti, Samuel, and Elizabeth Hallam, eds. *Medical Museums: Past, Present, Future*. London: The Royal College of Surgeons of England, 2013.
Alberti, Samuel J. M. M., Piotr Bienkowski, Malcolm J. Chapman, and Rose Drew. 'Should We Display the Dead?' *Museum and Society* 7, no. 3 (2009): 133–49.
Allen, Judith A. *Sex & Secrets: Crimes Involving Australian Women since 1880*. Melbourne: Oxford University Press, 1990.
Allen, P. W. 'Adelaide's Blackbirding Pathologist'. *Annals of Diagnostic Pathology* 2, no. 3 (1998): 208–11.
Altick, Richard D. *The Shows of London*. Cambridge. MA: Belknap Press, 1978.
Anderson, Warwick. *The Cultivation of Whiteness: Science, Health and Racial Destiny in Australia*. Carlton: Melbourne University Publishing, 2005.
Annas, George J., and Michael A. Grodin, eds. *The Nazi Doctors and the Nuremberg Code: Human Rights in Human Experimentation*. New York: Oxford University Press, 1992.
Appadurai, Arjun. 'Introduction: Commodities and the Politics of Value'. In *The Social Life of Things: Commodities in Cultural Perspective*, 3–63. Cambridge and New York: Cambridge University Press, 1986.
Atkinson, Henry. 'The Meanings and Values of Repatriation'. In *The Long Way Home: The Meanings and Values of Repatriation*, edited by Paul Turnbull and Michael Pickering, 15–19. New York and Oxford: Berghahn Books, 2010.
Bakhtin, M. M. *Rabelais and His World*. Translated by Hélène Iswolsky. Bloomington, IN: Indiana University Press, 1984.
Barbian, L. T., P. S. Sledzik, and A. M. Nelson. 'Case Studies in Pathology from the National Museum of Health and Medicine, Armed Forces Institute of Pathology'. *Annals of Diagnostic Pathology* 4, no. 3 (2000): 170–3.
Barbian, Lenore, Paul Sledzik, and Jeffrey Reznick. 'Remains of War'. *Museum History Journal* 5, no. 1 (2012): 7–28.
Bates, A. W. '"Indecent and Demoralising Representations": Public Anatomy Museums in Mid-Victorian England'. *Medical History* 52, no. 1 (2008): 1–22.
Bennett, Brett M., and Joseph M. Hodge, eds. *Science and Empire: Knowledge and Networks of Science across the British Empire, 1800–1970*. London: Palgrave Macmillan UK, 2011.

Bennett, Tony. *The Birth of the Museum: History, Theory, Politics*. London and New York: Routledge, 1995.
Berkowitz, Carin. 'The Beauty of Anatomy: Visual Displays and Surgical Education in Early-Nineteenth-Century London'. *Bulletin of the History of Medicine* 85, no. 2 (2011): 248–78.
Bevers, Amanda. 'To Bind Up the Nation's Wounds: The Army Medical Museum and the Development of American Medical Science, 1862–1913'. PhD diss., University of California San Diego, 2015.
Biernoff, Suzannah. 'The Rhetoric of Disfigurement in First World War Britain'. *Social History of Medicine* 24, no. 3 (2011): 666–85.
Bleichmar, Daniela, and Peter C. Mancall, eds. *Collecting across Cultures: Material Exchanges in the Early Modern Atlantic World*. Philadelphia, PA: University of Pennsylvania Press, 2011.
Bonner, Thomas Neville. *Becoming a Physician: Medical Education in Britain, France, Germany, and the United States, 1750–945*. Baltimore, MD: Johns Hopkins University Press, 2000.
Bourdieu, Pierre. 'The Forms of Capital'. In *Handbook of Theory and Research for the Sociology of Education*, edited by John G. Richardson, 241–60. New York: Greenwood Press, 1986.
Bourke, Joanna. *Dismembering the Male: Men's Bodies, Britain and the Great War*. Chicago, IL: The University of Chicago Press, 1996.
Bourke, Joanna. 'The Battle of the Limbs: Amputation, Artificial Limbs and the Great War in Australia'. *Australian Historical Studies* 29, no. 110 (1998): 49–67.
Bouwer, Hope Ellen, Krisztina Valter, and Alexandra Louise Webb. 'Current Integration of Dissection in Medical Education in Australia and New Zealand: Challenges and Successes'. *Anatomical Sciences Education* 9, no. 2 (2016): 161–70.
Bracegirdle, Brian. *A History of Microtechnique: The Evolution of the Microtome and the Development of Tissue Preparation*. London: Heinemann, 1978.
Bridge, Carl, and Kent Fedorowich. 'Mapping the British World'. *The Journal of Imperial and Commonwealth History* 31, no. 2 (2003): 1–15.
Buklijas, Tatjana. 'Cultures of Death and Politics of Corpse Supply'. *Bulletin of the History of Medicine* 82, no. 3 (2008): 570–607.
Burke, Peter. *A Social History of Knowledge: From Gutenberg to Diderot*. Cambridge: Polity, 2000.
Burrell, Sean, and Geoffrey Gill. 'The Liverpool Cholera Epidemic of 1832 and Anatomical Dissection – Medical Mistrust and Civil Unrest'. *Journal of the History of Medicine and Allied Sciences* 60, no. 4 (2005): 478–98.
Callister, Sandy. '"Broken Gargoyles": The Photographic Representation of Severely Wounded New Zealand Soldiers'. *Social History of Medicine* 20, no. 1 (2007): 111–30.
Cay-Rudiger, Prüll. 'Pathology at War 1914–1918: Germany and Britain in Comparison'. In *Medicine and Modern Warfare*, edited by Roger Cooter, Mark Harrison, and Steve Sturdy, 131–61. Atlanta, GA: Rodopi, 1999.

Champney, Thomas H., Sabine Hildebrandt, D. Gareth Jones, and Andreas Winkelmann. 'BODIES R US: Ethical Views on the Commercialization of the Dead in Medical Education and Research'. *Anatomical Sciences Education* 12, no. 3 (2019): 317–25.

Charlier, Philippe. 'Naming the Body (or the Bones): Human Remains, Anthropological/Medical Collections, Religious Beliefs, and Restitution'. *Clinical Anatomy* 27, no. 3 (2014): 291–5.

Claes, Tinne. '"By What Right Does the Scalpel Enter the Pauper's Corpse?" Dissections and Consent in Late Nineteenth-Century Belgium'. *Social History of Medicine* 31, no. 2 (2018): 258–77.

Clarke, Tim. 'Sickles' Leg and the Army Medical Museum'. *Military Medicine* 179, no. 9 (2014): 1051.

Colligan, Mimi. 'Anatomical Wax Museums in Melbourne 1861–1887'. *Australian Cultural History* 13, no. 1 (1994): 52–64.

Condé, Anne-Marie. 'Imagining a Collection: Creating Australia's Records of War'. *ReCollections: Journal of the National Museum of Australia* 2, no. 1 (2007).

Conn, Steven. *Museums and American Intellectual Life, 1876–1926*. Chicago, IL: The University of Chicago Press, 1998.

Cooke, Robin A. 'Forgotten Bodies: Pathology Specimens from the Trenches'. In *Compassion and Courage: Australian Doctors and Dentists in the Great War*, edited by Jacqueline Healy, 85–92. Melbourne: Medical History Museum, University of Melbourne, 2015.

Coote, Anne. '"Pray Write Me a List of Species ... That Will Pay Me Best": The Business and Culture of Natural History Collecting in Mid-Nineteenth Century New South Wales'. *History Australia* 11, no. 2 (2014): 80–100.

Coote, Anne, Alison Haynes, Jude Philp, and Simon Ville. 'When Commerce, Science, and Leisure Collaborated: The Nineteenth-Century Global Trade Boom in Natural History Collections'. *Journal of Global History* 12, no. 3 (2017): 319–39.

Crone, Rosalind. *Violent Victorians: Popular Entertainment in Nineteenth-Century London*. Manchester: Manchester University Press, 2012.

Daley, Paul. 'Restless Indigenous Remains'. *Meanjin* 73, no. 1 (2014).

Daston, Lorraine, and Peter Galison. 'The Image of Objectivity'. *Representations* 40, no. 40 (1992): 81–128.

Davenne, Christine. *Cabinets of Wonder*. New York: Harry N. Abrams, 2012.

Department of Pathology, University of Melbourne. *The Melbourne School of Pathology: Phases and Contrasts*. Parkville: University of Melbourne Department of Pathology, 1962.

Degueurce, Christophe. 'The Celebrated Écorchés of Honoré Fragonard, Part 1: The Classical Techniques of Preparation of Dry Anatomical Specimens in the 18th Century'. Translated by Philip Adds. *Clinical Anatomy* 23, no. 3 (2010): 249–57.

Del Río Parra, Elena. '"He Has No Pulse": Typologies of the Fear of Being Buried Alive in Preindustrial Spain'. *South Atlantic Review* 76, no. 3 (2011): 129–50.

Devine, Shauna. *Learning from the Wounded: The Civil War and the Rise of American Medical Science*. Chapel Hill, NC: The University of North Carolina Press, 2014.

Dittmar, Jenna M., and Piers D. Mitchell. 'From Cradle to Grave via the Dissection Room: The Role of Foetal and Infant Bodies in Anatomical Education from the Late 1700s to Early 1900s'. *Journal of Anatomy* 229, no. 6 (2016): 713–22.
Domańska, Ewa. 'The Return to Things'. *Archaeologia Polona* 44 (2006): 171–85.
Donlon, Denise. 'Aboriginal Skeletal Collections and Research in Physical Anthropology: An Historical Perspective'. *Australian Archaeology* 39 (1994): 73–82.
Dubow, Sara. *Ourselves Unborn: A History of the Fetus in Modern America*. New York: Oxford University Press, 2010.
Duden, Barbara. *Disembodying Women: Perspectives on Pregnancy and the Unborn*. Cambridge, MA: Harvard University Press, 1993.
Duden, Barbara. 'The Foetus on the "Farther Shore": Toward a History of the Unborn'. In *Fetal Subjects, Feminist Positions*, edited by Lynn M. Morganand Meredith W. Michaels, 13–25. Pennsylvania, PA: University of Pennsylvania Press, 1999.
Durbach, Nadja. *Spectacle of Deformity: Freak Shows and Modern British Culture*. Berkeley: University of California Press, 2010.
Ebenstein, Joanna. *The Anatomical Venus*. London: Thames and Hudson, 2016.
Eichhorn, Philip, Udo Andraschke, Fritz Dross, Carol I. Geppert, Arndt Hartmann and Tilman T. Rau. 'Restoration of an Academic Historical Gross Pathology Collection – Refreshed Impact on Current Medical Teaching?' *Virchows Archiv* 473, no. 2 (2018): 219–28.
Elmslie, R. G. 'Early Anatomists of the Adelaide Medical School'. *Australian and New Zealand Journal of Surgery* 57, no. 11 (1987): 865–9.
Fahy, Kathleen. 'An Australian History of the Subordination of Midwifery'. *Women and Birth* 20, no. 1 (2007): 25–9.
Farey, John E., Jonathan C. Sandeford, and Greg D. Evans-mckendry. 'Medical Students Call for National Standards in Anatomical Education'. *ANZ Journal of Surgery* 84, no. 11 (2014): 813–5.
Faulkhead, Shannon, and Jim Berg. *Power and the Passion: Our Ancestors Return Home*. Melbourne: Koorie Heritage Trust Inc, 2010.
Featherstone, Lisa. 'Becoming a Baby? The Foetus in Late Nineteenth-Century Australia'. *Australian Feminist Studies* 23, no. 58 (2008): 451–65.
Featherstone, Lisa. 'The Kindest Cut? The Caesarean Section as Turning Point, Australia 1880–1900'. In *Motherhood: Power and Oppression*, edited by Marie Porter, Patricia Short, and Andrea O'Reilly, 25–40. Toronto: Women's Press, 2005.
Feldman, Mark B. 'Remembering a Convulsive War: Whitman's Memoranda during the War and the Therapeutics of Display'. *Walt Whitman Quarterly Review* 23, no. 1 (2005): 1–25.
Ferber, Sarah, and Sally Wilde, eds. *The Body Divided: Human Beings and Human 'Material' in Modern Medical History*. Aldershot: Ashgate, 2011.
Fforde, Cressida. *Collecting the Dead: Archaeology and the Reburial Issue*. London: Duckworth, 2004.
Fforde, Cressida. 'From Edinburgh University to the Ngarrindjeri Nation, South Australia'. *Museum International* 61, no. 1–2 (2009): 41–7.

Fforde, Cressida, C. Timothy McKeown and Honor Keeler, eds., *The Routledge Companion to Indigenous Repatriation: Return, Reconcile, Renew*. London: Routledge 2020.

Finch, Lyn, and Jon Stratton. 'The Australian Working Class and the Practice of Abortion 1880–1939'. *Journal of Australian Studies* 12, no. 23 (1988): 45–64.

Findlen, Paula. *Possessing Nature: Museums, Collecting, and Scientific Culture in Early Modern Italy*. Berkeley: University of California Press, 1996.

Fontein, Joost. 'Between Tortured Bodies and Resurfacing Bones: The Politics of the Dead in Zimbabwe'. *Journal of Material Culture* 15, no. 4 (2010): 423–48.

Gandevia, Bryan. *The Melbourne Medical Students, 1862–1942: Being a Review of Their Numerous Activities, with a Summary of the History of the Medical School and a List of Office-Bearers in the M.S.S.* Melbourne: Melbourne Medical Students' Society, 1948.

Gatrell, V. A. C. *The Hanging Tree: Execution and the English People 1770–1868*. Oxford: Oxford University Press, 1994.

Geary, Laurence M. 'The Scottish-Australian Connection, 1850–1900'. In *The History of Medical Education in Britain*, edited by Vivian Nutton and Roy Porter, 51–75. Atlanta, GA: Rodopi, 1995.

Gillespie, James. 'Medical Markets and Australian Medical Politics, 1920–45'. *Labour History* 54 (1988): 30–46.

Glaskin, Katie. 'Anatomies of Relatedness: Considering Personhood in Aboriginal Australia'. *American Anthropologist* 114, no. 2 (2012): 297–308.

Golden, Janet Lynne. *Babies Made Us Modern: How Infants Brought America into the Twentieth Century*. New York: Cambridge University Press, 2018.

Good, Byron J. *Medicine, Rationality, and Experience: An Anthropological Perspective*. Cambridge: Cambridge University Press, 1994.

Gorman, Joshua M. 'Universalism and the New Museology: Impacts on the Ethics of Authority and Ownership'. *Museum Management and Curatorship* 26, no. 2 (2011): 149–62.

Gould, Bronte. 'The Professional Midwife: Adelaide's Destitute Asylum and Midwifery in South Australia, 1880–1900'. *Journal of the Historical Society of South Australia* 42 (2014): 5–16.

Grehan, Madonna. '"From the Sphere of Sarah Gampism": The Professionalisation of Nursing and Midwifery in the Colony of Victoria'. *Nursing Inquiry* 11, no. 3 (2004): 192–201.

Griffin, Graeme M., and Des Tobin. *In the Midst of Life … The Australian Response to Death*, 2nd ed. Carlton: Melbourne University Press, 1997.

Griffiths, Tom. *Hunters and Collectors: The Antiquarian Imagination in Australia*. Cambridge: Cambridge University Press, 1996.

Hafferty, Frederic. 'Cadaver Stories and the Emotional Socialization of Medical Students'. *Journal of Health and Social Behavior* 29, no. 4 (1988): 344–56.

Hallam, Elizabeth. *Anatomy Museum: Death and the Body Displayed*. London: Reaktion Books Ltd, 2016.

Hearder, Rosalind. 'Battlefield Legacies: The Australian Collection of WW1 Pathological Specimens'. *Australian Military Medicine* 8, no. 3 (1999): 24–8.

Hendriksen, Marieke M. A. *Elegant Anatomy: The Eighteenth-Century Leiden Anatomical Collections*. Leiden: Brill, 2014.

Herewini, Te Herekiekie. 'The Museum of New Zealand Te Papa Tongarewa (Te Papa) and the Repatriation of Kōiwi Tangata (Māori and Moriori Skeletal Remains) and Toi Moko (Mummified Māori Tattooed Heads)'. *International Journal of Cultural Property* 15, no. 4 (2008): 405–6.

Highet, Megan J. 'Body Snatching & Grave Robbing: Bodies for Science'. *History and Anthropology* 16, no. 4 (2005): 415–40.

Hobbins, Peter. '"Outside the Institute There Is a Desert": The Tenuous Trajectories of Medical Research in Interwar Australia'. *Medical History* 54 (2010): 1–28.

Hodder, Ian. *Entangled: An Archaeology of the Relationships between Humans and Things*. Malden, MA: Wiley-Blackwell, 2012.

Hoffenburg, Peter. '"A Science of Our Own": Nineteenth Century Exhibitions, Australians and the History of Science'. In *Science and Empire: Knowledge and Networks of Science Across the British Empire, 1800–1970*, edited by Joseph M. Hodge and Brett M. Bennett, 140–59. London: Palgrave Macmillan, 2011.

Hooper-Greenhill, Eilean. *Museums and the Shaping of Knowledge*. London: Routledge, 1992.

Hopwood, Nick. '"Giving Body" to Embryos: Modeling, Mechanism, and the Microtome in Late Nineteenth-Century Anatomy'. *Isis* 90, no. 3 (1999): 462–96.

Hopwood, Nick. 'Producing Development: The Anatomy of Human Embryos and the Norms of Wilhelm His'. *Bulletin of the History of Medicine* 74, no. 1 (2000): 29–79.

Huistra, Hieke. *The Afterlife of the Leiden Anatomical Collections: Hands On, Hands Off*. London: Routledge, 2019.

Hurren, Elizabeth T. *Dissecting the Criminal Corpse: Staging Post-Execution Punishment in Early Modern England*. London: Palgrave Macmillan, 2016.

Hurren, Elizabeth T. *Dying for Victorian Medicine: English Anatomy and Its Trade in the Dead Poor, c. 1834–1929*. Basingstoke: Palgrave Macmillan, 2012.

Hutchinson, Erin F., Beverley Kramer, Brendon K. Billings, Desiré M. Brits, and Nalini Pather. 'The Law, Ethics and Body Donation: A Tale of Two Bequeathal Programs'. *Anatomical Sciences Education* 14, no. 4 (2019): 1–8.

Jalland, Patricia. *Australian Ways of Death: A Social and Cultural History 1840–1918*. South Melbourne: Oxford University Press, 2002.

Jalland, Patricia. *Death in the Victorian Family*. Oxford: Oxford University Press, 1996.

Jefferies, Ryan. 'War Wounds'. In *Compassion and Courage: Australian Doctors and Dentists in the Great War*, edited by Jacqueline Healy, 130. Melbourne: Medical History Museum, University of Melbourne, 2015.

Jenkins, Tiffany. *Contesting Human Remains in Museum Collections: The Crisis of Cultural Authority*. New York: Routledge, 2011.

Jenkins, Tiffany. '"Who Are We to Decide?" Internal Challenges to Cultural Authority in the Contestation over Human Remains in British Museums'. *Cultural Sociology* 6, no. 4 (2012): 455–70.

Jones, D. Gareth. *Speaking for the Dead: Cadavers in Biology and Medicine*. Aldershot: Ashgate, 2000.

Jones, D. Gareth, and Maja I. Whitaker. 'Engaging with Plastination and the Body Worlds Phenomenon: A Cultural and Intellectual Challenge for Anatomists'. *Clinical Anatomy* 22, no. 6 (2009): 770–6.

Jones, D. Gareth, and Maja I. Whitaker. 'The Contested Realm of Displaying Dead Bodies'. *Journal of Medical Ethics* 39, no. 10 (2013): 652–3.

Jones, D. Gareth, R. Gear, and K. A. Galvin. 'Stored Human Tissue: An Ethical Perspective on the Fate of Anonymous, Archival Material'. *Journal of Medical Ethics* 29, no. 6 (2003): 343–7.

Jones, Michael. 'From Catalogues to Contextual Networks: Reconfiguring Collection Documentation in Museums'. *Archives and Records* 39, no. 1 (2018): 4–20.

Jones, Ross L. *Anatomists of Empire: Race, Evolution and the Discovery of Human Biology in the British World*. Melbourne: Australian Scholarly Publishing, 2020.

Jones, Ross L. 'Cadavers and the Social Dimension of Dissection'. In *The Body Divided: Human Beings and Human 'Material' in Modern Medical History*, edited by Sarah Ferber and Sally Wilde, 29–52. Aldershot: Ashgate, 2011.

Jones, Ross L. 'Medical Schools and Aboriginal Bodies'. In *Power and the Passion: Our Ancestors Return Home*, edited by Shannon Faulkhead and Jim Berg, 50–5. Melbourne: Koorie Heritage Trust Inc, 2010.

Kelly, Laura. 'Irish Medical Student Culture and the Performance of Masculinity, c. 1880–1930'. *History of Education* 46, no. 1 (2017): 39–57.

Kenny, Stephen C. 'The Development of Medical Museums in the Antebellum American South: Slave Bodies in Networks of Anatomical Exchange'. *Bulletin of the History of Medicine* 87, no. 1 (2013): 32–62.

Kevin, Catherine. '"I Did Not Lose My Baby … My Baby Just Died": Twenty-First-Century Discourses of Miscarriage in Political and Historical Context'. *South Atlantic Quarterly* 110, no. 4 (2011): 849–65.

Kevin, Catherine. 'Maternal Responsibility and Traceable Loss: Medicine and Miscarriage in Twentieth-Century Australia'. *Women's History Review* 26, no. 6 (2017): 840–56.

Klestinec, Cynthia. *Theaters of Anatomy: Students, Teachers, and Traditions of Dissection in Renaissance Venice*. Baltimore, MD: Johns Hopkins University Press, 2011.

Knoeff, Rina. 'The Visitor's View: Early Modern Tourism and the Polyvalence of Anatomical Exhibits'. In *Centres and Cycles of Accumulation in and around the Netherlands during the Early Modern Period*, edited by Lissa Roberts, 155–75. Berlin: Lit, 2011.

Kopytoff, Igor. 'The Cultural Biography of Things: Commoditisation as Process'. In *The Social Life of Things: Commodities in Cultural Perspective*, edited by Arjun Appadurai, 64–94. Cambridge: Cambridge University Press, 1986.

Korf, Horst-Werner, Helmut Wicht, Robert L. Snipes, Jean-Pierre Timmermans, Friedrich Paulsen, Gabriele Rune, and Eveline Baumgart-Vogt. 'The Dissection Course – Necessary and Indispensable for Teaching Anatomy to Medical Students'. *Annals of Anatomy* 190, no. 1 (2008): 16–22.

Kornmeier, Uta. 'Almost Alive: The Spectacle of Verisimilitude in Madame Tussaud's Waxworks'. In *Ephemeral Bodies: Wax Sculpture and the Human Figure*, edited by Roberta Panzanelli, 67–81. Los Angeles, CA: Getty Research Institute, 2008.

Kristin D. Hussey, *Imperial Bodies in London: Empire, Mobility, and the Making of British Medicine, 1880–1914*. Pittsburgh: University of Pittsburgh Press, 2021.

Kraft, Alison, and Samuel J. M. M. Alberti. '"Equal though Different": Laboratories, Museums and the Institutional Development of Biology in Late-Victorian Northern England'. *Studies in History and Philosophy of Biological & Biomedical Sciences* 34, no. 2 (2003): 203–36.

Krmpotich, Cara. 'Remembering and Repatriation: The Production of Kinship, Memory and Respect'. *Journal of Material Culture* 15, no. 2 (2010): 157–79.

Krmpotich, Cara, Joost Fontein, and John Harries. 'The Substance of Bones: The Emotive Materiality and Affective Presence of Human Remains'. *Journal of Material Culture* 15, no. 4 (2010): 371–84.

Kubicki, Francesca. 'Recreated Faces: Facial Disfigurement, Plastic Surgery, Photography and the Great War'. *Photography and Culture* 2, no. 2 (2009): 183–94.

Landes, Joan B. 'Wax Fibers, Wax Bodies, and Moving Figure: Artifice and Nature in Eighteenth-Century Anatomy'. In *Ephemeral Bodies: Wax Sculpture and the Human Figure*, edited by Roberta Panzanelli, 41–65. Los Angeles, CA: Getty Research Institute, 2008.

Laqueur, Thomas W. *The Work of the Dead: A Cultural History of Mortal Remains*. Princeton, NJ: Princeton University Press, 2018.

Larsson, Marina. 'Restoring the Spirit: The Rehabilitation of Disabled Soldiers in Australia after the Great War'. *Health and History* 6, no. 2 (2004): 45–59.

Larsson, Marina. *Shattered Anzacs: Living with the Scars of War*. Kensington: UNSW Press, 2009.

Lawrence, Susan C. 'Educating the Senses: Students, Teachers and Medical Rhetoric in Eighteenth-Century London'. In *Medicine and the Five Senses*, edited by W. F. Bynum and Roy Porter, 154–78. Cambridge: Cambridge University Press, 1993.

Layne, Linda. *Motherhood Lost: A Feminist Account of Pregnancy Loss in America*. New York: Routledge, 2003.

Leavitt, Judith Walzer. '"Science" Enters the Birthing Room: Obstetrics in America since the Eighteenth Century'. *The Journal of American History* 70, no. 2 (1983): 281–304.

Leavitt, Judith Walzer. 'The Growth of Medical Authority: Technology and Morals in Turn-of-the-Century Obstetrics'. *Medical Anthropology Quarterly* 1, no. 3 (1987): 230–55.

Leavitt, Sarah A. '"A Private Little Revolution": The Home Pregnancy Test in American Culture'. *Bulletin of the History of Medicine* 80, no. 2 (2006): 317–45.

Lee, Ruth L. *Woman War Doctor: The Life of Mary De Garis*. Melbourne: Australian Scholarly, 2014.

Leonetti, G., M. Signoli, A. L. Pelissier, P. Champsaur, I. Hershkovitz, C. Brunet, and O. Dutour. 'Evidence of Pin Implantation as a Means of Verifying Death during the Great Plague of Marseilles (1722)'. *Journal of Forensic Sciences* 42, no. 4 (1997): 744–8.

Lester, Alan. 'Imperial Circuits and Networks: Geographies of the British Empire: Imperial Circuits and Networks'. *History Compass* 4, no. 1 (2006): 124–41.

Lewin, Roger. 'Extinction Threatens Australian Anthropology'. *Council for Museum Anthropology Newsletter* 9, no. 3 (1985): 7–9.

Lewis, Milton J. 'Medicine in Colonial Australia, 1788–1900'. *The Medical Journal of Australia* 201, no. 1 Suppl (2014): S5–10.

Lucas, A. M. 'Specimens and the Currency of Honour: The Museum Trade of Ferdinand von Mueller'. *Historical Records of Australian Science* 24, no. 1 (n.d.): 15–39.

Lyford, Amy. 'The Aesthetics of Dismemberment: Surrealism and the Musée du Val-de-Grâce in 1917'. *Cultural Critique* 46 (2000): 45–79.

Lyford, Amy. *Surrealist Masculinities: Gender Anxiety and the Aesthetics of Post-World War I Reconstruction in France*. Berkeley, CA: University of California Press, 2007.

MacDonald, Helen. 'A Dissection in Reverse: Mary McLauchlan, Hobart Town, 1830'. *Lilith: A Feminist History Journal* 13 (2006): 12–24.

MacDonald, Helen. 'A Scandalous Act: Regulating Anatomy in a British Settler Colony, Tasmania 1869'. *Social History of Medicine* 20, no. 1 (2007): 39–56.

MacDonald, Helen. '"Humanity's Discards": The New South Wales Anatomy Act 1881'. *Mortality* 12, no. 4 (2007): 365–82.

MacDonald, Helen. 'The Anatomy Inspector and the Government Corpse'. *History Australia* 6, no. 2 (2009): 40.1–40.17.

MacDonald, Helen. *Possessing the Dead: The Artful Science of Anatomy*. Carlton: Melbourne University Press, 2010.

MacDonald, Helen. 'Procuring Corpses: The English Anatomy Inspectorate, 1842–1858'. *Medical History* 53, no. 3 (2009): 379–96.

MacKenzie, John M. *Museums and Empire: Natural History, Human Cultures and Colonial Identities*. Manchester: Manchester University Press, 2009.

Maerker, Anna. 'Between Profession and Performance: Displays of Anatomical Models in London, 1831–32'. *Histoire, Médecine et Santé* 5, no. 2 (2014): 47–59.

Mangham, Andrew. 'Buried Alive: The Gothic Awakening of Taphephobia'. *The Journal of Literature and Science* 3, no. 1 (2010): 10–22.

Maple, Eric. *Magic, Medicine & Quackery*. London: Hale, 1968.

Margócsy, Dániel. 'Advertising Cadavers in the Republic of Letters: Anatomical Publications in the Early Modern Netherlands'. *The British Journal for the History of Science* 42, no. 2 (2009): 187–210.

Marie Porter, Patricia Short, and Andrea O'Reilly. '"The Value of the Victorian Infant": Whiteness and the Emergence of Paediatrics in Late Colonial Australia'. In

*Historicising Whiteness: Transnational Perspectives on the Construction of an Identity*, edited by Jane Carey, Leigh Boucher, and Katherine Ellinghaus, 445–53. Melbourne: RMIT Publishing, 2007.

Maroske, Sara. '"A Taste for Botanic Science": Ferdinand Mueller's Female Collectors and the History of Australian Botany'. *Muelleria* 32 (2014): 72–91.

Martyr, Philippa. *Paradise of Quacks: An Alternative History of Medicine in Australia*. Paddington: Macleay Press, 2002.

Mason, Michael. *The Making of Victorian Sexuality*. Oxford: Oxford University Press, 1995.

Mazzolini, Renato G. 'Plastic Anatomies and Artificial Distinctions'. In *Models: The Third Dimension of Science*, edited by Nick Hopwood and Soraya de Chadarevian, 43–70. Stanford, CA: Stanford University Press, 2004.

McCall, Vikki, and Clive Gray. 'Museums and the "New Museology": Theory, Practice and Organisational Change'. *Museum Management and Curatorship* 29, no. 1 (2014): 19–35.

McCalman, Janet. *Sex and Suffering: Women's Health and a Women's Hospital*. Carlton: Melbourne University Press, 1998.

McCorristine, Shane. *The Spectral Arctic: A History of Dreams and Ghosts in Polar Exploration*. London: UCL Press, 2018.

McCracken-Flesher, Caroline. *The Doctor Dissected: A Cultural Autopsy of the Burke and Hare Murders*. Oxford: Oxford University Press, 2012.

McKernan, Michael. *Here Is Their Spirit: A History of the Australian War Memorial 1917–1990*. St. Lucia, QLD: University of Queensland Press in association with the Australian War Memorial, 1991.

McLaughlin, Loretta. *The Pill, John Rock, and the Church: The Biography of a Revolution*. New York: Little, Brown and Company, 1982.

McLeary, Erin. 'Science in a Bottle: The Medical Museum in North America, 1860–1940'. PhD diss., University of Pennsylvania, 2001.

McMeeken, Joan. 'From Massage to Physiotherapy: The Emergence of a Profession'. In *The First World War, the Universities and the Professions in Australia 1914–1939*, edited by Kate Darian-Smith and James Waghorne, 77–93. Carlton: Melbourne University Press, 2019.

McWilliams, Rob. 'Resting Places: A History of Australian Indigenous Ancestral Remains at Museum Victoria', 2016. https://museumsvictoria.com.au/media/4273/resting_places__history_of_ancestral_remains_25_aug_2016.docx (accessed 3 February 2023).

Melrose, Craig. 'The Australian War Memorial and the "Culture Wars": The Representation of Triumph and Sacrifice in Inter-War Commemoration'. *ACH: The Journal of the History of Culture in Australia* 26 (2007): 211–32.

Michaels, Meredith W., and Lynn M. Morgan. 'The Fetal Imperative'. In *Fetal Subjects, Feminist Positions*, 1–12. Pennsylvania, PA: University of Pennsylvania Press, 1999.

Moore, Wendy. *The Knife Man*. London: Bantam, 2005.

Morgan, Lynn M. *Icons of Life: A Cultural History of Human Embryos*. Berkeley, CA: University of California Press, 2009.

Morgan, Lynn M. '"Properly Disposed Of": A History of Embryo Disposal and the Changing Claims on Fetal Remains'. *Medical Anthropology* 21, no. 3–4 (2002): 247–74.

Morgan, Lynn M. 'The Rise and Demise of a Collection of Human Fetuses at Mount Holyoke College'. *Perspectives in Biology and Medicine* 49, no. 3 (2006): 435–51.

Morison, Patricia. *J. T. Wilson and the Fraternity of Duckmaloi*. Amsterdam: Rodopi B.V., 1997.

Morton, Sarah. 'The Legacies of the Repatriation of Human Remains from the Royal College of Surgeons of England'. PhD thesis, University of Oxford, 2018.

Nash, Catherine. 'Making Kinship with Human Remains: Repatriation, Biomedicine and the Many Relations of Charles Byrne'. *Environment and Planning D: Society and Space* 36, no. 5 (2018): 867–84.

Neale, Kerry. '"Without the Faces of Men": The Return of Facially Disfigured Veterans from the Great War'. In *When the Soldiers Return Conference Proceedings, Brisbane, November 2007*, 114–20. Brisbane: University of Queensland, 2007.

Norman, Heidi and Anne Maree Payne. 'Nowhere Else but Home: A National Resting Place for Indigenous Australian Ancestral Remains'. *The Museum Journal* 65, no. 4 (2022): 817–34.

Nutton, Vivian, and Roy Porter, eds. *The History of Medical Education in Britain*. Atlanta, GA: Rodopi, 1995.

O'Sullivan, Lisa, and Ross Jones. 'Two Australian Fetuses: Frederic Wood Jones and the Work of an Anatomical Specimen'. *Bulletin of the History of Medicine* 89, no. 2 (2015): 243–66.

Pacitti, Eugenia. 'Dissecting the Student Experience at Australian Medical Schools, 1884–1912'. *Social History of Medicine* 34, no. 1 (2021): 467–88.

Park, Katharine. 'The Life of the Corpse: Division and Dissection in Late Medieval Europe'. *Journal of the History of Medicine and Allied Sciences* 50, no. 1 (1995): 111–32.

Parker, Lisa M. 'Anatomical Dissection: Why Are We Cutting It Out? Dissection in Undergraduate Teaching'. *ANZ Journal of Surgery* 72, no. 12 (2002): 910–2.

Parsons, Christopher M., and Kathleen S. Murphy. 'Ecosystems under Sail: Specimen Transport in the Eighteenth-Century French and British Atlantics'. *Early American Studies: An Interdisciplinary Journal* 10, no. 3 (2012): 503–29.

Patel, Salil B., Daniel Mauro, James Fenn, Dermot R. Sharkey, and Conor Jones. 'Is Dissection the Only Way to Learn Anatomy? Thoughts from Students at a Non-Dissecting Based Medical School'. *Perspectives on Medical Education* 4, no. 5 (2015): 259–60.

Penfold-Mounce, Ruth. 'Consuming Criminal Corpses: Fascination with the Dead Criminal Body'. *Mortality* 15, no. 3 (2010): 250–65.

Penny, H. Glenn. *Objects of Culture: Ethnology and Ethnographic Museums in Imperial Germany*. Chapel Hill, NC: University of North Carolina Press, 2002.

Pensabene, T. S. *The Rise of the Medical Practitioner in Victoria*. Research Monograph (Australian National University. Health Research Project) 2. Canberra: Australian National University, 1980.

Petch, Alison. 'Collecting Immortality: The Field Collectors Who Contributed to the Pitt Rivers Museum, Oxford'. *Journal of Museum Ethnography* 16 (2004): 127–39.

Petrow, Stefan. 'The Last Man: The Mutilation of William Lanne in 1869 and Its Aftermath'. *Aboriginal History Journal* 21 (2011): 90–112.

Pickering, Michael. '"The Big Picture": The Repatriation of Australian Indigenous Sacred Objects'. *Museum Management and Curatorship* 30, no. 5 (2015): 427–43.

Pickering, Michael. 'Policy and Research Issues Affecting Human Remains in Australian Museum Collections'. In *Human Remains and Museum Practice*, edited by Jack Lohman and Katherine Goodnow, 42–7. New York: Berghahn Books, 2006.

Pickering, Michael. 'Where Are the Stories?' *The Public Historian* 32, no. 1 (2010): 79–95.

Pietsch, Tamson. 'Between the Nation and the World: J. T. Wilson and Scientific Networks in the Early Twentieth Century'. In *Science and Empire: Knowledge and Networks of Science Across the British Empire, 1800–1970*, edited by Joseph M. Hodgeand Brett M. Bennett, 140–59. London: Palgrave Macmillan, 2011.

Pietsch, Tamson. *Empire of Scholars: Universities, Networks and the British Academic World, 1850–1939*. Manchester: Manchester University Press, 2013.

Pietsch, Tamson. 'Wandering Scholars? Academic Mobility and the British World, 1850–1940'. *Journal of Historical Geography* 36, no. 4 (2010): 377–87.

Pomian, Krzysztof. *Collectors and Curiosities: Paris and Venice 1500–1800*. Cambridge: Polity Press, 1990.

Ponce, Rachel N. '"They Increase in Beauty and Elegance": Transforming Cadavers and the Epistemology of Dissection in Early Nineteenth-Century American Medical Education'. *Journal of the History of Medicine and Allied Sciences* 68, no. 3 (2013): 331–76.

Porter, Roy, and Lesley Hall. *The Facts of Life: The Creation of Sexual Knowledge in Britain, 1650–950*. New Haven, CT: Yale University Press, 1995.

Porth, Emily F. 'When Women Birthed Mooncalves and Moles: The Display of Fetal Remains and the Invisibility of Females in Museums'. *Humanimalia: A Journal of Human/Animal Interface Studies* 4, no. 1 (2012): 1–44.

Purcal, Nita K. 'The Politics of Midwifery Education and Training in New South Wales during the Last Decades of the 19th Century'. *Women and Birth* 21, no. 1 (2008): 21–5.

Quigley, Christine. *Dissection on Display: Cadavers, Anatomists, and Public Spectacle*. Jefferson, NC: McFarland & Co., 2012.

Quigley, Christine. *The Corpse: A History*. Jefferson, NC: McFarland, 1996.

Qureshi, Sadiah. *Peoples on Parade: Exhibitions, Empire, and Anthropology in Nineteenth-Century Britain*. Chicago and London: The University of Chicago Press, 2011.

Reagan, Leslie J. 'From Hazard to Blessing to Tragedy: Representations of Miscarriage in Twentieth-Century America'. *Feminist Studies* 29, no. 2 (2003): 357–78.

Redman, Samuel J. *Bone Rooms: From Scientific Racism to Human Prehistory in Museums*. Cambridge, MA: Harvard University Press, 2016.

Reinarz, Jonathan. 'Learning to Use Their Senses: Visitors to Voluntary Hospitals in Eighteenth-Century England'. *Journal for Eighteenth-Century Studies* 35, no. 4 (2012): 505–20.

Reinarz, Jonathan. 'The Age of Museum Medicine: The Rise and Fall of the Medical Museum at Birmingham's School of Medicine'. *Social History of Medicine* 18, no. 3 (2005): 419–37.

Richardson, Ruth. *Death, Dissection, and the Destitute*. London: Routledge, 1987.

Richardson, Ruth. *The Making of Mr. Gray's Anatomy*. Oxford: Oxford University Press, 2008.

Richardson, Ruth, and Brian Hurwitz. 'Celebrating New Year in Bart's Dissecting Room'. *Clinical Anatomy* 9, no. 6 (1996): 408–13.

Roberts, Lissa. 'Accumulation and Management in Global Historical Perspective: An Introduction'. *History of Science* 52, no. 3 (2014): 227–46.

Roginski, Alexandra. *The Hanged Man and the Body Thief: Finding Lives in a Museum Mystery*. Clayton: Monash University Publishing, 2015.

Roginski, Alexandra. *Science and Power in the Nineteenth-Century Tasman World: Popular Phrenology in Australia and Aotearoa New Zealand*. Cambridge; New York: Cambridge University Press, 2023.

Rose, Deborah Bird. *Nourishing Terrains: Australian Aboriginal Views of Landscape and Wilderness*. Canberra: Australian Heritage Commission, 1996.

Rosner, Lisa. *The Anatomy Murders: Being the True and Spectacular History of Edinburgh's Notorious Burke and Hare and of the Man of Science Who Abetted Them in the Commission of Their Most Heinous Crimes*. Philadelphia, PA: University of Pennsylvania Press, 2011.

Russell, K. F. *The Melbourne Medical School, 1862–1962*. Carlton: Melbourne University Press, 1977.

Russell, K. F. 'Richard James Arthur Berry, 1867–1962'. In *Festschrift for Kenneth Fitzpatrick Russell: Proceedings of a Symposium Arranged by the Section of Medical History, A. M. A. (Victorian Branch), 25th February 1977*, edited by Geoffrey Kenny and Harold Atwood, 25–45. Carlton: Queensberry Hill Press, 1978.

Russell, Lynette. 'Reflections on Murray Black's Writings'. In *Power and the Passion: Our Ancestors Return Home*, 56–63. Melbourne: Koorie Heritage Trust Inc, 2010.

Sappol, Michael. *A Traffic of Dead Bodies: Anatomy and Embodied Social Identity in Nineteenth-Century America*. Princeton, NJ: Princeton University Press, 2002.

Sarah Ferber and Sally Wilde. *Humanity's Mirror: 150 Years of Anatomy in Melbourne*. South Yarra: Haddington Press, 2007.

Sarah Ferber and Sally Wilde. 'The Master Potter and the Rejected Pots: Eugenic Legislation in Victoria, 1918–1939'. *Australian Historical Studies* 29, no. 113 (1999): 319–42.

Schnalke, Thomas. 'Dissected Limbs and the Integral Body: On Anatomical Wax Models and Medical Moulages'. *Interdisciplinary Science Reviews* 29, no. 3 (2004): 312–22.
Schultka, Rüdiger, and Michael Viebig. 'The Fate of the Bodies of Executed Persons in the Anatomical Institute of Halle between 1933 and 1945'. *Annals of Anatomy – Anatomischer Anzeiger*, Special Issue: Anatomy in the Third Reich, 194, no. 3 (2012): 274–80.
Seidemann, Ryan M. 'NAGPRA at 20: What Have the States Done to Expand Human Remains Protections?' *Museum Anthropology* 33, no. 2 (2010): 199–209.
Selleck, R. J. W. *The Shop: The University of Melbourne 1850–1939*. Carlton: Melbourne University Press, 2003.
Servitje, Lorenzo. 'Birthed from the Clinic: The Degenerate Medical Students of Edward Berdoe's St. Bernard's'. *Critical Survey* 27, no. 2 (2015): 21–35.
Shapin, Steven. 'The Invisible Technician'. *American Scientist* 77, no. 6 (1989): 554–63.
Sheard, Heather, and Ruth Lee. *Women to the Front*. Sydney: Random House Australia, 2019.
Simpson, Donald. 'The Adelaide Medical School, 1885–1913: A Study of Anglo-Australian Synergies in Medical Education'. PhD thesis, University of Adelaide, 2000.
Simpson, Donald. 'English Roots of Medical Education in Australasia: Kenneth F. Russell Memorial Lecture'. *Australian and New Zealand Journal of Surgery* 70, no. 12 (2000): 843–50.
Smith, Andrew. *Victorian Demons: Medicine, Masculinity and the Gothic at the Fin-de-Siècle*. Manchester: University Press, 2004.
Smith, Laurajane. 'The Repatriation of Human Remains – Problem or Opportunity?' *Antiquity* 78, no. 300 (2004): 404–13.
Stephens, Elizabeth. *Anatomy as Spectacle: Public Exhibitions of the Body from 1700 to the Present*. Liverpool: Liverpool University Press, 2011.
Strachan, Glenda. 'Present at the Birth: Midwives, "Handywomen" and Neighbours in Rural New South Wales, 1850–1900'. *Labour History* 81 (2001): 13–28.
Strange, Julie-Marie. *Death, Grief and Poverty in Britain, 1870–1914*. New York: Cambridge University Press, 2005.
Squire, Michael. *The Art of the Body: Antiquity and Its Legacy*. New York: Oxford University Press, 2011.
Taylor, William M. 'War Remains: Contributions of the Imperial War Graves Commission and the Australian War Records Section to Material and National Cultures of Conflict and Commemoration'. *National Identities* 17, no. 2 (2015): 217–40.
Tuggle, Lindsay. 'The Afterlives of Specimens: Walt Whitman and the Army Medical Museum'. *Walt Whitman Quarterly Review* 32, no. 1–2 (2014): 1–35.

Turnbull, Paul. 'Anthropological Collecting and Colonial Violence in Colonial Queensland: A Response to "the Blood and Bone"'. *Journal of Australian Colonial History* 17 (2015): 133–58.

Turnbull, Paul. 'British Anatomists, Phrenologists and the Construction of the Aboriginal Race, c. 1790–1830'. *History Compass* 5, no. 1 (2007): 26–50.

Turnbull, Paul. *Science, Museums and Collecting the Indigenous Dead in Colonial Australia*. Basingstoke: Palgrave Macmillan, 2017.

Vergo, Peter. *The New Museology*. London: Reaktion Books, 1989.

Waddington, Keir. 'Death at St Bernard's: Anti-Vivisection, Medicine and the Gothic'. *Journal of Victorian Culture* 18, no. 2 (2013): 246–62.

Waddington, Keir. 'Mayhem and Medical Students: Image, Conduct, and Control in the Victorian and Edwardian London Teaching Hospital'. *Social History of Medicine* 15, no. 1 (2002): 45–64.

Waghorne, James. 'Growth and Specialisation: The Medical Profession in Interwar Australia'. In *The First World War, the Universities and the Professions in Australia 1914–1939*, edited by Kate Darian-Smith and James Waghorne, 29–47. Carlton: Melbourne University Press, 2019.

Walkowitz, Judith R. *City of Dreadful Delight: Narratives of Sexual Danger in Late-Victorian London*. London: Virago, 1992.

Warner, John Harley, and James M. Edmonson. *Dissection: Photographs of a Rite of Passage in American Medicine, 1880–1930*. New York: Blast Books, 2009.

Weindling, Paul. '"Cleansing" Anatomical Collections: The Politics of Removing Specimens from German Anatomical and Medical Collections 1988–92'. *Annals of Anatomy* 194, no. 3 (2012): 237–42.

Weindling, Paul. 'From Scientific Object to Commemorated Victim: The Children of the "Spiegelgrund"'. *History and Philosophy of the Life Sciences* 35, no. 3 (2013): 415–30.

Willis, Chris. 'A House for the Dead: Victorian Mausolea and Graveyard Gothic'. *Victorian Gothic: Leeds Centre for Working Papers in Victorian Studies* 6 (2003): 155–65.

Winter, Jay. 'Museums and the Representation of War'. *Museum and Society* 10, no. 3 (2012): 150–63.

Withycombe, Shannon. *Lost: Miscarriage in Nineteenth-Century America*. New Brunswick, NJ: Rutgers University Press, 2019.

Withycombe, Shannon. 'Slipped Away: Pregnancy Loss in Nineteenth-Century America'. PhD thesis, University of Wisconsin, 2010.

Wittman, Laura. *The Tomb of the Unknown Soldier, Modern Mourning, and the Reinvention of the Mystical Body*. Toronto: University of Toronto Press, 2011.

Wolf, Jacqueline H. *Cesarean Section: An American History of Risk, Technology, and Consequence*. Baltimore, MD: Johns Hopkins University Press, 2018.

Young, J. A., Ann Jervie Sefton, and Nina Webb. *Centenary Book of the University of Sydney Faculty of Medicine*. Sydney: Sydney University Press, 1984.

# Index

achondroplasia xi, 87
*An Act for Regulating Schools of Anatomy* 13
AIA. *See* Australian Institute of Anatomy (AIA)
Alberti, Fay Bound 26
Alberti, Samuel 5, 45, 49, 53, 61, 99, 112, 168 n.75
Allen, Harry Brookes 1–2, 4, 6–7, 33–50, 56–64, 68–9, 85, 88–9, 100–1, 103, 105, 108–9, 117, 119, 121, 129, 136, 159 n.14
amateur collectors 35, 38, 49–51, 122, 161 n.33
American Civil War 105, 110
AMM. *See* Army Medical Museum (AMM)
anatomical models 57, 62, 66, 68
anatomist 6–7, 9–25, 41, 47, 123, 127
anatomy
    museum 43, 61, 71–3, 85, 89, 95, 106, 110, 121, 145
    persistent culture of 121–4
    public 69–74
Anatomy Act, Britain (1832) 12–13, 18
Anatomy Act, New South Wales (1977) 140
Anatomy Act, South Australia (1884) 15–16, 121
Anatomy Act, Victoria (1862) 13–16, 18, 40
Ancestral Remains 2, 4, 120, 123–5, 128–31, 133–4, 140, 143
anencephaly xi, 75
Anzac/ANZAC. *See* Australian and New Zealand Army Corps (ANZAC)
aortic aneurysm xi, 54
*Archaeological and Aboriginal Relics Preservation Act*, Victoria (1984) 125, 129, 184 n.27
*The Argus* 18–19, 22–3, 41–2
Army Medical Museum (AMM) 110–12

Ashworth, Louis 44–5
Atkinson-Wood, W. 88
Australian and New Zealand Army Corps (ANZAC) 97, 113–15
Australian Army Medical Corps (AAMC) 100, 102–4, 114, 178 n.49
Australian Institute of Anatomy (AIA) 108–9, 123
Australian Medical Association (AMA) 126
Australian War Memorial (AWM) 112, 115–17
Australian War Records Section (AWRS) 97, 99, 102, 115
Auzoux, Louis 67–8

Bakhtin, Mikhail 55
Barry, Redmond 17
Basedow, Herbert 89
Bates, A. W. 71–2
Beadles, Cecil 104
Bean, Algernon Carter 101
Beck, Samuel 72
Bell, Charles 166 n.48
Bennett, George 122
Bennett, Tony 70
Berg, Jim 125–6, 132
Berry Collection 134–5
Berry, Richard 22–3, 36, 67–8, 119, 123, 134–5
Bevers, Amanda 105
Biernoff, Suzannah 114
bioethical climate 135–41
bioethics 7, 120, 135, 141, 145
Black, George Murray 123
body parts 39–45, 49, 55–60, 74–5, 110–13, 127–8, 130
boro-salicylic powder xi, 39
Bourke, Joanna 113–14
British General Medical Council 57, 164 n.18
British Medical Association (BMA) 37, 107

Burke, William 12
Byrne, Charles 47, 138–9, 189 n.83

cadaver poem 25–30
Carnegie Institute 84, 87
Charlier, Philippe 138
childbirth 44, 76–81, 83, 85–6, 94–5
clastiques 67
cleansing 188 n.80
clinical gaze 21, 127, 130
Cohen, B. Stewart 44
Colligan, Mimi 71
*Compassion and Courage* exhibition 97, 99, 117–18
Conn, Steven 61
corrosion casts xi, 56
craniotomy xi, 94–5
Crowther, William 122–3
cultural value 43–4
culture of anatomy 8–9, 30–1, 121–4
Cuscaden, W. G. 94, 105

Daley, Paul 131
Daston, Lorraine 163 n.13
Declaration of Helsinki 135
decolonization 7, 120, 124–31, 133, 145
Department of Anatomy, University of Melbourne 125–6, 129, 134
Devine, Shauna 110
Dickens, Charles 22
disfigurement 114
dissecting room 7, 19–24, 26–8, 30, 59, 68, 146–7
dissection xi, 10–15, 21–30, 145–7
dividual body 61
Donlon, Denise 126
Dowling, Norman 39, 45–6
Drummond, John R. 102–3
dry specimens xi, 54
Dubow, Sara 88
Dunshea, Claude 114

Electoral Act, Victoria (1863) 13–14
Elmes, John 81, 83
encyclopaedia of the body 60–2
extra-uterine foetation xi, 81–2, 85, 94

Farmer, P. W. 29
Featherstone, Lisa 88
Feldman, Mark B. 110

Fetherston, Richard 79–80, 100
fibrodysplasia ossificans progressiva (FOP) xi, 58, 121
First World War 7, 97, 99–101, 105–6, 108–9, 111, 113, 115–18, 145, 175 n.16
foetal remains and specimens 7, 45–6, 66, 74–91, 93–5, 119
foetuses 75–6, 78–9, 173 n.67
    preserved in isolation 87–90
    preserved in situ 90–5
Fowler, Walter 40, 44–5, 60
'freak shows' 70, 110

Gandevia, Bryan 47
Garis, Mary de 94–5
gigantism xi, 47
Glisson's capsule xi, 57
'Government corpses' 121
Gray, Henry 55
grotesque body parts 55–60, 74

Hagens, Gunther von 139
Halford, George Britton 17–19, 41–2
Hallam, Elizabeth 61, 165 n.29
Hare, William 12
Harrison, Christopher 41
Harry Brookes Allen Museum of Anatomy and Pathology 2, 7, 34, 56, 68, 74–5, 82, 86–7, 91, 98–9, 118–20, 129–30, 137, 139
Haynes, E. J. A. 79
Head, Claud 113
Hearder, Rosalind 99
Hertig, Arthur T. 84
historic specimens 3, 120, 134–9, 141, 148
His, William 86
Hobbins, Peter 100
Howse, Neville Reginald 102
Hughes, Wilfrid Kent 114
Huistra, Hieke 53, 168 n.75
human body, collection of the 10–16
humanity 28, 30, 39, 91, 110, 114, 122–3, 127, 147–8
*Human Tissue Act*, New South Wales (1983) 140
*Human Tissue Act*, Victoria (1982) 136, 139
Hunterian Museum 43, 47, 122, 138, 189 n.83

Hunter, John 43, 47
Hunter, William 25, 49, 57
Hurren, Elizabeth 24
hydatid cysts xi, 54
hydrocephalus xi, 1–2, 8, 33–4, 37, 40–1, 44, 46–7, 58, 60, 69, 119, 143

Inglis, Keith 103–9, 117
insanity 41
in-vitro fertilization (IVF) 76

Jermyn, David 84–5
Johnston, H. O. 86
Jones, Ross L. 2–4, 89
Jordan, Henry Jacob 72–3

Kelly, Laura 24, 44
Kidd, J. S. 40–1
Kings Domain 128, 131–2, 185 n.42
Knoeff, Rina 46
Knox, Robert 12
Kreitmayer, Maximilian 71–2

Lanne, William 122–3
Larsson, Marina 113, 115
Lawrence, Carmen 117
Lawrence, Susan C. 62
Legge, Frank R. 46
Lendon, Alfred 78
Lewin, Roger 126
Lidwill, Mark 48
lithotomy xi, 28
Little, E. Marjory 107, 178 n.49
Loch, Henry 55
Lyford, Amy 111, 179 n.71

MacCallum, Peter 107–8
MacDonald, Helen 4, 12, 182 n.7
Mackenzie, John M. 160 n.25
Mall, Franklin Paine 87
Martyr, Philippa 73
Mason, Michael 71
Maund, John 85
McCalman, Janet 78–9
McKenzie, Colin 108
McLeary, Erin 5, 53
Medical Act, United Kingdom (1858) 54
medical authority 76–85, 93
medical museums 4–6
medicine, history of 4–6

Melbourne Advanced Facial Anatomy Course (MAFAC) 190 n.8
Melbourne Hospital 17, 36, 38–9, 54, 60, 86
Melbourne Medical School 4, 13, 16–19, 25, 29, 33, 40–4, 51, 54, 62–3, 65, 90, 100, 105, 119, 129–30
Melbourne Medical Students' Society (MSS) 23–4, 65, 73
Mendelson, Bryan 190 n.8
meningoencephalocele xii, 54
Menkin, Miriam 84
midwife 78–81
midwifery 44, 79
military medicine 97, 100–10, 116–17
Mollison, Crawford Henry 42–3
'monsters' 69–70
Moore, Wendy 57
Morgan, Lynn M. 85, 172 n.38
moulages 111, 115
Mueller, Ferdinand von 35
Murder Act, Great Britain (1752) 10
Murray Black Collection 125–31, 134
Museum of Victoria 1, 125, 128, 184 n.25, 184 n.27
*Mycobacterium ulcerans* xii, 126

National Museum of Australia (NMA) 109, 112, 116, 133, 136
National Resting Place 133
Neale, Kerry 114
Newland, Henry 103–5, 117
Nuremberg Code 135

Obscene Publications Act, United Kingdom (1857) 72
obstetrics 70, 80
omentum xii, 28, 158 n.104
O'Sullivan, Lisa 2–3, 89
ovarian pregnancy 78
Owen, Richard 17

Paget, James 17
paid collectors 35, 49–51
Pickering, Michael 130, 133
Pietsch, Tamson 6
podalic version xii, 94
polydactyly xii, 89
Ponce, Rachel N. 21
Porth, Emily F. 88

post-mortem examination xii, 11, 24, 37–9, 44–5
pregnancy 7, 76–8, 82–6, 91–5
prosectors xii, 59
provenance 131–4, 138

quickening xii, 78–9

RAMC. *See* Royal Army Medical Corps (RAMC)
Ramsay, John 48–50, 60
*Real Bodies: The Exhibition* 139–40
Reinarz, Jonathan 5, 53, 62, 166 n.42
repatriation 4, 7, 120, 124–36, 139–40, 184 n.24
Richardson, Ruth 14
Robertson, James 67, 163 n.10
Roberts, William 13
Rock, John Charles 84
Roginski, Alexandra 123
Royal Army Medical Corps (RAMC) 102, 107, 112, 178 n.49
Russell, Kenneth 64
Ruysch, Frederick 57
Ryan, Graeme 126–7, 129

Salmon, H. R. 24
Sappol, Michael 24
Second World War 108, 135
Shelley, Mary 12–13, 26
'shell shock' 101
Sickles, Daniel E. 110
Smith, William Ramsay 15–16, 121, 182 n.7
socialization 21, 30
specimens
    collecting and medical discourse 86–7
    foetal 7, 45–6, 66, 74–91, 95, 119
    pathology 43, 51, 55, 57, 86, 106, 108–12, 115–16, 118–19
    as pedagogical tools 62–9
    preparation techniques 56–9
    transforming patient into 38–41

*Speculum* (journal) 23–5, 27, 29–30, 60, 63, 65, 67, 73
Spencer, Walter Baldwin 89
Stephens, Elizabeth 71
St Vincent's Hospital 38
Sydney Medical School 39, 55, 59, 63, 103, 108, 136
Syme, G. A. 28–9, 89

Tebbutt, A. H. 101
Thomson, W. 92
Thorburn, J. O. 86
Towne, Joseph 57
Treloar, John 115
Turnbull, Paul 123

University of Adelaide 58, 65, 121
University of Melbourne 4, 42, 106, 119, 124, 135
University of Sydney 105–6

Val-de-Grâce hospital museum 111, 115–16, 179 n.71

Waddington, Keir 22
war wounds 97, 99, 108–9, 113, 115–16, 118, 134, 136
Watson, Archibald 1, 33, 37, 40–1, 46–7, 58, 65, 69, 119, 121
wax and papier-mâché models 62, 66–7
Weindling, Paul 188 n.80
wet specimens xii, 54
Willis, J. R. H. 45
Wilson, James Thomas 14–15, 39–40, 121
Withycombe, Shannon 82
Wittman, Laura 112
Wolf, Jacqueline H. 80
Women's Hospital 38, 44, 79–80, 83–4, 92, 94
Wood-Jones, Frederic 90
*Wunderkammern* 61